To Ron + Connie

The best to you always

Diana Burkhart

FACTS DON'T MATTER

BY DIXIE BURKHART

Eloquent Books
New York, New York

Copyright © 2008
All rights reserved — Dixie Burkhart

No part of this book may be reproduced or transmitted in any form or by any means, graphic, electronic, or mechanical, including photocopying, recording, taping, or by any information storage retrieval system, without the permission, in writing, from the publisher.

Eloquent Books
An imprint of AEG Publishing Group
845 Third Avenue, 6th Floor – 6016
New York, NY 10022
www.eloquentbooks.com

ISBN/SKU: 978-1-60693-336-7   1-60693-336-1

Printed in the United States of America

Cover Design: Peggy Ann Rupp, *www.netdbs.com*

Photographer: Amy Becker

Book Design: Denise Johnson, Dedicated Business Solutions, Inc.

DISCLAIMERS

The author of this book was involved in certain court proceedings surrounding a legal contract. The facts recited herein come from actual court documents presented in said legal dispute. The author believes the facts are correct as supported by said legal documents. But cautions that any opinions recited herein by the author are her own opinions and are not to be relied upon by any individual relating to his or her own legal transactions.

The publisher, its employees and agents do not accept any responsibility or liability, whatsoever, for any error, omission, interpretation or opinion which may be present, however it occurred, nor for the consequences of any decision based on the information supplied in this publication. The publisher, its employees and agents expressly disclaim al liability to any person relying on the whole or any part of this publication. The information contained herein is completely the authors opinion and the publisher has acted only as a production company in this regard.

To my husband, Steve, who was passionate in his support throughout the legal proceeding and in writing this book. He made it possible to see it through to the end.

CONTENTS

Acknowledgments		xi
Introduction		xiii

Chapter

1	In the Beginning	1
2	A Seed is Planted	7
3	Due Diligence and Buying In	11
4	Getting Started	16
5	A New Partner and New Format	22
6	A Partner Leaves	28
7	Personal Changes and a Prelude to a Fall	33
8	A Partner Falls	37
9	A Strange Proposal and Goodbye to Mike	44
10	Thoughts of Selling Out and the Trouble Begins	48
11	The Coup	54
12	The Fight Begins	62
13	Fighting Back	70
14	The Injunction Hearing Begins	76
15	The Injunction Hearing Continues	87
16	Kuhens Takes the Stand	92
17	Kuhens Cross-Examined	101
18	A Break	105

19	The By-Laws and Surprise Witnesses	108
20	The Affidavit	118
21	Taking a Stand	122
22	The Decision	127
23	Regrouping in a Mud Storm	135
24	The Trial Begins	137
25	Dennison Confronted	144
26	More Lies	149
27	Noyes Fires Back and I Take the Stand	162
28	The Trial Ends and Wait Begins	172
29	The Bomb Drops	177
30	One Step Forward, One Step Back	186
31	Three Strikes, You're Out	190
32	Restitution and Theft	193
33	Now and the Future	196

APPENDIX

1	By-laws of MediaComm, Inc.	204
2	Stock Transfer Agreement (May 20, 2003)	217
3	Time Brokerage Agreement (August 21, 2003)	221
4	30 Day Notice of Right to Cure Default of Stock Purchase Agreement (July 16, 2003)	231

5	MediaComm, Inc. Board Meeting Minutes (August 18, 2003)	232
6	Burkhart Letter to Kuhens cc Dennison, Beaver (August 18, 2003)	233
7	Beaver Letter to Kuhens (August 18, 2003)	234
8	Wiegel letter to Squires (November 5, 2003)	235
9	30 Day Notice of Right to Cure Default of Stock Purchase Agreement (December 9, 2003)	236
10	Dennison Letter to Burkhart (December 31, 2003)	237
11	Letter of Agreement (effective January 1, 2004)	238
12	Letter of Noyes to Squires Requesting Dennison to Vacate (January 7, 2004)	239
13	Bogus Corporate Resolution to Pilot Grove Savings Bank (January 8, 2004)	240
14	Affidavit of Governor Thomas J. Vilsack	241
15	Business Account Agreements with Pilot Grove Savings Bank	243
16	Foreclosure Sale Ad	248

FACTS DON'T MATTER

Acknowledgments

I received council from several attorneys in the journey to find justice in the judicial system.

Alanson Elgar represented me when the initial corporate documents were written. Safeguards were in the agreements to protect me if major changes occurred in the corporation.

Fred Beaver, our corporate attorney who relentlessly attempted to get the original active partners to correct their ways to avoid tax problems. Eventually, he would try to enforce the original corporate documents. He would be forced from his position as corporate attorney because of conflict of interest. He could not do what he was hired to do in the end.

Rande McAllister gave me correct council when he advised me to be involved with KILJ on a day to day basis after one of the original active partners had been found to be embezzling.

Gary Wiegel represented the bank that held the KILJ stock in escrow. He refused to just hand over the stock at the Dennison's whim. Instead, waited for the courts to rule.

Mike Noyes with the firm Lane & Waterman, LLC who originally thought we could bring things back to where they were prior to the indiscretions of the active partner and the prior owner His views would change as we proceeded.

Nathan Clark, a new associate with Lane & Waterman, would assist at the injunction hearing. He would give a power point presentation giving timelines and documentation to the case. One would think we could not loose after seeing that!

Stacey Hawke, who replaced Nathan Clark when he moved on, worked on my case behind the scene with Mike Noyes in the later phases.

In the end, it did not matter how good the council was. We could not win! Facts did not matter.

Introduction

This is the cautionary tale of what can go wrong in business. The best of planning, the best of council, the best of corporate documents, the best of everything can be to no avail. Why? We have many good laws on the books. However, if common sense and the appropriate laws are not applied, all justice in the judicial system is lost. If judges abuse judicial discretion or if inappropriate political intervention occurs, the letter of the law is lost. We become a lawless nation.

This book is written for the "little people", the common man and woman on the street who start up businesses and assume if something goes wrong, the courts will bring justice. There will always be winners and losers in all cases, but you should be able to assume that the appropriate facts and the appropriate laws will prevail.

In this case, a jury trial was denied as the judge said it was a foreclosure issue. She later would say there were "too many issues to deal with." This was not just a foreclosure issue. If it had been, there would have been no law suits and this book would not have been written. There was no justice in the judicial system.

Chapter 1

In the Beginning

Mt. Pleasant, Iowa, is a deceptively low-key place on the surface. Located about fifty miles from Iowa City and two hundred-thirty miles from St. Louis, it's the kind of place you'd picture when someone asks you what a small, Midwestern town looks like. It's a picturesque town where life revolves around the churches and schools and where everyone knows everyone.

We've got a population of between eight thousand five hundred and nine thousand, a town square with a memorial fountain, businesses, restaurants and a Wal-Mart Supercenter. Mt. Pleasant also has a strong manufacturing presence, though that's changing. The Blue Bird school bus factory is no longer here, the same with the Motorola factory that once called Mt. Pleasant home. We've got new industry now and though farming has changed over the years, there are still many people in this town who still make a living at it.

It was a big deal for us when Sam Walton came to town to open a Wal-Mart distribution center, and you won't find too many of the "fine" arts here, though we have the Southeast Iowa Symphony and we also have support for the arts at Iowa Wesleyan College, including displays and music.

My name is Dixie Burkhart and I was born here in Mt. Pleasant on October 15, 1946 and lived with my mother and father on a small farm fifteen miles outside of town with my two sisters and younger brother. One sister was three years older, the other was thirteen years younger and my brother was eleven years younger than I was. My father was a full-time farmer when I was young but he later went to work as a corrections officer at the Iowa State Penitentiary in Fort Madison while farming part-time. We lived about a half mile from any of our neighbors and like a lot of kids, my siblings and I kept busy with pets and the farm animals my father had. It was a simple life and none of us knew any different.

And I've stayed in Henry County, where Mt. Pleasant is located, my whole life, attending high school in New London and college at Iowa Wesleyan College. I earned my degree in business and economics and married my late husband the summer before my sophomore year. After graduating I went to work at the Iowa Department of Job Services.

Looking back now at the life I led as a young woman, I realize how naïve I was. Beneath the beautiful town square named Central Park and the tree lined streets, Mt. Pleasant has some ugly skeletons in its closet. Take, for example, that fountain I just mentioned. It's in honor of our former mayor, Ed King, who was murdered in 1987 during a City Council meeting. The killer was Ralph Davis, a disgruntled citizen who also wounded two other officials that night.

Tom Vilsack, an attorney and a rising star in local politics became the new mayor; he worked his way up the ladder, eventually becoming Iowa's governor (and, briefly, a candidate in the 2008 presidential election, running mostly in 2007). Little did I realize what impact Vilsack's influence would have on me in the future, or how the intertwined lives of the people here in Mt. Pleasant would come back to haunt me during the most difficult days of my professional life.

You see, the best and worst thing about this town is that, as I've said, everyone knows everyone. While that lends the town a closeness and a sense of community it also means that no one's business is their own. And when there's trouble, everyone hears about it.

There's a lot to reflect on about this town, a lot that makes you think, and that's just what I was doing in November 2006. The leaves had fallen off of the trees here and a brisk wind whipped them around my home, located about three miles from downtown. There was a nip in the air and that gave me a good excuse not to go outside and instead work in the confines of my home office.

The office is in my basement, where I run a small insurance business. I mostly work as a consultant now, but there was a time when I had a full-fledged insurance business selling life insurance, group benefits and at one point I even worked with 401(k)s when I was a registered representative. I started in the insurance business after seventeen years with the Iowa Department of Jobs Service because I felt like I'd done all I could there without leaving the area.

My office is a homey kind of place with wood filing cabinets, pictures of my current husband, children and grandchildren, telephone, computer and printer, appointment book and other necessities. There's also a radio, and on that cold morning in November, sipping on my coffee (black, of course!), I turned it on for some background music.

Flipping through the stations, I accidentally landed on KILJ, a locally owned outlet. I froze for an instant, and then quickly turned the knob. A flood of memories swept through me and I couldn't change the station fast enough. My involvement with KILJ and its owners, Paul and Joyce Dennison, still affects me greatly and it's changed my views on both our legal system and the weight that the facts and law carry when opposing parties take their cases to the courts.

My involvement with the Dennisons and my investment partners would cost me thousands of dollars and leave me with nothing to show for it but some useless stock in a parent company that once owned KILJ. It would also shatter any notion I had that greed and corruption are only big-city problems; something that couldn't be here in Mt. Pleasant, Iowa, with its small town values.

KILJ AM/FM has been around since 1970, broadcasting news, music and local high school sports. The station has a range of about fifty miles and is known by everyone as "our" local station. Today the FM band plays memory music. They also play some more contemporary songs. AM continues to play country. Again, on the surface, KILJ seems like a congenial broadcast outlet with something for everyone, and anyone who wasn't familiar with how the station came into the hands of the Dennisons again, after my partners and I bought it in 1991, would probably think that it was a calm and familial place of business.

I know better. You see, I was involved with KILJ starting in 1991 as an owner and continued in some capacity with them until it all fell apart in a slow, chaotic spiral during the early 2000s. I started off as an investor, looking for a stable business where I could enjoy myself and invest some of the insurance money from my first husband's death. I thought I could make some money in the process of helping a local institution. In theory, our local radio station seemed like an ideal setup. The reality was something completely different, and I turned the whole thing over in my head as I sipped my coffee that November day.

Thinking back on the cast of characters I dealt with at KILJ is a lesson in the human character, and how some people have more of it than others do. There were the "former" owners, the Dennisons, who held a tight grip on the station, never letting go of their baby regardless of any legal sales agreements they had signed. Paul Dennison, it turned out, was not the business minded radio station owner I thought he was. His collusion with another character would help to pull the radio station out from under me when we all ended up in court. His co-conspirator, John Kuhens, was, and probably still is, considered the "voice" of KILJ, a man who started at the station when he was seventeen—over thirty years ago. He had risen to the position of general manager of the station and was responsible for almost everything that went on the air at KILJ. He covered sports and wrote advertisements; he did the morning drive time shows and even read the news.

John is the kind of guy who's easy to like. He's jovial and humorous and he likes to be liked. He's usually the life of the party, and when I first went into business with him and my other partners I couldn't have known what he was capable of doing.

One of the people John really wanted to like him was Paul Dennison, and when they were together you could tell that Dennison was the one in charge, even though he's not that much older than John. That relationship would be the bane of my existence when things finally came to a head, and it explains how I lost hundreds of thousands of dollars in an effort to keep the radio station alive and in my hands.

While they share a close relationship with each other, Paul's style is different from John's. He dresses in expensive suits and has an air about him that lets people know he's in charge. He's been described as looking like a TV evangelist and in some ways he shares the same attributes. He can convince people to give him their money when he's dealing with advertisers and he's also good at spinning a message, which played a big part in how the public viewed my confrontation with him. John is jovial, but looks more frumpy, with glasses and some extra weight added to his frame in recent years.

John remained loyal to the Dennisons, even during the years he co-owned the station through our parent company, and nothing would ever get in the way of that loyalty—despite his contracts with me. There were partners and other investors, marked by varying degrees of honesty, but regardless of their positions, it seems in retrospect that my original KILJ partners all had something in common: they were connected in a web of deceit, questionable business practices and downright unethical behavior.

I got caught up in this web, an often-frustrating place where unscrupulous activities seemed to be the standard operating procedure, and my story is something I think can help others when they decide to put their money into the hands of other people. Anything and everything you can imagine happened behind the scenes at KILJ, from bogus bookkeeping to clandestine romances, mixed in with a plethora of backbiting, chicanery and lies, and it all ended up in a series of lawsuits and countersuits that would shake my faith in the legal system of even a small town in Iowa.

Looking back, I realize now my first mistake was that of believing that people you do business with want to succeed and are inherently respectful of everyone they work with. It's a natural thing; we all want to think everyone is honest. Sure, office politics are bound to happen in any workplace, and radio is notoriously rife with that, but in the end you want to think everyone can rise above their egos for the overall good of the operation. I played by the rules during my time as an owner of KILJ, did my job and expected others would do the same. In the end, my attorney explained to me, my problem was I was dealing with "a bunch of crooks." Ironic, isn't it? A small town full of pleasant images and pleasant people and I ended up the victim of crooks.

My second blunder? I believed that the judicial system was there to correct errors and punish dishonest people. Thinking over my long history with KILJ, I sat back in my chair, took another sip of coffee and came to a simple conclusion: I was amazingly naïve. If you get anything out of my story, I want you to understand that the legal system *does* work—although not always for what we think are its intended purposes. Sometimes the fix is in from the start, regardless of how you adhere to the rules and connections, ignored conflicts of interest and labyrinthine twists in the legal processes can ultimately result with down being up and up being down—never mind logic.

You might think you have all your ducks in a row, that you're a savvy business operator and that you couldn't be duped by the people you work with. But you'd be surprised how easily your ducks can be shot down.

As you read my story, I don't want you to think that I'm whining or complaining about unfair treatment. What happened to me over the course of a few years was a nightmare journey, and while it was a long, difficult and sometimes maddening road, when I reached the end, I realized I'd learned some hard lessons in the process.

Look at my story as a cautionary tale about how facts and the law can be ignored or circumvented by people determined to get what they want. Understand, also, that there are people out there, sometimes working right along with you, who don't have your best interests at heart. I don't want you losing all faith in humanity, but learn from my story and seriously consider who it is you're doing business with. If only I had recognized the warning signs from the get-go, I could have saved myself a lot of time, energy, money and most importantly, gained enormous peace of mind.

Chapter 2
A Seed is Planted

My dealings with KILJ began in 1991. My husband of twenty-five years, Jerry Norton, was diagnosed with lung cancer. Jerry and I were married on June 5, 1965, right here in Mt. Pleasant. We had two children, Patty, a high school student, and Steve, who was married with one child and a second on the way. Both of our kids live in Henry County just as I did growing up.

The cancer took its toll on Jerry and was very aggressive. He had just turned forty-seven when the cancer struck and because it was so aggressive the treatments were also aggressive. Though he'd quit smoking recently, he'd also been a welder and it's conceivable that the things he'd been inhaling over the years, metal dust and the like, could have contributed to his cancer.

First Jerry had surgery and within three weeks was back on the tractor, mowing our lawn. In the meantime, I maintained my insurance business, periodically heading to the office I kept uptown to check mail and do paperwork. But as the cancer quickly progressed, Jerry was forced to undergo several rounds of chemotherapy and then some radiation. The treatment was sometimes worse than the disease, and it took a terrible toll. Wanting to make the most of the time we had left together, I became his main caretaker. Finally, just ten months after the date of diagnosis, we faced the worst possible outcome. Jerry died on February 6, 1991 at the age of forty-seven, just four months shy of our twenty-sixth wedding anniversary.

I was forced to ask myself some hard questions after Jerry died. I wasn't sure what to do next in my life and I decided to give myself a few months to mourn. I then began to look at what possibilities I could explore for myself. In the meantime, I had my insurance business to keep me busy. The summer after Jerry died I earned my CLU (Charted Life Underwriter) and CHFC (Chartered Financial Consultant) certifications in order to build on my skills. I also decided to return to school for a master's degree in financial services as part of my lifelong education. And I began looking for investment opportunities for the insurance money I'd received after Jerry passed away. I was fortunate that my involvement with the insurance industry had educated me to the needs of surviving family members in the case of an early death, and Jerry and I had prepared ourselves well.

I did have some mutual funds, but I also was interested in local businesses. One day, I ventured to the Mt. Pleasant Chamber of Commerce to see if there were any prospects in the area. It had been a while since I'd been close to the daily activity in Mt. Pleasant's business community and I felt meeting with someone at the Chamber of Commerce would be the best way to get my feet wet.

"Funny you should ask," the official at the Chamber told me. "Mike Stoffregen is looking for investors in KILJ."

Stoffregen's name was familiar to me, although I didn't know him personally. He'd been working for the local savings and loan in our downtown area and was involved in the community through the Kiwanis Club and other organizations. The savings and loan Stoffregen worked for had changed hands several times, with him being a mainstay throughout. Mike was vice president and managing officer of the Iowa regional offices and was in charge of nine offices throughout Iowa for the savings and loan he worked at. He was considered a high achiever, even in a failing company. Finally, though, in the wake of the national Savings & Loan scandals of the 1980s, his employer folded.

Now, like me, he was looking for new opportunities. The official at the Chamber of Commerce told me that Stoffregen was looking for investors who could put together $500,000 to purchase our local radio station. Paul and his wife, Joyce, knew Mike, and he had inquired of Paul about what it would take to buy him out of the radio station. Paul came up with a number and Mike accepted, surprising the Dennisons and allowing them to take an early retirement.

Now that sounded like a smart idea to me—everyone knew KILJ! I really wanted to get involved with our area, and KILJ was considered a sound business. The Chamber of Commerce official suggested I go to the chamber's monthly gathering, Alive After Five, so that I could get back into the flow of what was going on in the community. I had been to the gatherings before and was familiar with the atmosphere.

The event was a social gathering where Mt. Pleasant business people could network, exchange business cards, meet new members of the Chamber of Commerce and learn what was happening in the community. It didn't hurt that Alive After Five also included a well-stocked buffet.

It wasn't long before I heard about an Alive After Five meeting at an area business. I decided to go just to get an idea of what the pulse of the community was. That night, I socialized with different people, exchanging chitchat and small talk. As I moved from group to group, I eventually found myself in conversation with the man himself, Mike Stoffregen.

He was a professional looking individual, thin, well-dressed and clean cut, with light brown hair and glasses. Despite his recent setback, Stoffregen exuded confidence. We made a little small talk and then switched our conversation to his plans for KILJ.

The Dennisons, who'd been running KILJ since 1979, still owned the station and the station's building. In fact, their house was built right next to the station. Stoffregen wanted into the radio business and was looking for other people who were interested in going in with him on a partnership.

The Dennisons wanted $500,000 to get the deal running, though the final purchase price would be something like $1.5 million paid to the Dennisons over eighteen years. Of the $1.5 million, approximately $1 million would be financed through the Dennisons themselves, who chose to accept payments over time. One of Stoffregen's potential partners was another member of KILJ's "family," John Kuhens. As I said earlier, Kuhens started at the radio station when he was just seventeen years old. Over time he'd developed into its on-air personality. He worked as announcer, newsreader and disk jockey and as a bonus for his long service Paul Dennison had given him $25,000 in KILJ AM stock. Unlike many people who start in small markets like ours before moving into bigger venues, Kuhens had stuck with KILJ throughout his many years in radio.

Upfront, Stoffregen's plan sounded good. I listened regularly to the station, as did just about everyone else in the area, and I liked that it was a local station rather than part of a media conglomerate. It seemed like an ideal proposition for someone like me who was looking to invest locally rather than in some far away business to which I had no connection.

Obviously, I didn't give Mike a yes or no that night I met him at the Alive After Five party. I listened as he told me of his plans, taking in every word with deep consideration. Initially, however, I liked what I was hearing. His plan seemed like just the kind of local interest I was looking to invest with.

Now, I may have been naïve in some parts of my life, but I had no intentions of investing my money on just a leap of faith. Stoffregen provided me with more information on his plan through a prospectus he'd put together. I wanted to know who the other prospective investors were, what the business plan was and where he saw the station developing.

Looking back, I can only think to myself: it seemed like a good idea at the time. But then, all disasters look good upfront. No one wants to create a bad business; people want to make money and do good work. And of course I was going to ask other professionals, including an attorney, an accountant and a business owner for their thoughts before I put any money into KILJ.

The night I met Mike Stoffregen, my schooling began. Though I couldn't have known it at the time, I would ultimately get some very hard lessons in how some business people and the court system operate. I would also learn that slick presentations and a professional appearance do not a good business partner make.

Chapter 3

Due Diligence and Buying In

When Stoffregen delivered the prospectus for the purchase of KILJ, I was pretty excited. It represented a chance to invest in my hometown! Not only would I be giving back to my community, I would be investing my money into what was considered a real community bedrock: our local radio station.

Radio in rural Iowa is something of a lifeline to the community. In Mt. Pleasant, we do pick up strong signals from several stations broadcasting out of larger towns like Burlington (about thirty miles from my town), which provides access to more choices in music, regional shows and nationally syndicated talk formats.

We also listen to stations out of Des Moines, including WHO-AM, the radio station where former President Ronald Reagan got his start in the broadcasting business (Des Moines is about one hundred twenty miles from Mt. Pleasant). But KILJ was a local station in the truest sense of the term. In addition to its AM and FM music formats, KILJ also provided news that was strictly local, such as what the school lunches were going to be for the day, births and deaths in the community and a talk show devoted to farming interests.

You see, around here, everyone is a little bit like a farmer. You check the weather, hope for a good season and a good crop, even if you aren't directly involved in farming the land. The station was conceived as and thrived as a unique niche outlet for Mt. Pleasant and the surrounding region of fifty miles, which was about as far as its signal stretched into the area.

Mike's prospectus looked good on the surface, very professionally laid out and put together in a nice looking binder. The proposal was typed on letterhead from the company Mike had created in order to purchase KILJ FM and KILJ AM from the Dennisons: MediaComm. Stoffregen had labeled MediaComm as marketing specialists, and in his proposal he detailed how he wanted his company to become a marketing company that would also own KILJ.

In his introduction to the proposal, Stoffregen explained that he'd begun discussion with the Dennisons in March of 1991 and that a "definitive Stock Purchase Agreement was entered between MediaComm and the existing owners on July 19, 1991." Stoffregen planned to install himself as president of MediaComm with John Kuhens acting as executive vice president. Stoffregen also detailed the history of KILJ, it's projected cash flows under the ownership of MediaComm and the payment schedule he planned for paying the Dennisons. He included resumes for himself and Kuhens and explained the shareholder agreement that would end up pertaining to me.

Just paging through it, I could see Stoffregen was serious about the potential deal. Every document looked good, with all the legal pieces in place. While it looked very much like something I wanted to a part of, from my business background in the insurance industry I knew darn well that if I was going to be a partner in the KILJ purchase, I had to do more homework!

The deal wasn't something I could enter into on just a whim. Yet, I told myself, unless something in the prospectus came up as a potentially devastating loophole or red flag, I was ready to make the move. After all, I did want to invest my money locally and KILJ was the only company in the area looking for buyers. Before I jumped in, though, I decided to consult with some businesspeople to make sure the deal was a sound one.

Immediately, I thought of Arnie Arledge, a local businessman who worked in Burlington. Arledge was a real character, with his fingers in a lot of different successful pies. One thing he really liked was running his own companies! For many years, he ran a thriving trucking firm that shipped various goods all over the country. He decided to retire and sold the trucking business. But Arledge was one of those guys who just couldn't sit back in his easy chair, watch football on television and think that that was the ultimate good life in his post-work world!

Eventually, Arnie bought himself a car dealership and parlayed that into another successful business venture for himself. The dealership had quite a reputation in the area, proving there's no such thing as retirement for the active person.

Eventually, however, Arledge decided he'd had enough of running his automobile dealership and he eventually sold that too. This time he downsized himself into a business that really was more of a hobby for him. He opened a store that specialized in selling old, refurbished jukeboxes, slot machines and pinball machines. Arledge just loved those kinds of gadgets. The store was more like a hangout for him rather than a business—although, to no one's surprise, this was another successful venture for him as well.

So naturally, when I wanted a businessman to look over Stoffregen's proposal, Arledge was my number one choice as a consultant. I drove out to Burlington one day, binder in hand, and stopped in on his shop. "Arnie," I said, "I have something I'd like you to look over. I'm thinking about investing in KILJ, and I'd appreciate it if you could read over the paperwork here to make sure they're on the up-and-up."

Being an old pal, Arledge was glad to help. Like me, he was impressed by the overall layout of the material. He carefully looked through each section of the prospectus, reading each page like a diamond merchant determining the carat value of a newly found stone. When he was done, he offered his advice.

"Dixie," he said, "I think they've done a good job here. Everything seems to be in order. I don't see any reason why this wouldn't be a good investment."

"But don't forget," he continued, "there's always a certain amount of risk with any business. You don't need me to tell you some great outfits have gone belly up despite their good intentions. There are market forces that just can't be controlled. But like I say, this one looks good."

Still, Arledge suggested, I should have an accountant look over the prospectus as a matter of course. He suggested I send it to a friend of his in St. Louis, Missouri. I agreed, of course.

After all, it made sense to send the proposal to a moneyman since I was considering investing my personal savings into the venture and buying in would cost me $150,000! In fact, it would cost me more than that because I ended up helping the other partners buy in, but more on that later.

I sent Stoffregen's materials to the accountant and waited on his advice. It was not long before I heard from him with his thoughts on the matter. Like Arledge, the accountant thought the deal was sound; everything was in order with nothing out of place as far as he could see. He did think that perhaps I was paying a little too much for my part of the investment, but that was just his opinion. A different accountant quite easily could have had another entirely different opinion. And like Arledge, he pointed out that there is always some risk when one invests money in a business, but that of course is standard no matter what you choose to sink your money into.

With two experts down, I decided it was time to go to my third adviser. My choice was Lanny Elgar, a man known around Mt. Pleasant as a highly respected attorney with a good reputation when it came to corporate law. Again, like any prudent potential investor, I was determined to seek out the best advice I could possibly find. As with my first two counselors, Elgar liked what he saw. He repeated what the others had told me and warned me that any kind of investment always carried the risk of failure. Yet, there was nothing out of the ordinary as far as he could see. And from what he knew about the popularity of the station with everyone in town, KILJ seemed like a logical choice for a local investor.

Once I gathered all this advice, I sat down for a few days to think over the decision. All three of my advisers found nothing wrong with the prospectus; it seemed as sound as sound could be. I certainly thought it was a good deal, myself! No one had found any red flags or potential legal or financial landmines buried within the carefully worded proposal. So, with all this in mind, I decided to move forward with the deal. What a moment that was for me. I was going to be an owner of the local radio station!

What no one could foresee, of course, was that I was getting involved with dishonest and unscrupulous people. Even with flawless documents and an ironclad contract you just can't predict the intentions people have in their hearts. You can't see that someone is without a moral compass based on a presentation inside of a folder. And on the surface everyone I was going into business with had a solid reputation. Again, in a small town you usually hear if someone isn't scrupulous. Unfortunately for me, bad people don't exist on well-written legal documents. My carefully researched decision would turn out to be one of the biggest mistakes of my life.

Once I made my decision, I told Stoffregen that I was ready to get in on his enterprise. He told me he was glad to have me aboard. Ideally, he told me, he and Kuhens were looking for four investors to put in $125,000 apiece, as stated in the prospectus. But we had an unforeseen problem when one of the potential investors had to back out because he was unable to tap his inheritance in time to get in on the deal. (He would later become a Class C stockholder with about $15,000 in stock and would eventually have to write his off, but more about that later.) The investor's situation was entirely understandable, and no one held any animosity toward him about this. However, we were now an investor short and more money was needed.

Chapter 4

Getting Started

Ultimately, we didn't find another investor, but that didn't stop us from going forward with the deal.

All in all, purchasing the station seemed like a great business investment—one that would be a sound financial deal as well as giving back to our community through a locally owned radio station. With the increase in syndicated radio and corporate owned stations, local ownership meant a lot to KILJ listeners. This was *their* station where people knew that *their* concerns and interests were important.

By the late summer of 1991, everything was finalized. What an exciting time that was! Of course, investing in KILJ was like any other business deal. There was, as you can probably imagine, a forest full of paperwork that had to be approved by lawyers and signed by all participants. And I needed to be sure there were no hidden clauses or loopholes that would cause me problems somewhere down the road. Since I had run everything by my advisors, I was sure this would be a good investment. After all, all the facts were there, for anyone to see, in a solid legal agreement.

Under the agreement, KILJ would exist as a subsidiary of MediaComm, the firm that Stoffregen wanted to grow into a thriving parent company. MediaComm would own all stock from KILJ and all stock purchases would be done through MediaComm. The stocks broke down into different categories. Stoffregen and Kuhens were considered "Class A" stockholders. This meant they collectively had sixty percent of voting power on decisions made on behalf of the company on a day-to-day basis, or in other words, Class A voters comprised sixty percent of the voting power to the forty percent from the Class B holders when it came to day-to-day decisions. The reason I was given forty percent initially was because they were worried that someone who wasn't involved in the day-to-day operations would come in and tell them how to run a station.

Mike and John also were responsible for guaranteeing payments to Paul and Joyce Dennison, as well as our bank loans. The Dennisons were given shares of KILJ stock as collateral, which was held by the bank in an escrow account. This meant that any default in payment to them could result in a return of KILJ's stock to them. They would get the company back. That is where our problems would lie many years down the road, but for now we were just getting things set up.

According to our agreement, Mike and John could outvote me on issues revolving around day-to-day station operations. However, there was a clause, put in by our corporate attorney, Fred Beaver, which he added as a protection to me: Should there be any major decisions there had to be unanimous approval by all board members, *i.e.*, the owners. Major decisions would include such things as selling the station out from MediaComm or agreeing to lease the station to another broadcast company.

The first set of papers, which involved the stock purchase, was signed in July. Personally, I was ready for a little break after all of the research and preparations I'd done. But, knowing I was in good hands with my partners, I went with Stoffregen to Elgar's office. At that time, I gave Elgar the power of attorney to sign off all documents in my absence. I also provided him with a personal check for part of the amount, then came back later to put in the balance. These payments were placed into an escrow account he could access for business involving the KILJ purchase.

Paul and Joyce Dennison's legal representation at the signing was a local attorney by the name of Tom Vilsack. Does that name sound familiar to you? Remember, after our mayor Ed King was murdered, Vilsack was elected as the new Mt. Pleasant mayor. This was the launch of his political career. He later became our state senator, and in 1999 was elected Governor of Iowa. He served two terms, and then in November 2007 announced his candidacy for the 2008 Democratic Presidential nomination. This final campaign was short lived. Three quick months later, he dropped out of the running, citing problems raising funds in what was already a very crowded field.

At the time of the signing, I had respect for Vilsack. He was a talented up-and-comer, with a lot of confidence and obvious legal talent. Years later, he would use his political influence against me when the deal with the Dennisons went bad and ended up in court, but that was years later. For now, I was happy with the way things were going.

With confidence that all would go well, my daughter and I headed for a little rest and relaxation in Florida. We vacationed along the Gulf Coast of Florida and of course paid a visit to Mickey and his pals at Walt Disney World. That was a great place for me, showing me just how far the power of good imagination can take you. Little did I realize that the total opposite of Disney World was forming in Iowa; the forces of a bad mindset were getting started without me.

Of course, I wouldn't find out about this for years. At no point was I naïve in my early dealings—other than operating under the concept that my partners in this deal were ethical and honest. But who wouldn't think such a thing about their fellow investors at the beginning of any business venture, except, perhaps, Don Corleone? Like my advisors said, all business dealings involve some level of risk, and to me the risk seemed minimal after the research I'd done and the agreement I'd signed. It seemed ironclad to me.

Another signing took place in September when we had to do some additional paperwork. My attorney gave me wine and cheese for an impromptu celebration at the station and it was a happy time for everyone. At last, I was a radio station owner! We would celebrate at the station with the staff.

The days and months following the purchase of KILJ were a wonderful time for me and my family. I was investing in a radio station that had been a local presence for years, and I felt like I was supporting Mt. Pleasant while also doing something for us.

Public reaction to the sale was good. People liked the idea that the station would stay in local hands. I was a silent partner so many people didn't really see me associated with the station on a day-to-day basis. I was more in the background when compared with John and Mike and that was just fine with me. I looked forward to my new adventure and I felt good about the research I'd done.

Our roles at the station were quickly established. Kuhens, with his many years behind the microphone, was our on-air talent. He worked as our disk jockey, sports announcer, and had other broadcasting duties, making him the voice of KILJ. Stoffregen was the sales, business and marketing guy. Why not? He had put together the deal with an excellent prospectus and had marketing in mind the whole time.

Stoffregen's vision was for MediaComm to become an all-encompassing marketing company that provided services to local and regional businesses looking to advertise. Plus, he'd worked for many years in banking and marketing, attaining skills that made him a respected local figure in these fields. Me? I was the silent partner. As I said before, the stock agreement gave me forty percent voting rights. Consequently, with no background in radio (other than as a listener!) it was a wise idea for me to sit back while my partners ran the show. Well, at least it seemed like a wise idea at the time.

These positions were never really discussed. It was all "understood" as a sort of handshake agreement that we would assume the different roles. There was no need to get this on paper, and in retrospect, I guess there never was a need to formally spell out who was responsible for which position. It wouldn't have changed a thing when it came to our different duties. Other than perhaps some brief descriptions in the employee manual, we all knew what was expected from one another. No contracts were necessary either, since this was all "at will" employment.

Thus, my involvement in the radio business got underway. Although I was not involved in the day-to-day operations, I did have a presence at the station. I was invited to move my insurance business into KILJ. The building where we broadcast from was a pretty small operation. There was a basement for offices and storage, the main floor for radio operations and other offices and an empty loft space just upstairs. As a partner in the station, I was made an amazingly cheap rental rate on the loft space as the base for my insurance business.

During this time I shared office space with Mike and our working relationship was a good one. Mike was always professional and courteous and we had regular meetings that were structured and well run.

There was one problem with the meetings, though. The financial statements we were given by Mike were often incorrect. The man we'd hired to do our bookkeeping often complained of one problem or another with our finances. He would complain that he wasn't getting the information he needed to do the books as he'd like, and Mike was always insistent that he would fix the problem and get the bookkeeper the information he needed. I was also insistent that the problems be fixed.

Maybe the fact should have a red flag that our bookkeeper was always running into problems, but at the time I really just viewed the situation as a breakdown in the channels of communication between Mike and the bookkeeper. We were sending our monthly financial statements to our corporate attorney, Fred Beaver, and so it never actually entered my mind that there was anything to be really concerned with. Mike was a professional and he had every interest in making the operation work successfully. Things were not as they seemed, though, but I wouldn't find out about that for several years. For now I was glad to have cheap office space and a significant piece of a local landmark.

In addition to having cheap office space, there were other perks to owning part of MediaComm, such as having KILJ employees answer my phone and take messages so I wouldn't have to hire a secretary. Again, this was not written out in any sort of contract, just a verbal agreement that everyone thought was a good idea.

Keep in mind that just because I had offices upstairs in the KILJ building, that didn't mean that I had any kind of oversight on the day-to-day life of KILJ. However, I definitely was a presence in the office and employees knew who I was. I was always considered an "outsider" of sorts because I was really just a moneyman, so to speak. I wasn't one of the daily operators interacting with the staff, so my position was less of a known quantity to everyone. I was just one of the owners and I had no problem with that.

One thing that did surprise me, though, was the attitude of Kuhens's wife, Susie. I knew her vaguely from around town (in a small town, everyone knows who *everybody* is!). She was the clerk of court at the Henry County courthouse (another coincidence that would come back to play a part in my fight with the Dennisons). Once I came into the deal, however, she began treating me with a very cold shoulder. It was as though she resented my involvement, albeit just monetary, in KILJ. That made no sense to me. After all, if neither Stoffregen nor her husband needed my involvement then why did they ask me to make a six-figure investment? Occasionally, she made snide remarks in my direction, things along the lines of, "Well, it *is* your money!" She also had complete faith in her husband's talents and was convinced he could have moved to a larger market had he chosen to.

Regardless, I took her attitude as just a small annoyance to be tolerated and generally ignored. Looking back now, I couldn't have possibly realized at this point exactly how Susie Kuhens would ultimately have a devastating effect on my financial stakes in KILJ.

Chapter 5
A New Partner and New Format

Not much really changed with the radio station once we took over operations that fall. We all fell into our routines fairly quickly. Kuhens continued on the air as if no changes had gone on behind the scenes, which KILJ listeners liked just fine. In the meantime, I did learn a few things about the radio business that I had never considered before.

One involved exactly how advertising works. Not all of our advertisers necessarily paid for their commercials in cash; rather, we had relationships that were called "trade outs." A trade out, which is a common business practice for local stations nationwide, involves businesses exchanging goods and services in exchange for on-air advertisements. It was a good business arrangement that KILJ had going for many years.

In fact, the Dennisons had many of them on the books when we bought. They also had quite a few accounts receivable on the books and they took minimal income while they owned the station. They were able to do so because they were able to trade for a lot of their needs and sometimes even had KILJ pick up their personal expenses.

Of course, it's not like trade outs are just fair exchanges without consequence. They are considered legal transactions. I always tallied up the costs of the goods I received as a result of a trade out and put it on my IRS statements at the end of the year using W-9 forms. To me, it was the only way to operate. This *was* income in a sense that I was being provided an economic benefit and it would be unethical of me not to declare it. Having run my own business, I knew all the ins and outs of what the IRS demanded. A company and its employees do have specific responsibilities to the tax codes—John and Mike received a leased company car, which I did not. Instead, I would receive trade outs equal to the value of the costs associated with their cars.

Other people at the station felt I was foolish to be writing out W-9s for the trade outs. After all, it was so easy to let something like that "slide," as it were. People do it all the time, right? But at the end of the day, it's dishonest and I didn't want that kind of thing on my conscience.

Then there were standard advertising sales. During all their years as owners, the Dennisons had a single sales person. Her job was to meet with different clients, tell them why KILJ was a great place to advertise, and what we could do for them to generate new—and consistent—business. Paul Dennison himself also did a lot of advertising sales, working mainly with people he had known for a long time. Paul had built up a pretty regular client base that we took over when we became owners.

After taking over the station, Stoffregen and Kuhens decided it was time to develop a more vigorous sales department. They hired several people and carved up our broadcast range into different territories. As an incentive, we had all of our sales people work on commission. The harder they worked and the more sales they made, the more they could make.

Unfortunately, what we didn't realize at the time was that small market radio makes for extremely tough sales. There are only so many places to try and sell advertising within our broadcast range. While they tried their best, our sales staff found it difficult to make enough in commissions to stay on the job. The sales people came and went rather quickly, and we ended up going through several people during our first years of ownership.

Meanwhile, Stoffregen was doing his best to build the marketing side of MediaComm. As I said before, MediaComm was designed to be a marketing firm first that happened to own a radio station. There is a lot of work that goes into a marketing business, especially trying to start one from scratch. Trust me, I know all this just from running my own small insurance firm.

Now Stoffregen had good experience as a marketer, or so he said. He had space at the radio station to work on the marketing end of MediaComm and he split his duties between sales and marketing. Stoffregen had a lot of energy and faith in what he was doing, and we had no reason to doubt this aspect of the business would be a great success.

In late 1992, a new man came on board to our group of investors. Steve Staebell was a smart, talented man with a strong background in all aspects of radio. He was well known in Iowa radio and he'd developed a strong reputation at a Burlington station, an important market for the state with many stations for listeners to choose from. Staebell was a multi-talent. He knew it all: sales and promotion, program formats, production and technical areas in the medium. What he didn't have was ownership and that's where Stoffregen thought we might have a chance in bringing Staebell to KILJ.

So Stoffregen went to Burlington to meet Steve and see if he could bring him on board. He provided him with a lot of information on the station, telling him how it was an exciting time to be with a developing broadcast outlet in a small, but loyal market. Staebell liked what he heard. With his extensive knowledge of the radio business, it was a logical career move for Steve to become a co-owner of a station.

Rather than come into the deal like the rest of us, Steve took a different route. He had a self-directed Individual Retirement Account that allowed him to invest in anything he wanted to and after consulting his business and financial advisors, he decided to use his IRA to invest in MediaComm with a contribution of $125,000, with some of that money coming in the form of a loan from me. Like me, he would be a Class B stockholder and would share in the collective forty percent vote Class B stockholders had in decisions by the board of directors. I didn't have a problem with any of the conditions bringing Steve to our team and neither did John or Mike. So, Steve signed up on the dotted line and soon was a part of the KILJ family.

Like John and Mike, however, Steve was short of the needed funding to meet the requirements of the subscription agreement. I was the only investor who had all of the needed money up front. I was able to put $150,000 into purchasing KILJ stock through MediaComm. John Kuhens had $25,000 in KILJ AM stock that the Dennisons had given him as a reward for his loyal service. He put that toward the purchase and also borrowed $70,000 from the bank, which is what Stoffregen did as well, since he only had $25,000 in cash to put toward the purchase.

Now in the beginning, when we first purchased the radio station from the Dennisons, this wasn't considered a problem; we knew they were good for the money eventually. But the time had come for each of them to fulfill their commitments.

Now, because I was convinced that the purchase of the radio station was a sound investment, and because I had confidence in my business partners, I had no problem lending the remaining money to Mike, John and Steve. I ended up loaning to each of them about $23,000, with the loans guaranteed by MediaComm. At the time it didn't seem like a problem. But that was because I was still under the impression that my new business partners were able businessmen.

Now, this wasn't something I did just on a whim. That would have been a huge mistake, which obviously I knew! However, I did have the money and did believe in my partners and our future together. I approached them with the idea, and to no surprise, Mike, John and Steve agreed to take my offer. But we agreed if it was going to happen, then we had better follow legal channels so we would all be protected.

I went to Fred Beaver, our corporate attorney, rather than my regular attorney. It made a lot of sense, since he was the corporate attorney for KILJ and MediaComm. Keep in mind, he'd done all the paperwork for us on the initial deal. And what's more, I knew from my interactions with Fred, he was an honest man who would look out for everyone's best interests.

In retrospect, this was a smart move on my part. Had we just drawn up a simple compact between partners, I could have been stiffed for as much as $69,000! Nobody wanted that—or at least I thought so at the time. So, Fred wrote into the contract that MediaComm as a corporation would guarantee the loan. This turned out to be a good move in the end even though at the time I didn't think it was necessary.

This guarantee was good business ... and in the long run an unintentionally intelligent move in light of how my relationship with KILJ was hijacked by unscrupulous partners. Ultimately, it was the only safeguard I had to get back the money I had loaned in good faith to a pair of dishonest individuals in Mike and John.

From the start, everyone liked Steve. He was a good guy, easy going and brimming with ideas. It made for an interesting time and lots of good development for the future of the station.

At the time, KILJ was broadcasting country on our AM side and oldies music on our FM band. That would change after Steve came on board and a decision was made to switch the arrangement so that FM was broadcasting some of the newer country music that was becoming popular at the time.

The world of country music was changing in the early 1990s, just like the rest of the modern pop world. New singers were replacing the old guard and selling CDs by the millions, winning new legions of fans to the Nashville style. But our station had yet to catch up. Where were the Clint Blacks, the Martina McBrides and the Mary Chapin Carpenters on our station? The new country was what people were listening to, but not what was being played at KILJ. It was a new wave of country vocalists taking the nation by storm. No matter how much people adored Patsy Cline or Buck Owens, new sounds were a must if we were going to keep up with what the market demanded.

What's more, by broadcasting our country music on the AM dial, we were limiting our audience. And what's more, the AM side was what's called a sun-up to sun-down station, which means our time to impact our audience was already limited. Have you ever driven under a bridge when you're a few miles shy of a radio station's broadcasting power while listening to something on AM? That's right, the sound gets all fuzzy and you get annoyed quickly!

As for the oldies music on our FM side, that was good stuff, but not as big a draw as modern country. Sure, every person has his or her favorite rock 'n' roll songs. But oldies music is definitely a limited market and doesn't have the fresh appeal to draw in new listeners. Basically, oldies cater to a well-established market, where the developing trends in country music in the early 1990s gave us the opportunity to widen our audience.

So we decided on a simple and obvious idea: We would flip the oldies music to the AM side and the country to the FM. The guys figured it would only help further the KILJ brand within the community and generate plenty of new listeners. And we could keep our regular features our audience expected from us, like news, weather reports, high school sports scores and what was being served for lunch at the local schools.

Now that we had the format changes with a potential for new listeners, it was decided that we should up our range. We'd always broadcast within a fifty-mile radius of Mt. Pleasant. If we could increase the size of our radio tower, the KILJ signal would stretch a little farther. It was hoped that this would increase both listenership and potential sales markets. This change was approved by the KILJ board of directors (John, Mike, Steve and me), and Fred Beaver drew up the legal papers. We had to have approval from the FCC to increase our tower's capability, so it was a bit of work to do it.

During this period it was a wonderful time to be a part of KILJ. We were moving forward as a station despite stagnant advertising sales. Part of the reason our funds were low, though, were because we were paying three partners large salaries by small station standards. Because the Dennisons had not taken large salaries and had traded for a lot of things, they had managed to keep expenses down. I still thought the future looked very bright!

Chapter 6
A Partner Leaves

Despite positive changes made during Steve's tenure, we still weren't increasing our sales. Though we weren't in dire financial straits, it became obvious something needed to be done to help out the KILJ books.

Clearly some sacrifices would have to be made. Perhaps jobs would be cut, while remaining staff members took on additional duties. It seemed like a logical choice, one made by companies throughout the world regardless of what kind of business they were involved in. At least such a move would save money on payroll.

What happened next came as a surprise to everyone at the station. One day John and Mike made an announcement to the staff. "We are taking salary reductions," we were told. It was implied by them that they were making personal sacrifices on behalf of the station. They were both going to reduce their salaries from an annual rate of $50,000 down to $37,000. Now, $13,000 is quite a salary reduction, particularly in a rural area. Both men insisted it was for the good of the station, and that it was just their part in working towards the long-term success of KILJ.

Steve wanted nothing to do with the salary reductions and kept out of the matter. I know these salaries don't sound like a lot, and they weren't. Small market radio does not pay well, though it does offer some benefits.

As a board member, I knew about Mike and John's decision. I didn't know, however, that they didn't plan to follow proper procedures when it came to taxes. And, their decision raised more questions. How would they make ends meet in light of a salary reduction? It turns out that Mike had that all figured out, as well.

Helped by his background in banking, Mike had obtained personal loans for both John and himself when they first bought into the radio station. They had each borrowed something like $70,000 to help cover the subscription agreement. The loans were personal loans, but they had MediaComm pay back the loans for their benefit out of the company's monthly revenues. The overall amount each of them would have had to pay back to the bank per year was the same amount as the pay cuts they had taken. Essentially, Mike and John would pay back the loans they'd received directly from the MediaComm coffers, as opposed to paying themselves the $13,000 and then writing personal checks to pay the bank. It was all MediaComm money anyway, and so it didn't make sense for them to write checks from MediaComm to themselves, only to turn around and write out personal checks for the same amount.

In effect, John, Mike and I were MediaComm, so it wasn't like they were taking the money illegally or without anyone's knowledge. Because they each owned a significant portion of MediaComm, any profits were theirs, anyway. But the arrangement wasn't exactly the self-sacrificing act that they said it was, it was more like a shift in the way that money was being routed back to the bank to cover the loan.

This arrangement would not change any day-to-day operations at the station, nor would it affect the voting status John and Mike had as board members. It all seemed like it was on the up and up, if not less than altruistic.

What we learned, however, is things are often not as they appear—especially when it comes to money.

Because the company was paying back the money, these loans were technically considered as an economic benefit for the pair. Though their salaries were now smaller, the bank loans were helping them get by with MediaComm at their back. Still, with the loans considered as a personal economic benefit, Mike and John both were supposed to pay taxes on them at the end of the year. It should have been declared on their income taxes at the end of the year because they got an economic benefit from it.

As the deal went through, Fred offered the two several options for paying what was due to the IRS. One way, he suggested, was to have them take "paper raises" which technically would have kept their salaries at the lower rate while the loan would be considered additional income. I felt that a payroll deduction might also be a good approach to paying back the loans. People did that for all sorts of reasons, such as car payments, child support or school loans. Or they could go with the most obvious choice: declare the loans as income using W-9 statements when filing personal tax returns.

Instead, both Mike and John ignored the issue. Periodically, Fred would stop by the station. "You know," he would say, "you really need to take care of this. You don't want to end up paying any penalties." Having run my own business, I knew exactly what he meant. The IRS is not exactly the most forgiving of federal agencies.

However, in the long run, this tax issue was Mike and John's problem, not mine. They ultimately were the ones responsible for making sure their personal books were in order.

It was shortly after Mike and John decided to take their pay cuts that Steve decided to leave the radio station. I don't think it was because of anything in particular, but he decided to head back to Burlington.

Though his improvements had really changed KILJ for the better, Steve decided to return to the stations he'd come from. Opportunities had opened up for him in Burlington, and Steve really wanted to get back to that market. There was also a problem with Steve's salary. When he was first approached by Mike, he was offered $50,000 as an annual salary. Steve felt confident that it was worth it for the company because he believed he could produce enough sales to cover his salary and then some. Unfortunately, he didn't meet his sales goals. When Steve decided to leave the partnership, we had to make closing financial arrangements with him.

Mike obtained a bank loan so Steve could be paid back his money. As for me, I agreed to take stock in MediaComm in lieu of Steve paying back the money he owed to me. It was a good deal that everyone agreed to, even though we would all miss Steve a lot.

Years later, it struck me that maybe Steve—with his many years in radio—had some kind of intuition about the operations at KILJ. I wish that I had had the same intuition if that was the case. It would have saved me a lot heartache and money.

Looking back, I again realize how naïve I was. I had assumed—wrongly—that when people commit to a business deal they do it on a fair, above-board basis. I just couldn't fathom anyone wanting to cheat on his or her taxes, particularly when the money amounted to a fairly substantial sum. Remember, I was the one who declared W-9 forms for the trade outs I received.

I should have realized that the same attitude that made people tell me that I was foolish for declaring the trade outs was the same attitude that led Mike and John to ignore the fact that MediaComm paying back their bank loans was an economic benefit that was taxable as income.

Fred continually dogged Mike and John throughout the years as they continued to let MediaComm pay back the loan while not taking any steps to fix their taxes. "You really do need to take care of this," he continually told them.

One day, after Fred left the building, Mike closed the door. He looked at no one in particular and said, "Sometimes you do what you've got to do."

Meanwhile, Mike's dream of turning MediaComm into a marketing company was falling short—very short. He put a lot of time and energy into the effort. Things weren't going any better on the KILJ side, either. Our advertising sales continued to remain flat. Sales people quit, and those who had some meager successes were ultimately let go as a cost-cutting move. Though some times were better than others and we always had enough money to pay the bills, we still lagged on advertising income.

Mike tried his hand at sales to pick up the slack, but he didn't get too far with it. "Sales just isn't my thing," he would explain. The truth, he told us, was that he really was a marketer.

Consequently, while he continued to run the business end of the radio station, Mike spent more time trying to develop the marketing end of the business than anything else.

Though Mike managed to get a few clients here and there, the MediaComm marketing division proved to be a sieve for money. There was never any more than $25,000 in gross revenue despite Mike's efforts. And this barely covered the expenses in time and production costs. Mike may have thought he was a great marketer, but no one at MediaComm ever saw any evidence of it.

Chapter 7

Personal Changes and a Prelude to a Fall

As we developed our professional lives, big changes also came in my personal life. On December 31, 1993, I was remarried to my current husband Steven Burkhart and changed my name from Norton to Burkhart. It was a wonderful moment for my family and me, a fresh start after the tragedy of my first husband's death. I continued to run my insurance business from the KILJ loft, but was rethinking where I wanted to go in life.

Finally, I made a big decision. Having always worked in business, I decided I wanted more education. I already had my bachelor's, my master's and several industry certifications. Why not take it all a step further and earn a Ph.D.? I consider myself a lifelong learner and this was part of that journey for me.

My husband agreed and supported my decision. I made a few changes to my insurance business, deciding to cut back on work so I would have more time for my education. Obviously, working for a Ph.D. in business was going to take a considerable amount of work, and it was important that I balance my time effectively.

So in early 1995, I moved out of the loft space at KILJ to my home and began working towards my doctorate. Prior to moving into the KILJ building I had had office space uptown. As a silent partner in KILJ, I really didn't need to be on hand for the day-to-day operations. When I had been at the office working my insurance business, I was in touch with the daily pulse at KILJ. I saw Mike on a regular basis, and we had regular meetings that kept everyone informed.

While I was working on my Ph.D. I didn't go to the station very often. The frequency of my visits depended on circumstances, but I would sometimes get reference material from the local library when working on my Ph.D. and go the station to use the copier. I didn't really see any reason to be at the station, and the lack of information coming to me from Mike and John was something I considered a good thing. No news is good news, right?

And besides, even though I'd spent considerable time around the station I was always considered the outsider. I was only there because I put up the money to buy the station. I could feel that I was an outsider from the staff, and it was sometimes even mentioned to me outright. Susie Kuhens made snide remarks about me being there simply because of the money. I think she thought that John should be the only owner, probably because of all the time he'd put into the station. She had mentioned several years earlier that he should have moved on to a bigger market, and I got the impression that KILJ wasn't enough for her.

And again, I naturally assumed that the people I was working with had everyone's best interests at heart and that working towards mutual success benefited everyone. Despite the periodic financial difficulties, we all thought things looked good. My lack of involvement would ultimately come back to haunt me.

Over the years, our regular board meetings had gradually diminished. This didn't seem like a big deal to anyone. For one, I was spending a lot less time at the station, just dropping by periodically to say hello or see how everyone was doing. After I left, I never got another call from Mike or John saying it was time for another board meeting. I assumed that the two of them were talking things over at the office, and that I would be informed should anything major happen.

Not having regular board meetings proved to be a major error. If we had met on a semi-monthly basis, or even quarterly, I might have had a much better handle on what was transpiring. But the reality was I didn't have a clue what was going on. I can't vouch for whether or not anyone else did. If anyone did know that something was going on they sure didn't say anything about it to me. I felt comfortable that things were going as they should have, though. We sent our financials to

Fred Beaver monthly, and though we sometimes had months where we paid the Dennisons late, it was always worked out.

* * *

Before I go any further, let me fill you in on a few things that should have been red flags to me. For one, John always considered himself a radio guy and not a manager. He never wanted to be a manager and didn't have the personality or the talents that it took to run a radio business. No, he knew his place was behind a microphone, reading the news and providing the information that would help listeners know what was happening in the Mt. Pleasant area.

He never took charge during our meetings, never really provided much input and maintained a close personal relationship with the Dennisons. This never struck me as odd; after all, he'd been their employee for many years, and deep friendships certainly can develop under those circumstances.

I never asked myself why on earth a man with John's personality would take such a strange turn and want to become involved as an owner, particularly when he showed no apparent interest in the business side of radio.

I did not take a closer look at how Mike ran the company. Why should I? His initial prospectus was great. My advisors said it looked like a smart investment. Mike certainly was an ambitious man, with a strong background in both the banking industry and marketing. Hadn't he been suggested to me by the Chamber of Commerce?

What no one could have realized, however, was that John's loyalties didn't always line up with his so-called business interests—or, that Mike put on a good show for the world, only to be running a different production when he thought no one was looking.

* * *

Not paying taxes on the loans turned out to be a good thing for Mike—or at least he thought so. In essence he was taking the money as tax-free income, while letting everyone at the station think he and John were making great sacrifices on their behalf. John, being the follower, never questioned Mike's motivation. He figured it would all work itself out.

It was, as things turned out, one of Mike's many schemes.

And as he worked on his schemes, I worked on my Ph.D. for a couple of years. Things were going well with my downsized business, and I was happy in my second marriage. I thought MediaComm was doing all right. My radio was always tuned in to KILJ AM or FM, and life was good. Then life came crashing down around me and things changed forever.

Chapter 8

A Partner Falls

It was late autumn of 1997. It was one of those Midwestern Novembers: bleak and grey and full of barren trees and a desolate landscape. Though Thanksgiving was around the corner, you would be hard pressed to find a roadside stand.

I was working at home, pouring through my books. The work on my doctorate was moving right along. I could see all the effort was definitely going to pay off. What could possible go wrong?

Then the phone rang.

It was Fred Beaver, our Des Moines-based corporate attorney. I hadn't heard from him in quite some time, so his phone call came as something of a surprise. I figured he was checking in with me just to shoot the breeze and catch up on where I was at in my life.

I couldn't have been more wrong.

"Look Dixie," he told me. "I have some bad news."

"What is it?" I asked. This phone call was definitely taking an unexpected switch in tone.

What he said next shook me to my core.

"Listen," he continued, "we've got a problem."

"Problem? What kind of problem?"

"I think Mike Stoffregen has been embezzling money from KILJ."

For a moment I couldn't speak. It seemed impossible! Sure, Mike had his faults like anyone else, but embezzlement? That just couldn't be!

"Yes, that's what I wanted to think," he said. I knew that Fred and Mike were friends from childhood. Their families had been close since they were boys. As a result, it dawned on me, what Fred was telling me wasn't something he would say lightly and without thorough investigation.

"Go on," I said.

Fred, in addition to being MediaComm's attorney, did financial work for us such as working on tax issues. He had spoken at length with Todd Wibben, KILJ's bookkeeper. Todd had found something strange: a KILJ savings account came up with a negative balance! Keep in mind, a checking account whether personal or business can have a negative balance if you overdraw from your funds. But savings accounts, no matter what the situation, always show something in the books. If all the money is taken out, then the account should have a balance of zero. Negative balances for savings accounts were unthinkable for any one or any business!

When Todd found these anomalies in the MediaComm books, he immediately informed Mike about it. Don't worry, he was told. I'll get it fixed. I'll get you the information you need, and we'll take care of this thing right away.

But, as Mike said before, sometimes you do what you've got to do. And time after time he simply didn't come through with the financial information Todd requested. Something was definitely wrong.

"What do you think is happening?" I asked Fred. I could feel a knot in my stomach. It was growing larger and larger as the minutes dragged on.

"What do I think?" Fred replied. "I think Mike has been cooking the books from day one. I think he's been skimming loans from MediaComm and diverting the money into his personal funds."

I couldn't believe it. Why would Mike do such a thing? I thought about the tax situation. *Well Dixie*, I thought to myself, *I don't know why he would do it, but I think Fred is on to something here. Fred may be Mike's long time buddy, but he's also an attorney and wouldn't make statements he couldn't back up with facts.* Despite their relationship, I felt in my bones that Fred was an attorney first, friend second and that rule of law should never be compromised by personal relationships.

He laid out the details for me. It wasn't pretty.

Evidence showed that Mike had set up the financial arrangements of MediaComm from the very beginning to provide himself with an emergency source of funding. Having gone through two divorces, as well as dealing periodically with layoffs when his places of employment shut their doors, Mike knew he needed alternative resources for cash. He also had child support payments to make for three children.

Fred explained the details. When Mike set up the original accounts for MediaComm, he made it so that he could siphon funds into his personal checking account. Essentially, when Mike found himself short of funds the MediaComm account could be tapped for a "loan" of sorts. Rather than have overdrawn checks, MediaComm money would be channeled directly into Mike's account whenever there was a zero balance. It was like overdraft protection for Mike, but instead of coming from the bank, it was coming from MediaComm.

Mike had set up this scheme when MediaComm and the new KILJ ownership was in its infancy, well before we had put our money into the investment. So, from day one, Mike was thinking about doing this. He knew that there was a possibility that he would siphon funds from MediaComm. None of us had a clue that this was going on. We had trusted Mike's business acumen, not realizing what was really going on. He had set things up so that only his signature was required on MediaComm and KILJ checks.

"Is there anything else to this?" I asked.

"Yes," Fred told me. It appeared that Mike had dipped into the corporate till more than once. A close examination of the records indicated that Mike had initially taken money from MediaComm once, then returned almost the entire amount. But for whatever reason, Mike decided to divert more money from the business right into his personal checking.

As things stood, the very founder of MediaComm was stealing money from the rest of us. It was to be the first in a long line of slights against the company from varying sources. But to have the president of the company turning his back on his fellow investors for his own personal gain was a real blow. Until this point, things had gone pretty smoothly with the operation of MediaComm and radio station.

We'd been operating for about six years at this point and as far as I knew, everything was going okay. I knew that Mike and John had not heeded Fred's advice in fixing the tax situation, and I knew that Mike was struggling to get the non-KILJ side of MediaComm off the ground. But does anyone ever want to believe that their business partner is stealing money from them? I was devastated.

But Mike hadn't just stolen money from MediaComm's principal earnings. Things were worse than that. Because MediaComm was a fairly new company, we'd had to take several bank loans in the beginning to take care of various expenses. Since Mike was the business chief at the station, he was in charge of all the paperwork involved. Once each loan was approved, Fred told me, Mike had skimmed money off the top, then doctored the paperwork and deposited the smaller amount into our corporate accounts.

I suppose if Mike had just used the accounts as an overdraft protection that things might have been easier to handle. Maybe he could have justified his actions by saying that he was in trouble financially or that he needed the money to support his kids. But to find that he had thought about doing so long enough in advance to set up the paperwork while MediaComm was in its infancy, and that he had gone further and stolen money from loans to the corporation was just too much.

"Okay, Fred," I said. "What happens next?"

"I think we all better get together," he told me.

The meeting happened about a week or so later. Fred wanted to get all the paperwork together. Plus, everyone wanted some much needed time and space to process the terrible news. We wanted a calm meeting, not a shouting match or angry confrontation.

The warm beauty of the previous week had taken quite a different feel now that December had come. You had the feeling there was some kind of early snow coming on, with a chilly air that manifested itself both in nature and our emotions. No one wanted to be a part of this, yet it was something that had to be taken care of. We couldn't just ignore what was happening and hope it would go away.

Fred, John and I drove to Mike's home in separate cars, arriving pretty much at the same time. Mike let us in and we took seats in the living room. The tension was thick and the mood somber. It was eerie, kind of like the atmosphere in a surreal funeral parlor. We were there, yet we were not there.

We exchanged nervous glances, and then Fred finally began to speak. He spelled out all the charges we were bringing against Mike, one by one. The only item left off the table was Mike's tax scheme.

Mike was quiet and not the least bit confrontational. He knew the evidence against him was overwhelming. "I shouldn't have done it," he mumbled over and over. That wasn't really a confession, but it certainly was no denial. Finally, after what seemed like an eternity, Fred finished up.

A silence hung over the room.

Mike was apologetic and seemed very humble. The man I knew, the go-getter who had put together a terrific business proposal, now seemed shrunken. If the floor could have opened up and swallowed him, I think Mike would have been eternally grateful.

There was an obvious question that had to be answered: Now, what do we do?

I spoke up. "I think you should turn in all your stock," I said. "And I think you should leave Mt. Pleasant."

When we left, it seemed like everyone was in a state of shock. It was like a bad dream that we couldn't wake up from. Here was our colleague, our friend, reduced to a shattered individual thanks to his own dishonesty. We couldn't speak. There was nothing anyone could say.

Though we were all hurting, I think Fred took Mike's betrayal the hardest. In the many years he had been friends with Mike, Fred had developed a deep and trusting relationship. Now, after a matter of minutes, their many years together had suddenly vanished.

Though the general terms were agreed to at this meeting, there was still some legal wrapping up that would be necessary before making our final agreement with Mike. Of course, he never came back to the station.

Mike's theft from the station was news in the town of Mt. Pleasant. Though the radio station's business was never really open to the public, things get around a small town pretty quickly. Everyone had been glad that the station was staying in local hands when the Dennisons sold it and to have one of those local owners, a man who had held prominent positions in the local business community, turn out to be a thief was a topic of gossip. But the story the public saw was rarely the whole story, and what was let out was often spun by one of the interested parties to garner a better public image.

I wasn't really worried about the public perception at this point, though. I was worried about one of my partners stealing money from MediaComm and how we were going to recover from that. It was a hard ending to a year that, up until that point, had gone well.

At last 1997 was coming to a close. I could only hope that the New Year would be a better one for MediaComm, KILJ, my colleagues and me.

Though I was still considered a silent partner, my personal attorney at the time, Randy McAllister, advised me to become more actively involved in the business on a day-to-day basis so I could see what was going on. After the fiasco with Mike, Randy felt it was important that I see exactly what was going on at the station. It seemed a smart move to me as well.

That morning I went into Mike's office to clean it out. I was more than a little shocked at what I found. There were still bills that needed to be paid. What's more, Mike's desk was filled with checks we had already written to settle some of those bills!

It was unbelievable, yet in light of what we had just gone through, I guess I wasn't that shocked at the mess. I took control of the accounts receivable and calculated that we owed more than $120,000 to various parties. I would work to reduce that number over the next several years and made good progress, reducing the $120,000 to under $20,000. In addition, I was able to pay off much of the bank loan we had taken to buy Steve out when he left; there was only $35,000 left due on the loan by the time I last worked at MediaComm. But bigger problems were looming just over the horizon, and Mike's sins would be eclipsed by the sins of others.

CHAPTER 9

A STRANGE PROPOSAL AND GOODBYE TO MIKE

Though I was now in the office in a much different capacity, the staff treated me with respect. They knew I was coming in to help make things right again, and everyone wanted to make sure KILJ would get back on track. After all, we were a community radio station, operating in our small niche market. We didn't have time to fool around.

I continued working, when an unannounced visitor came into my office. I looked up to see John standing in front of me. Well, why not? He and I were still partners. We had to continue our working relationship, regardless of what Mike had done.

John didn't even bother to say "hello" or something like, "Can I talk to you for a minute?" No, he was a man with a mission this morning. "Dixie," he said abruptly, "how much will it take to buy you out?"

Boy, was I surprised! John never liked the duties that came with ownership and performed them with great reluctance. His offer to buy me out wouldn't have been unwelcome if he'd had the money to pay me a reasonable sum.

"Look John," I replied. "If I had put my money into just about any other business I could have doubled it by now."

He didn't respond.

"If you want to buy me out, then I want $350,000."

He didn't comment.

Around this time, I asked that I be made a Class A stockholder. Like John, I wanted to be an A Class owner with majority voting rights because I was working in the business every day, and I also had more money in the business than anyone. John said he wouldn't go along with it. There was no way he was going to relinquish the control he had.

Maybe it was a blessing that John didn't allow me to become a Class A stockholder; otherwise I may have had to guarantee the loans to the Dennisons and to the banks. Though if I had full voting we probably never would've ended up in court. I would have had more control over what happened to the company.

My hopes for a happy new year were quickly dashed. Rather than a great investment, KILJ had turned into a migraine of seemingly epic proportions.

After that strange encounter, John and I continued as if nothing had been said between the two of us. He continued reading the news; I continued to mop up the mess Mike had left behind. Then John and I had another discussion.

Since he and I were now the only board members, he pointed out, what was the point of having regular meetings? If we had anything to discuss relating to the station operations and ownership, we could just talk in our offices or even in the hallway. Why be so formal, when it was so much easier to make things casual?

In retrospect, agreeing to this was a big mistake. No matter how big or small your company board is, you *must* have formal meetings that include taking of notes about what is discussed. Those meeting minutes provide a very public and ultimately invaluable record of what is said. It's just good business sense to make things official, rather than make important decisions in simple hallway conversations. What's more, if there're any legal difficulties encountered, those meeting minutes can provide important documentation.

But in my case, as I was to discover soon enough, it really didn't matter whether John and I carried out our discussions formally or informally. As I'd learned the hard way already, when you're dealing with dishonest people, facts really don't matter.

* * *

The final wrap-up with Mike was held in March of 1998. As things turned out, McAllister offered the conference room at his law office for that final discussion. That was fine with everyone. At last we could put the matter behind us once and for all, then move forward with business.

Fred represented everyone at MediaComm/KILJ, while Mike's attorney was Mary Anne Brown. Ultimately, Mike's choice in legal representation had deeply ironic repercussions for my own troubles with the station, though obviously there was no way I could have known that at the time.

I arranged to meet Fred at the KILJ building before the meeting so we could go together in the same car. Though John and I were the majority stockholders now that Mike was gone, John had no intention of attending this final meeting. That was totally in character, since he hadn't liked his management role from the start. He didn't have much to say before Fred and I left. As we drove off, another staff member heard John mutter, "Well, there goes Fred and Dixie, off to do battle. I should go with them . . . but I just can't." John had no guts for confrontation. Anything that required a little backbone he couldn't do.

We arrived at McAllister's office and were led to the conference room. Everyone took their seats at the table—Fred, Randy and I on one side, Mike and Mary Anne Brown on the other. Fred had certainly done his homework. A large sheaf of papers emerged from his briefcase as he and Brown began to hash out what would be involved in officially separating Mike from MediaComm.

I was amazed at the amount of legal work that went into the preparation. Though Mike clearly was guilty of embezzlement, Brown wanted to get her client the best deal she could. Throughout the negotiations, she would consider what Fred offered, then huddle with Mike. Periodically, the two of them would get up from the table and go into the hallway where they could have a private conference. It made sense though, since what was transpiring in the room would be a matter of public record. With Mike's reputation seemingly destroyed, Brown was determined to salvage anything she possibly could.

As for me, I felt a mixture of anger, resentment and deep disappointment. In my mind's eye, I flashed back to that Alive After Five event. It seemed like yesterday when I first met Mike. He was so animated, so eager . . . and so forthright. I turned over the pieces of that night in my head. Was there something—anything—in his behavior that I should have seen that could have served as a warning sign? I'd been recommended to meet with him by the Mt. Pleasant Chamber of Commerce, so obviously he was considered trustworthy by people I knew were responsible in their own business dealings. What's more, I thought, Mike and I had something in common during that first meeting. We both wanted to do something with the potential to bring revenue to our town, while succeeding in an exciting new venture ourselves.

No, I told myself, *no. There was nothing I could have seen, nothing that would have possibly foreshadowed what Mike was up to.* As I've said before, who wants to enter into a business deal thinking that a potential partner is actually a dishonest individual?

Finally, after Fred and Brown had spent the afternoon seesawing back and forth, a deal was agreed on. Mike would get credit for his initial $125,000 in stock. He also agreed to pay back all the money he had stolen that was still outstanding which amounted to $79,600. In addition to that, he had to pay ten percent interest on the sum, for a grand total of $87,560. As further protection for MediaComm interests, Mike agreed he could not bail on us by declaring bankruptcy for at least one year. The final legal document stated that Mike was considered guilty in a judgment by confession, which meant that he was publicly stating he had wronged his partners and employees at KILJ and MediaComm.

There was also the matter of the loan I had given to Mike when we first put our investment capital together. That loan was guaranteed by MediaComm and so would become a debt to the company.

Leaving town was a no-brainer for Mike. Obviously, Mike had no desire to hang around Mt. Pleasant.

And I, for one, was grateful Fred had made sure MediaComm would cover my loan to Mike. Though our former partner had taken us for a ride and then some, at least I was going to be getting back the money I'd provided him.

Of course, I thought that would be an easy process. I didn't realize what I was up against. Nor did I think I would ever have to deal with Mike Stoffregen ever again.

Chapter 10

Thoughts of Selling Out and the Trouble Begins

So there we were. Mike was gone for good and other than our odd conversation shortly after the beginning of the year, John and I seemed to have a fairly good working relationship. Yet, still there were problems to be faced in the daily operations, let alone the fallout from Mike's underhanded dealings. One of those challenges was something neither John nor I could have predicted.

In the late 1990s, radio was really starting to change. With the rise of syndication, it became infinitely cheaper for broadcast outlets to pay for popular national radio shows rather than hire local professionals as on-air talent. It seemed like the only things you couldn't get from the large syndicates were weather and traffic reports, though you never knew!

Even though we were a small market niche station, we still felt the financial pinch that bigger outlets were receiving in cities like Burlington and Des Moines. More money had to be saved, which meant more jobs were combined as radio stations continued to lay off their employees.

Our sales staff, never a success at KILJ as I said before, was completely eliminated. Even the long-time sales staffer hired many years before by the Dennisons had to be let go. It came down to John and me sitting in my office one day, divvying up the accounts, deciding which of us would try to sell advertising to what area or business.

Because of my background in the insurance and financial industries, I told John those were markets I didn't want to take. I felt there could be potential conflict of interest. Looking back, again I see that I was foolish to adhere to what we had learned as school children, that "honesty is the best policy." While it certainly is best practice (and really the only moral choice!) to be honest in your business dealings, I was operating in a way that would prove to be in total opposite to

Kuhens, his wife, Paul and Joyce Dennison and ultimately, the legal system.

I felt uncomfortable selling to industries where I thought there would be conflict of interest. I was an insurance agent and for me to go to other insurance professionals and try to sell advertising would have been awkward. It turned out, though, that the radio business is a lot looser than the insurance business or any other that I had seen to that point. There were not set prices for advertising like you might think there would be. It was pretty much an on-the-spot negotiation when trying to get someone to advertise on radio, and least at our station, and prices were as flexible as the people selling the advertising.

John had new problems. Remember that $70,000 loan he had taken to show his "sacrifice" to employees? When Mike left, the money owed from that loan was absorbed into the agreement he signed. But like Mike had done before he was caught embezzling, John had also skipped paying taxes on his $70,000. It seemed like he was following Mike's example, using the loan money as a way of avoiding taxes. Somehow, John had dragged out the process a lot further than Mike ever had, even though Fred Beaver had given him several options and opportunities to take care of the problem. It could have been as simple as paying the taxes on the loan, which would have been much cheaper than an IRS audit.

Finally, desperate to pay off his debt, John turned to his old friends, Paul and Joyce. I don't know what transpired; all I know is that they wrote him a check and suddenly the loan was no longer hanging over John's head. It made no sense whatsoever, at least from a business perspective. Why on earth would someone you were theoretically buying a business from loan you money to pay off a loan? Particularly a personal loan directly related to your salary at the business you were buying?

While on paper, it is a confounding way to operate, the reality was that John always had this kind of relationship with Paul Dennison. John was a follower, not a leader and liked his position. He *did* love working in radio and the Dennisons gave him that opportunity. Since he'd first come to the station as a teenager, John had relied on the Dennisons and once again he came to them. Once again, they happily assisted.

I couldn't understand it! Why didn't John take out a W-9 as Fred originally suggested, or go with a payroll deduction? It made no sense to pay off one loan (particularly a salary and business related loan!) by going further into debt. What's more, the debt was being taken care of by his former employers, the very people John had bought the radio station from! The whole situation reminded me of a little kid who tries to start a lemonade stand to earn some money; if the lemonade doesn't sell then the kid runs right back to mommy and daddy to collect his weekly allowance.

I'd had enough experience running my own business, plus studying how corporations are run in my doctoral work to know that something wasn't right about the situation. Was this another secret like the one Mike had been hiding? Or was this something deeper than a "mere" embezzlement?

I couldn't know at the time, and so I didn't object to what was going on between John and the Dennisons. We had other problems to worry about.

In 2001, the market was not good for radio advertising. New media was taking away revenues and we were hit like every other station. We'd already let our advertising staff go and were doing it ourselves. Though we were doing okay and treading water, John and I thought at this point about selling the radio station.

We figured that if we could get some good money for it at that point, then we could avoid any further slumps in the market. We'd owned the station for a decade and things hadn't gone well for the few years leading up to this point, with Mike's embezzlement and the decline in the market.

John and I contacted a broker we knew and let it be known that we were interested in selling the station if the price was right. We attracted a few parties interested in the station, but only one of them turned out to be serious in their inquiries.

They came to the station to take a look at it, and we even met with them and the Dennisons together. Paul Dennison was not opposed to the idea of us selling the station at this time, and neither was I. If the suitors had offered me a decent amount for my stock, I would gladly have sold.

Unfortunately, the offer we received was not what we were looking for. The offer would have left us breaking even once we'd paid all of our debts to the Dennisons and the banks. So, we turned it down.

It was around this time that things got even stranger than they had been up to that point. Paul Dennison approached John and me about employment selling ads for us. This was the man MediaComm was purchasing the station from, the one who had allowed us to finance the $1 million needed to purchase the station beyond the $500,000 we raised and he was coming to us for employment. We offered to let him sell some of our more difficult accounts, and he confirmed that he'd had problems with them when he was owner of the station. Ultimately, he didn't come to work at the station and things stayed as they had been for the next couple of years: MediaComm struggling to make payments on a rigid schedule, but enough money to cover what we needed.

Beginning in 2003, my problems would start down a slippery slope, the end of which would see my relationships with my remaining partners crumble and my ownership of KILJ disappear.

Despite problems we'd had with Mike and the tax situation with John, I still felt that MediaComm and its main asset, KILJ, were viable and worth saving. I'd entertained the idea of selling, but when that didn't work I committed myself to working at the station and doing my best to make it succeed.

I felt that part of the problem we'd had was our commitment to paying so many partners an owner's salary. At one point we'd had Mike, Steve and John collecting as owners, and that was radically different from the minimalist operation Paul Dennison had run, where his deals with advertisers covered many of his personal expenses and he took a minimal salary.

Now that Mike and Steve were out of the picture, I felt we could still save the station, despite our staff cuts and tough advertising market. We just needed to get past the problems of our past.

I found out soon enough that our real problems were smack dab in front of us and their names were John Kuhens and the Dennisons.

John deliberately withheld payments to the Dennisons in May and June of 2003, successfully creating a default. Because of that, the Dennisons filed a request with the bank in May to have the KILJ stock transferred back to them because of the default on the loan. Unbeknownst to me, John signed that paperwork and agreed to the proposed transfer of the stock. He never told me about doing this and we never had a meeting or even discussed the possibility of doing so. John signed the paperwork on May 20, 2003, even before the May payment to Dennison was due. John's plan of withholding payments worked, and we were hit with a notice to cure the default on the payments for May and June.

In the notice of default to MediaComm, the Dennisons requested not only the payments for May and June, but for July as well, which wasn't even due yet. The Dennisons were the financiers in the business transaction between themselves and MediaComm. They essentially agreed to take payments for the radio station and as collateral, MediaComm agreed to put the KILJ stock in escrow with the local bank.

Well, MediaComm missed payments to the Dennisons in May and June because of John, and the Dennisons requested that the shares be released to them as a result. The bank refused to release the stock, and so the Dennisons filed suit. The bank verbally refused to do so and so Paul filed suit asking the courts to release the stock. But in between Paul Dennison's first request that the shares be released and any court action, all hell broke loose at the station.

As bad as Mike's transgressions were against the station, there was a far more insidious plot building right under my nose. Despite the fact that I was spending more time at the station on the advice of my attorney, John Kuhens was now the president and was taking care of the day-to-day operations. I was working as an advertising sales person, trying to bring some much-needed revenue into KILJ and MediaComm.

I always knew that John wasn't very interested in the duties that came with being a co-owner in MediaComm. It was obvious that he much preferred being the on-air personality and that he would almost have rather stayed that way instead of becoming an owner. I had a pretty good relationship with John, but I made a few mistakes in the way I let the radio station operate.

When Mike left the station in 1997, we didn't replace him on the board of directors. The MediaComm by-laws stated that we were to have three members on the board of directors at all times, two of which were to represent Class A stockholders. The by-laws also stated that we were to have annual meetings with all of the shareholders invited and that the meetings had to be formally announced in advance, with a written roster of all shareholders and an agenda.

My lack of insistence on the formality of how we ran things was about to cost me a lot of time, money and would rid me of much of the naiveté that I was still operating under, even after the incident with Mike Stoffregen. Because we didn't have regular meetings things were allowed to get further out of hand and culminated in a major blowout just a couple of months after Paul Dennison first requested a transfer of shares from the bank. John had insisted that we could just discuss things on a casual basis rather than having formal meetings. John had said he didn't want to have a bunch of meetings.

Chapter 11

The Coup

In August 2003, I sat at my desk on the main floor of the KILJ building. I was working on some advertising sales and other paperwork; just another normal day at the office. Suddenly, I was interrupted.

It was Susie Kuhen, John's wife. She told me I was wanted downstairs in John's office, and that I had to come immediately. Okay, I told her. I had no idea what was going on. But in my bones I knew something strange was about to happen. Susie didn't bust into my office without a good reason!

When I got to John's office, I was greeted by a strange sight. There he was, my partner, sitting on a stepstool of all things, perched high above his desk. Why on earth was he sitting on a stepstool rather than his regular desk chair? It made no sense. It struck me that John had inadvertently made himself look like a toad sitting on a rock.

I sat down on the couch in John's office. Susie took a seat next to me. A moment later Paul Dennison entered the office and sat down. This did not look good. Something clearly was about to come down, with yours truly on the receiving end!

Rather than say something like, "Let's call this meeting to order," John surprised me with his totally unprofessional behavior. "That's it!" he exclaimed. "I can't take it anymore! I can't take it physically, financially, emotionally. Call me a quitter if you want to, but I'm a realist."

So, that's what was happening! John wanted out. That was no surprise. As I've said, John was never cut out for the management side of the business. Still, I felt sick to my stomach. I had no idea where any of this was going, but it sure seemed like I was on the verge of disaster.

With the difficulties we'd had in advertising, Mike's betrayal and the need to release our advertising staff, the Media-Comm journey had not been an easy one. It turned out to be too much for John, who had no inclination to be a manager in the first place. Now, he was announcing, without any formal notification, that he wanted out of the ownership business. Good thing his good buddy, Paul Dennison was standing by to pick him up out of his hardship.

Having already sued the bank to get the KILJ stock released to him, it seemed now that Paul was orchestrating things behind the scenes in order to assure that he would regain control of the station. How I had ever gotten to this point was beyond me. I instantly regretted the day I ever heard of KILJ.

Dennison was the next to speak. He wanted to know if there were enough funds to cover the current payment due him. Of course there were, and even if we didn't have the funds, I could pay them with my personal funds. It's not as if I hadn't done that before! Surely everyone in the room knew that I had loaned money to John, Mike and Steve not that long ago.

"That's not good enough," said Paul. I had no idea what he meant. I knew we had enough for two month's payments in MediaComm's accounts and there would be more coming if my theory about property tax payments proved to be true.

When I'd examined MediaComm's books, I'd noticed that at times in the past, MediaComm had paid property taxes on some of the empty lots around the station's buildings. Because we didn't own these lots, it wasn't right that we paid the property taxes. If we were able to recoup that money, we could pay Dennison his money easily. Dennison had pulled another fast one.

It seemed that John was dead set on giving the station back to the Dennisons and Paul was dead set on taking it. *It wouldn't be that easy*, I thought as I sat there in John's office. The stock was being held by the bank and so John would have to somehow get the board of directors, himself and me to vote to transfer the FCC license over to Paul. But there was no way I was doing that and John knew it. That didn't stop him, though, and it turned out he'd already thought of that.

Why do you think his wife and the former owner were in the room?

This entire meeting had clearly been orchestrated in an attempt to throw me off guard, so John and Paul could intimidate me into submission. Well, they weren't going to get away with anything that easily!

With the facts on my side—I firmly believed—this blatantly illegal move would easily be overruled by me, regardless of who held what percentage of the voting. Even John's sixty percent over my forty percent couldn't outweigh that we could easily cover the payments to the Dennisons. And Paul, who was no longer the owner or supposedly active in the KILJ operations, did not have a say in the matter. John needed to have unanimous approval from the board (that means me) to move forward.

I knew that from their long relationship, John always looked up to and followed whatever the Dennisons did. My gut feeling was that the three of them, along with Susie, had hashed out this plan and were doing everything they could to intimidate me. What was *she* doing there? Susie had no legal interest in the station, other than the fact that her husband was an owner and member of the board. Something ugly was definitely afoot.

Okay, I thought. You people want to play hardball? Well, don't try and sneak a fastball past this batter.

I decided that a call should be immediately placed to Fred Beaver, our corporate attorney. If anybody could settle this argument, I knew that he was the man. He'd been looking out for everyone's best interests in a fair and ethical manner from day one. I was sure he'd agree with me; what was transpiring was in strict violation of the legal agreement everyone in the room had signed more than a decade before.

Paul, who was the only Dennison in attendance during what would turn out to be a two-part meeting, left for our phone call with Fred. Susie stayed in the room and later, after we took a lunch break, Paul returned with Joyce.

Over the phone, Fred confirmed my feelings to the letter. John's attempt to transfer ownership back to Paul was considered a major change to the station and there had to be a unanimous vote in order for it to pass. John could not get rid of me and go back with the Dennisons without my consent. I knew John and his confederates wouldn't like the situation and would probably try something else down the road. However, for the moment I had them. Facts are facts, particularly when put down in a legal agreement. They couldn't deny what they had signed with me when we all bought into the station!

After we were done with Fred, John and I took a lunch break. He wasn't happy and I knew he was ready to tell the Dennisons what had just transpired—kind of like a whiney schoolyard brat telling the teacher on another kid he felt had wronged him. When our lunch break finally ended, around one o'clock, we went back into the room for a second round. While I knew they weren't going to give up this fight, Fred's strict admonition that everyone stick to the agreement weighed strongly in my favor.

What happened next was another complete surprise. It turned out that John and the Dennisons had an alternative plan in case I wasn't willing to play ball. John motioned that Susie be placed on the board for KILJ. I couldn't believe it. This just couldn't be happening. Not only was it unethical and unscrupulous, it was totally illegal!

Like that bull in the china shop, smashing everything in sight, John roared onward. He called for a vote to hand KILJ back to the Dennisons. The outcome was a given. With his sixty percent and my forty percent, I would clearly be outvoted. However, our corporate documents stated that if a substantial change was made it had to be unanimous among the board members. It was illegal on all counts.

All in favor? John. All against? Dixie. Motion carries and Susie is now on the board. And to hell with anything we had legally signed on to years ago. To paraphrase Forrest Gump, *unscrupulous is as unscrupulous does.*

You see, Susie couldn't legally be appointed to the board of directors for two reasons. First, new members to the board had to be voted in by a majority of the directors. Since there were only two members of the board, then a majority would have to be the both of us. There's more on that later. Second, according to the by-laws, even though special meetings of the board can be called by the board of directors or by "holders of not less than ten percent of shares," it also requires that those meetings be announced to non-voting shareholders and that notice be given to them so that they can attend the meetings.

At the time of the meeting, we did have non-voting shareholders and they were not given notice. Also, the by-laws state in Article Two, section three that, "Written notice stating the place, date, hour and the object of the shareholder meeting shall be given to each shareholder not less than ten nor more than sixty days before the date of the meeting. The notice shall be delivered by mail or personally at the direction of the President of the Corporation."

As you can imagine, no notice was delivered to me prior to the meeting telling what the object of the meeting was. If it had been you can imagine that I would have been a little more prepared to defend my position than I was on that day in August. Also, since John was the president of the corporation, notice of the meeting would have had to have been given at his direction. Since he was planning on taking KILJ out from under MediaComm to give back to the Kuhens, he had no incentive whatsoever to follow the dictates of the by-laws—but back to the meeting.

Now that Susie was installed, the battle increased to a two against one fight, and an unfair fight at that! A new motion was made. The FCC license and the KILJ stock would be handed over to the Dennisons, who would now be handling all operations for KILJ under what's called a time brokerage agreement. The time brokerage agreement gave Paul Dennison control over all available broadcast time allotted to KILJ by the FCC, which was essentially control over the entire station. He didn't have the right to hire and fire people and do some other things, but if you have control over the entire revenue producing asset of a radio station—its air time—then you effectively control the whole thing.

John and Susie voted in favor, and of course I voted against it. Remember how every major decision about the station had to be approved by all the board members? Well, I guess that fact no longer mattered, either.

Now, John couldn't just give the shares of KILJ back to the Dennisons; it's a lot more complicated than that. The shares were being held in escrow at the US Bank NA, and they refused to transfer the stock until the issue was decided in court. And even after the transfer of the stock was complete, the FCC license still had to be transferred.

The reason he had to sue the bank to release the stock was because the bank refused his verbal request to do so. So, until that was decided in court, MediaComm—in the form of John and Susie—could only attempt to allow Dennison to take control under the time brokerage agreement that is included in the FCC paperwork. But the FCC license couldn't be transferred until the stock was transferred and the station was put up for auction, both of which would take place months later. The time brokerage agreement, however, would be called into question—but again, more on that later.

I could see I was overpowered and beaten down. The Dennisons and the Kuhens had developed their scheme perfectly, albeit less than legally. And there I was, the only one left in the room who wanted to live up to what Mike, John and I had all said should be done in the first place. Mike was the first to pull something; now—it seemed to me—John was taking his turn. What's more, his old pals, the Dennisons, were leading him perfectly by the nose.

It was such a ridiculous scene: John perched on the stepstool like some low-level poobah, Susie on the couch with me, and the Dennisons playing the dual role of Lord High Poobahs-in-Chief off to the side. That left me as the unwilling dupe to their nefarious plot. Immediately following the meeting, John would sign FCC paperwork to begin the transaction process. To think that he and the Dennisons weren't in cahoots, but just happened to have FCC paperwork ready is just ridiculous. Who just walks around with FCC paperwork?

Joyce Dennison was still there sanctimonious as one could be considering the circumstances. She turned, and in her most condescending tone, burst out, "Well, at least you still have your house. We know people who have lost millions."

What on earth was she thinking? Her snide remark had nothing to do with business, and certainly nothing to do with me! Whether they liked it or not, I was still a member of the board, still a co-owner of the station and still had the law on my side! And again, to my surprise, it turned out Joyce had more to say.

"And at least you didn't get a letter in the mail, like we did when we lost our money in the dairy!"

This was a surreal moment. She was in the process of stealing my business, and yet she felt it necessary to tell me that I was fortunate to have a place to live. *Well, too darn bad!* I thought. They were the ones who had invested in a dairy and it was no concern of mine when it failed. And what's more, it didn't matter how they were informed about the dairy going belly up. That certainly didn't mean they had the right to bulldoze me, or anyone else in any other business deal.

Well, obviously none of that mattered. As far as the majority of people in the room were concerned, the Dennisons were now in charge, Susie was on the board and Dixie was a disgruntled minority of one. There was no way in the world I was going to stick around for more of their battering. The meeting thankfully came to an end and I stormed back upstairs to my office. But before I left, I demanded that John provide minutes of the meeting.

I was furious, so mad and so angry I couldn't see straight. Who did these people think they were that they could change the rules as they pleased? I stormed into my office. There was no point in my staying. I might be an owner on paper, but that didn't matter at the moment. I threw my things into a bag, cleaning out my belongings from the office, and briskly walked out the door. I assume my actions were much to the delight of the hanging party downstairs!

I turned over the situation in my mind. John and Susie had voted to hand over the radio station to the Dennisons. I technically didn't own the radio station; my stock was in the parent company, MediaComm. But MediaComm *was* KILJ! In essence, the Kuhens gutted the corporation by giving its only source of income back to the former owners. I was a partner in the corporation, but now my stock was worthless in the eyes of everyone else involved in this outfit.

Chapter 12

The Fight Begins

I immediately drove home, got on the phone and called Fred for our second conversation of the day—this time just one to one. I spilled out the details, moment by moment, to a very shocked man at the other end of the line. As usual, his advice was sound. Every last move in that meeting was entirely out of line and completely illegal according to the original contract. Nothing had changed in that document, other than tightly written addendums when it came to loan matters.

Fred asked me to send him minutes of the meeting. I was insistent that we keep minutes at the meeting, otherwise they wouldn't have been written up. Looking it over, he denounced the whole shambles, calling the gathering a "purported meeting." The minutes of the meeting were less than all encompassing when they were delivered. But their curtness gives a good indication of how cold the whole thing had been. The minutes read as follows:

"The MediaComm board of directors held a board meeting August 18th, 2003 at one thirty-seven p.m. (The record doesn't mention the fact that Paul Dennison was there for the morning session or that both the Dennisons were at the afternoon session—or that we had two meetings at all) at KILJ studios. A phone conference was held with corporate (attorney) Fred Beaver concerning corporate laws and the transfer of ownership of the KILJ AM & FM stations (again, no mention that Fred Beaver was completely against the idea).

"President John Kuhens named Mary Susanna Kuhens (Susie) to the board of directors. The board then voted on a transfer of ownership agreement from Paul Dennison and Joyce Dennison. John and Susie voted in favor of the transfer with Dixie Burkhart casting a vote of no (I'll say). The measure passed. John Kuhens then proceeded to sign the agreement. The meeting was then adjourned at two ten p.m."

So, according to the minutes of the meeting, in the span of thirty-three minutes, a new director had been added to the board and the Dennisons were allowed to take over under the Time Brokerage agreement in the FCC paperwork, even though the license itself would not be transferred until after the injunction hearing and an auctioning of the station. Fortunately for me, the KILJ stock could not be transferred yet, even though John had secretly signed an agreement to transfer the stock in May. As I said before, the bank wasn't allowing it.

Upon reading the minutes of the meeting, Fred Beaver immediately sent a letter via fax and post mail to John, stating in part, "Please be advised that the action reflected in those minutes is contrary to the advice I gave earlier in the day during a telephone conference among Mrs. Burkhart, you and me. You also must be aware that the appointment of Mrs. Kuhens as a director by you in your capacity as president of MediaComm, Inc. is ineffective and contrary to section ten of Article Three of the MediaComm by-laws."

Now, section ten of Article Three of the by-laws, states, "Any vacancies on the board of directors may be filled by the affirmative voted of the *majority* of the remaining directors. Any director so elected shall serve the remaining term of the director being replaced." Well, clearly, what John had done did not involve a majority of the directors of MediaComm since there were only two of us and a majority of two isn't one. Part of the problem is that we had been in violation of our own by-laws by not replacing Mike Stoffregen when he resigned. Our by-laws required that MediaComm have three directors.

Fred continued on in his letter, pointing out each article and section of the MediaComm by-laws that had been violated. He also stated that not only had corporate agreements been broken, but also the attempted transfer of ownership to the Dennisons was in flagrant violation of Iowa laws. ". . . [Y]ou are not the corporate authorizer whatsoever to act upon Media-Comm's behalf when you signed and attempted to enter into the agreement referred to in the minutes," he firmly stated.

He advised that appropriate actions—such as declaring what had happened that day null and void—must be completed and soon. He closed by saying, ". . . be advised that further reliance upon the agreement or upon the actions purportedly taken or the authority purportedly granted at the meeting would in my opinion be legally inappropriate and ineffective."

Legally inappropriate and ineffective; that pretty much sums up the entire meeting if you ask me. In addition to being illegal under MediaComm's by-laws, John's actions had been illegal under Section 490.1202(1) and (2) of the Code of Iowa. Those sections state that, "A sale, lease, exchange or other disposition of assets, other than a disposition described in section 490.1201 (which is in the usual and regular course of business), requires approval of the corporation's shareholders if the disposition would leave the corporation without a significant continuing business activity."

I would say that divesting MediaComm of its only money-making asset, KILJ, would fall under those sections. I mean, after John gave away KILJ the only means of income was the building that KILJ was housed in, and even that didn't last. But, more on that later.

I wanted to make sure my feelings were recorded on paper following the meeting, and so I also wrote a letter that day to John Kuhens stating that I believed we had enough money to cover the thirty-day notice of right to cure default submitted by Paul Dennison. The right to default was something Dennison had every legal right to file. But we also had a right to respond with the funds he was requesting (see appendix).

The FCC transfer paperwork was what was signed at the meeting. The stock transfer paperwork had been done in May, but not a lot could be done for some time.

In the weeks following the meeting I stayed away from the station until I could decide what to do. It was at this time that I hired legal counsel in the form of Mike Noyes, an attorney from Davenport. Fred himself told me that he couldn't represent me any further in this matter since he had worked as corporate attorney and had a conflict of interest. After all, he was the MediaComm attorney and legally John and I were the owners. He couldn't play favorites should this fray move into a courtroom—which seemed to be a logical step farther down the road should we be unable to resolve the situation.

Davenport is about ninety miles from Mt. Pleasant, a safe enough distance from the chain of connections within Mt. Pleasant. It was also the hometown of my current husband. I made an appointment with Noyes and within a week or so was sitting in his office. I had a mountain of paperwork to show him, including the original prospectus, the contract between the Dennisons, Mike Stoffregen, John Kuhens and me, along with minutes from our board meetings (that is, when we had official meetings with someone taking the minutes!), and other ancillary materials. I had picked up most of this material from my personal attorney in Mt. Pleasant, Randy McAllister.

If you're ever in this kind of situation (and I hope you never are!), paperwork is vital. You need to show that people signed agreements, that corporate boards introduced and approved of various business items and all actions made by the company are beyond reproach—in other words, the facts. In my case, as I was ultimately to learn the hard way, even facts don't necessarily hold up when you're faced by different levels of corrupt people who have no boundaries for unscrupulous behavior. But still, I can't recommend strongly enough that you have it all there in black and white, every contract, every letter or fax, every e-mail printed out, meeting minutes and notes, even items jotted down on scraps of paper. Hopefully in your situation the facts *will* make a difference!

Noyes and I spread out the paperwork on his desk and he poured through it intently. Periodically, he would make a note or scribble something on a legal pad. I watched with great interest. His body language told me that he was finding exactly the items I needed to prevent the Dennisons from taking away KILJ.

"Well, Dixie," he said at last, "what they've done is obviously illegal. They didn't accept your payments, they claimed the station owed three payments to the Dennisons when you only owed two and they violated a lot of their own rules."

"Do you think we can fix everything?" I asked.

Noyes answered me directly and firmly. "I think we can get things back to the way they were," he replied.

That sounded good to me.

Getting things back to the way they were. It was a nice thought when I had it, but both Noyes and I realized it might be easier said than done. After all, at this point our backs were to the wall. Both the Dennisons and the Kuhens had acted illegally, so it was obvious they had no scruples when it came to their business dealings. Would that change when our battle came to a head in the legal system? That was hard to say, though experience had taught me that nothing was beneath these people. It was obvious that they had aided and abetted to this point. The Dennisons hadn't just dropped by in August and happened to have the FCC documents to sign.

I returned to the station after several weeks because I had been notified by my attorney that Dennison had gone home. I returned to find that the funds we'd previously had earmarked in MediaComm's accounts were gone. John had used them to pay other expenses, necessary expenses, but still not the Dennisons. It was something John seemed to do intentionally: he took money that he knew should have gone to the Dennisons and made sure it went elsewhere.

At this time I had checks written to myself to cover the loans I had made to Mike. MediaComm had been made a guarantor, and I felt it was completely within my rights to have the money paid to me. I can tell you that Paul Dennison didn't like that. John also signed the checks, and he was reimbursed $5,000 for having used his personal funds to make some repairs at the station.

In October, Paul decided to call a kitchen-table conference of sorts. He invited John and me over to his house from the station. We entered his home and sat in his kitchen as Joyce pretended to be busy in the kitchen.

Dennison looked at the both of us and said, "We've all spent a lot of money on attorney's fees, we can take care of all this."

His proposal was simple: we would cede control of the station back to him, in the form of the KILJ stock, and he would give us both jobs. Then, if he and Joyce decided to sell the station down the road, John and I would get a piece of any profits there might be.

I looked at Paul and I said, "You're trying to steal it," and I got up from the table and went back to the radio station. I was there maybe five minutes and John was there for another ten before heading toward town. It was ridiculous for Dennison to be offering me employment. I wasn't an employee, I was the owner.

Unfortunately, I would have to see Paul again, and soon. Because he had sued the bank and MediaComm all the way back in May to try and force a stock transfer because of default, John and I were forced to go to the Iowa City branch of Vernon Squires' (Dennison's attorney) firm, which was based in Cedar Rapids to be deposed for the suit. Joyce was so bored that she left early to go visit a friend. So, how did Paul get a ride home? With John. It was insane that a man—John—who was supposed to be the president of MediaComm was just throwing it all down the river and not thinking twice about it.

On December 9, 2003 we were given a thirty-day notice to cure the default for the months of May through November 2003. I would take a short vacation after receiving the notice, and I returned to the station on December 31. Very shortly after I arrived, Dennison walked into the station through the basement stairs, marched into my office and notified me that he was enforcing the time brokerage agreement that was signed in August. He also informed me that he had taken control of the accounts receivable at the station. Then he offered me employment once more, all while John was hiding out in the control room.

I contacted Noyes and asked him whether or not I should pay Dennison the money we owed him for the months of May through December.. He said that I wouldn't have a case in court if I didn't pay him at least that.

I left that day and returned on January 7, when I paid all of the back default owed to Dennison by MediaComm from May through December of 2003. The amount was $88,956.48 and it came from my own funds. This payment would later be lied about by Dennison in court when he said he believed it still didn't bring MediaComm current. He knew that it made us current, even though he didn't put it on the books until August of 2004.

Along with the payments for May through November, which covered the default notice, I also had the payment for December 2003. In addition I had a receipt and a letter from my attorney asking that Dennison leave the premises. I believed, and still do, that Paul had no right to be there under a time brokerage agreement. The meeting at which Media-Comm—John Kuhens—signed the agreement was illegal and therefore should not have stood. But Paul refused to leave, and that's where more problems started. Since he wouldn't leave, I decided that he wouldn't get paid by me. As far as MediaComm paying him, he had control of MediaComm's revenue stream, and therefore was in control of whether or not he got paid by them. But why should he have been paid when he'd taken illegal control of the corporation's only real asset? This, too, would become a major point of disagreement between the parties when we landed in court months later. But it was clear to me that the check cleared any default and that by staying at the station Paul was acting illegally.

The day after the confrontation with Paul, John took a letter to Pilot Grove Savings Bank saying that there was a board resolution and that I was no longer employed by the station or the corporation and that his signature was the only one needed on checks. It was all lies. There were no meetings and I was still on the board.

In January of 2004, around the same time that I was showing up with the money and the letter, John and Paul were devising a scheme that would put Paul in charge of the station and its management even in the even they should lose in court.

John, acting as president of MediaComm, signed an agreement to pay Mount Pleasant Management, LLC $3,000 a month plus twenty percent on all advertising sales revenue to manage the radio station. Who do you think was the owner and operator of Mount Pleasant Management LLC? If you guessed Paul Dennison, you win. The reason they went with a management agreement was due to their belief that the time brokerage agreement wouldn't hold up.

It was a powerful step in the coup that would see me left with nothing and see Paul Dennison the owner, once again, of KILJ. And it was all illegal.

Ironically, because Paul was now in charge of the accounts receivable along with John, they were both responsible for Dennison receiving the January payment and all subsequent payments. They chose not to allocate funds for those payments and so were responsible for any missed payments from then on.

Chapter 13

Fighting Back

The letter I'd sent to John following the August 2003 meeting, in which I stated that we did have the money to pay the Dennisons, went unanswered. Though I couldn't prove a thing, my gut feeling was that the Kuhens and the Dennisons might be plotting a new strategy to be rid of me. Undoubtedly, they must be consulting with an attorney other than Fred! I knew that they understood I wasn't going to go away quietly from all of this and that meant ending up in court. So, it was only prudent for them to be ready for that.

For our part, we filed for an injunction to have Paul Dennison cease and desist all actions at the radio station and to have things restored to the way they were, with MediaComm control of KILJ's FCC license and with the stock still under MediaComm's name, but still at the bank in escrow. We did not file our injunction until Paul was paid in full, there was no default and he had refused to leave the premises in January of 2004.

Well, because the petition in equity and the suit against the bank hadn't been heard yet, it was decided that those issues would be heard on the same day as our injunction request at the courthouse.

The Dennisons were convinced that the bank, Firstar Bank N.A. (which is now US Bank), should hand over the KILJ stock because they claimed the situation we were in met the terms of the escrow agreement; that MediaComm was in default and that they had provided authorization from MediaComm for transfer of the stock and that they had provided written notice to the bank as required by law.

In their complaint, the Dennisons claimed that the bank "orally refused to deliver the stock on October 30, 2003." They felt that they should control the KILJ shares during the lawsuit, since "MediaComm authorized the transfer by corporate action." Well, the "corporate action" involved only the president of the corporation and not the entire board of directors. That made it null and void in the eyes of the law. Or, so I thought heading into the injunction hearing.

Now, for those readers who might be confused about how the legal system works, let me explain what an injunction is. This aspect of the legal system is a court decision that is intended to prevent harm—often irreparable harm—between two parties. In other words, it asks one party to cease and desist from actions that being conducted that can be harmful to another party. So the injunction—in theory—can fix an on-going situation, such as I was experiencing with KILJ. In other words, injunctions are orders that one side refrain from or stop certain actions. Injunctions can be temporary, pending a consideration of the issue later at trial, which is what we were planning on later in the year. Noyes and I had agreed to file suit against the Dennisons and the Kuhens over all the turmoil and illegal activities that bulldozed over our tightly written original agreement to buy KILJ and create MediaComm.

Our hope was that the injunction would do what it was designed to to: *status quo ante*. That Latin term means to return things to the way they were, or to make whole again someone whose rights have been violated. So, in my case, the injunction was the perfect legal weapon for me and MediaComm, since our rights had been violated and we needed to be made whole again.

It was March 3, 2004. Noyes and I were ready. In fact, I was looking forward to it. On paper—legal agreements between the Dennisons, John Kuhens and me—the weight of the law was certainly on my side. After all, when a contract is signed, it's the legal obligation for everyone to live up to his or her respective end of the deal.

The judge for the injunction hearing was an interesting choice—Mary Ann Brown. Does the name sound familiar? She was the attorney for Mike Stoffregen when he was caught embezzling from MediaComm! I had no problem with her as our judge. In fact, both Noyes and I felt this was a potential asset. After all, she once was involved with the station through the legal procedure. It was our feeling that having delved extensively into Mike's crooked ways, she had a good sense of what was involved in the KILJ/MediaComm agreements. What more could we ask for?

We had no reason to worry about Judge Brown's prior involvement with the station and MediaComm. My attorney, Mike Noyes, had tried cases before her in the past and told me that she was fair and understood what she was doing. My only dealing with her was during the wrap up meeting with Mike Stoffregen, and she did not do anything unusual or alarming at the time. She was a solid advocate for her client and we got what we wanted during the meetings with her. I thought it was almost a plus to have her presiding over the injunction because she was familiar with MediaComm. We had no reason to believe that she wouldn't give us a fair shake.

Now, prior to the injunction, Judge Brown gave both parties the chance to object to her being the presiding judge. Because of her past involvement, it was understood that her objectivity could have been called into question. Neither party chose to contest her position, and so she was assigned to the injunction hearing. Judge Brown even mentioned at the beginning of the injunction that all parties agreed to have her there, and I believe she would have stepped down if either party had offered an objection.

The Mt. Pleasant courthouse is a classic rural American structure, three floors in a gray structure sitting on the southeast corner of the town square. The American flag flies out front and it's under the flag's watch where all the legal business for the area goes on. We were part of the Eighth District Circuit Court, so many trials and hearings went on there. Noyes and I arrived in the morning with Nathan Clark, a young attorney working with Noyes on the case. We were confident that the facts were on our side.

We entered the courtroom and saw that the Dennisons were already there with their lawyer, Vernon Squires. The injunction was to take place in one of several courtrooms in the building. It was moderate size.

The courtroom was like most in that it had a gallery for spectators, fronted by an area headed by the judge's stand. There were tables placed on the three open sides of this area, forming a square with the judge's stand. Mike Noyes and I sat at a table that faced Judge Brown from the left side of the courtroom, her right. The Dennisons were directly in front of her, with their table butted up against ours. There really wasn't that much distance between us in a physical sense, but the atmosphere between them and me was distant, and I was barely acknowledged by the pair during the injunction.

The Dennisons and I didn't make eye contact and Joyce refused to look at me during the whole proceeding. Paul eventually did look at me during my testimony, but Joyce acted as though the entire event was beneath her and even brought her knitting to the first day of the injunction hearing. It was as if she couldn't be bothered to engage.

Joyce is a little like Paul in that she dresses in expensive clothing, always keeping up appearances. She has short blonde hair, and as long as I've seen her role in their business dealings, it has seemed to me that she couldn't have cared less about what was going on. But the hearing was different. She pretended not to care, but she did.

John was present as a defendant and was representing himself. He had a local attorney early on then switched to an attorney in Des Moines, but decided to act as his own attorney before we got to court. He sat in the gallery of the courtroom for the entire hearing and elected not to make any presentation, question any witnesses or object to any of the testimony. He was really counting on the Dennisons carrying the day.

John seemed resigned to whatever the court had to say, and it seemed to me he just wished all of it would go away. As I said in Chapter One, John is usually the life the party and a fun guy to be around. But when it came to being confronted by a lawyer who was questioning his actions, he had no backbone for it.

The bank was also named as a defendant, but decided to concede to any decision the court made. They were holding on to the KILJ stock that Dennison wanted so badly, but were refusing to release it until the court made a decision on who should really be in charge of the station. Essentially, Paul Dennison was claiming that there was a default worthy of triggering a return of the KILJ stock to him, the financier of the purchase. Media-Comm, in the form of myself, was contending that there was no default and that Paul Dennison could have accepted payment in August of 2003 to cure any late payments there were.

Now, here's another interesting fact you should know, and that's the person who held the position of clerk at our courthouse. Again, just so you have the roles clear, the clerk of the court helps judges oversee the administrative duties at the courthouse, especially when it comes to managing the flow of cases through the court and maintaining court records.

The court clerk? Why, that was none other than Susie Kuhens!

It was another clear reminder of how small a town Mt. Pleasant can really be. The fact is, everybody deals with everybody else at some time. In my case, I was forced to deal with Susie Kuhens, a woman with whom I didn't exactly have the greatest relationship. I still can't forget the snide remarks she made to me about my presence at the radio station. I can still remember her saying, "It's your money," whenever I was involved in a decision at the radio station.

Though Susie's involvement was another potential conflict of interest in the injunction, neither Mike nor I felt this would be harmful to our case. After all, Susie was simply there to manage paperwork, not unduly influence the outcome of any trial, right? I mean, the clerk of court doesn't have any decision-making abilities during the course of a trial and she is there only to serve the judges, prosecutors and public in the managing of court documents.

But what about her official position versus her status in the case as an illegally elected member of the KILJ board of directors? We looked into it, but ultimately there were no legal conflict of interest or potentially damaging effects to our case just because Susie was handling paperwork on behalf of the court.

Should she try and pull any stunts, she could end up in serious trouble, herself! So while it was a rather strange set of circumstances, there really was nothing we could do. Ultimately, though it was a strange coincidence, we had no problem with Susie doing her regular tasks throughout our hearing. Obviously, the clerk would have regular interactions with the judge during a trial, but nothing obviously wrong took place.

Throughout the injunction hearing, Susie would come in to sit next to John, hold his hand and be supportive. I remember being on the stand, the two of them looking at me with somber eyes. She would occasionally take his hand, playing her role as loyal spouse, providing comfort for her wronged husband in his time of need. That was fine; it was something you'd expect in any trial.

The Kuhenses, unlike the Dennisons, would look at me throughout the hearing, but for the most part, they looked dead. They looked depressed, like there was no life in them, and they had blank stares on their faces. They sat in the gallery for the entire proceeding and looked as though they were the ones being victimized by the whole process.

As I said before, John had no legal counsel present. The first attorney John had approached about the case, in Mt. Pleasant, declined to go forward. She referred John to an attorney in Des Moines, who John eventually dismissed, choosing instead to represent himself throughout the injunction hearing and the subsequent trial.

In fact, since John wasn't interested in stopping the financier of the MediaComm deal, Paul Dennison, from illegally foreclosing on the company in order to reclaim KILJ's stock, I was forced to file a notice to intervene on behalf of the company. Here I was a Class B stockholder, and I was forced to act as representation for MediaComm because the president and co-owner of the company had no interest in defending against the actions of Paul Dennison. Hell, he was responsible for letting those actions go forward in the first place!

Chapter 14

The Injunction Hearing Begins

The injunction hearing began a little bit later than expected, as Judge Brown was held up in her chambers. It turns out she was concurrently overseeing a murder case in Burlington, which was keeping her *very* busy. I later thought she was more interested in working on that case than she was on our injunction, though of course I had no proof of that! But as a judge, the murder case had to have held more cache.

Because we had so many issues to deal with, Noyes had earlier suggested to me that we boil down our grievances at the injunction to their very essence of what we knew to be illegal about John and Paul's actions. Noyes felt that the less the judge had to deal with, the easier it would be to prove our case. I completely agreed with him. If we went through every nook and cranny of the original agreement, combined with all the illegal actions rammed through by the Dennisons and the Kuhenses, we could be there for an eternity—which would not go over well with Judge Brown during an injunction hearing! If the injunction dragged on and made me look like an embittered partner on the sour end of a business deal, I would be setting myself up for a major loss. This would put me in an uncomfortable position come our trial in the fall. Mike and I decided that it was better to save those myriad of other arguments for our later legal dealings with the Dennisons and Kuhenses.

Thus, our contention for the injunction was reduced to a simple fact: the Dennisons and Kuhenses had acted illegally when control of KILJ was turned over to Joyce and Paul. If any reasonable person looked over all the facts we had agreed on in a legally binding document, it was obvious that I was in the right. The goal of this injunction was to do exactly what Noyes told me we should be able to do, get things back to the way they were.

Judge Brown would preside over the injunction hearing and would make a ruling based on her own judgment as is the case in every injunction hearing. There are no juries present at injunctions, and Judge Brown said that the later trial would be a bench trial because she saw it as an equity issue.

Now, before we begin with the actual injunction hearing, it's important to examine Judge Brown's decision to look at the issue only as an equity case and not what we would have liked, which was a violation of the universal business code, the code of Iowa and the by-laws of MediaComm. Her decision was an indication that the violations of our corporation's strictures were less important to her than whether or not we were late on certain payments leading up the illegal acts. It was a devastating setback, and it was an abuse of judicial discretion, which allows judges the right to determine which issues of a case they will hear. Judge Brown focused on the default issue, but that ignored the fact that there was no default in January when Paul Dennison took control with John's help. They made sure that a default would take place after that. But I felt the facts were still on my side and that we would prevail, regardless.

Judge Brown's decision to have a bench trial later in the year would also turn out to be a negative, but at the time I felt that it was fine. She was familiar with the case and Noyes believed she was fair. Still, having the later trial be a bench trial only meant that I wouldn't be able to plead my case in front of a jury of my peers. The idea of having Judge Brown act as the only arbiter in this case would prove costly when all was said and done, because it opened the door to outside influences on her. I would learn quickly that political influencing and power grabs are as much a part of the law in Iowa as they are in other, big-city places.

With myself and Mike Noyes seated and not too far from the Dennisons, the injunction hearing began, and the defense was the first up on the stand because they filed suit first. Noyes always hated that. He felt that we would have been able to present a better case had we been able to go first.

The injunction hearing began with opening statements from both sides. Noyes was helped in his presentation by his assistant, Nathan Clark, who put together a Power Point presentation that so succinctly outlined where I had been wronged that I felt it would be impossible for Judge Brown to rule against us, regardless of how the testimony panned out, it was so good and so simple. There was no question about all the wrongs that had been done.

I think the presentation scared Paul Dennison because later, during the recess between the first and second days of the injunction, he called in some reinforcements to help make his case. But more on that later.

Paul Dennison was sworn in as the first witness by Vernon Squires, who, by the way, was always respectful to me, unlike his clients. Though I felt the facts were obviously on my side, I still could feel my heart beating against my ribs. After everything I had been through, now the story was about to unfold in a very public forum! And one where I could not be bullied or intimidated or shut out—or so I believed.

Paul sat on the stand, appearing confident and assured of his case, despite Clark's presentation. Paul is on the short side and heavy enough to have a double chin. But he is also confident and takes pride in his appearance. His hair is very thick and gray and he wears glasses, and both he and Joyce have always made a point of dressing nicely.

Squires opened the questioning by asking Dennison to give an overview of the history of his involvement with KILJ. Dennison explained the station began in October of 1970—nearly thirty-four years ago. During that time, Dennison added, he'd done just about everything you could imagine needed to be done at a small market radio station. "I've mowed the yard, I've done play-by-play, I've done talk shows, sold advertising," he said, explaining that advertising was his area of expertise. "So, that's been my main love and interest—in generating revenue," he concluded.

Squires asked Dennison whether he was currently employed at the station and he said yes, explaining, "Yes, I have an agreement with KILJ to sell advertising for them." This of course was the employee contract that he and John Kuhens signed after realizing that what they had done at the meeting wouldn't really stand up.

Dennison went on to explain that he had been hired because, "There was no one selling advertising and John sells some advertising if people call in, but he's on the air at six in the morning. He does basketball games at night. So there was no one selling advertising, so he needed help and that's my expertise. I've done it all my life since I was nineteen years old. So . . ."

Now, Paul wasn't telling the whole truth here, though what he said wasn't technically a lie. There was no one selling advertising at the radio station because I had left when he refused to vacate the premises. I had been working at the station since January 1, 1998 and only left after the bogus meeting in August, 2003, returning in September 2003 and working until December of 2003, shortly before Paul came on as an advertising salesman.

He then explained John's role at KILJ. "Really, you can go out the door and ask anybody on the street and they'll say he's Mr. Radio in Mt. Pleasant," Paul told the court. In that sense, Dennison was right. As the long time mainstay at KILJ, Kuhens was considered the public voice of the station.

I kept my eyes fixed on Dennison. So far he hadn't said anything that couldn't be refuted. These were plain and simple facts of how the station began and how John was viewed in the area.

Still, the meat of my case was quickly approaching. I felt each breath I took in.

Squires focused in on some of the financial affairs and the various loans the Dennisons had provided to us over the years. He also was asked about the $70,000 personal loan provided to Kuhens. He then stated that Kuhens put this money back into MediaComm to help pay off some loans—loans made by Dennison of course! Keep in mind, this was money the corporation had paid for John's benefit so he could fulfill his original subscription agreement for stock.

I mean, the whole thing was a bit ridiculous. If you lent money to someone and they were having trouble paying you, would you lend them money to cover their debt to you? It was circular logic, but that's the way Paul Dennison worked with John Kuhens. And I do mean worked *with*. They seemed to have a partnership to the very end, and John's bond to Paul was far stronger than his bond to MediaComm, as evidenced by his persistent lack of responsible behavior on behalf of the company.

Why was this loan made, Squires asked him.

"I still was not willing to admit that I was going to have to go back to work because I didn't want to go back to work, and I still don't want to."

Though neither Noyes nor I could say a word, every ounce of me wanted to scream, "That's not true and you know it!" After all, why was he trying to win back control of KILJ? Why had MediaComm been gutted? The facts just didn't fit with Paul's testimony. Why hadn't he just taken the money that was available for payment in August if he didn't want to go back to work?

On the stand, Paul consistently acted as though he were swooping in to save the station and that he had no choice. Though I'd made efforts to rectify any late payments we had, even offering my own funds, Paul made it difficult every step of the way. That told me he wanted back in. Yes, things would have been smoother had we made all of our payments right on time, but I felt that we were still viable as a business. That's why I kept putting more of my money into the enterprise.

Paul, though, felt that things were going downhill from the time Mike had been found out. He said, "Well, after Media-Comm had their problems with one of their investors—namely, Mike Stoffregen—it was the start of the kind of a downward spiral in both the revenue and in every way, management, all of that, because in spite of all of his faults, Mike might have had some management skills. So they lost all of that."

Well, Mike's management skills didn't make up for his skills at embezzlement. I'm not sure where Paul thinks that Mike helped the company. When he was "improving management" and trying to build the business, he was simultaneously working to undermine it for his own benefit. How we were better off with him is beyond me, but that was apparently what Paul thought.

Dennison then explained that he'd grown sick of sinking his money into KILJ and MediaComm, and John "sort of said, 'well, I agree.'" This confirmed in my mind that the two had colluded together to turn the station back over to the Dennisons and shut me out! After all, the Dennisons didn't just happen to drop by in August of 2003, and Paul Dennison hadn't just shown up after I returned from vacation at the end of December 2003 to tell me he had taken over while John hid in the control room. The time brokerage agreement didn't just appear in his hand, or the FCC transfer. These things were all planned out.

When asked if he'd had a similar conversation with me, Dennison replied, "You know, I don't actually remember."

Selective memory, I thought.

"She's always saying, 'oh, we have the money, we have the money.' Well, if we have the money, where is it? You know, where is it?" he said in reference to me.

Dennison knew exactly where the money was! Keep in mind, I'd told him I was willing to put my personal funds toward paying off the loan for the two payments we owed to him. Those were the payments he insisted during the surprise meeting that could not be paid off, regardless of what I said. There was always money to pay the Dennisons with cash in the bank. We had overpaid property taxes, and I had also agreed to make up any deficit personally in August.

And this was also regardless of the fact that I'd provided a cashier's check to make the payments in January 2004, which paid all back payments and the current payments. There was not default at this time and yet he refused to leave the station.

Paul was apparently under the impression that MediaComm was a complete bust that was without hope. He told Squires on the stand that, "This financial problem has been going on for several years and they also owed some of their other bills, they were behind on them."

Next came the issue of that surprise meeting, the one I believed had specifically been previously arranged to back me into a corner and force me out. Paul fiddled with the date, claiming he couldn't exactly remember when the meeting was held. Again, I felt nothing but anger and contempt. I heard an inner voice inside me ask, "Is this man capable of telling the truth, ever?"

Paul spooled out his version of the events. No, John could not pay. And three payments were needed to be made at the time, not two. Paul explained that he assumed that three payments needed to be paid at the August meeting because we were close to the July payment date. Paul had even given a notice to cure the default for three months, one of which wasn't due yet.

"Did MediaComm offer to pay that amount to you?" asked Squires.

Well, of course not! MediaComm, such that it existed during that point in the underhanded meeting, was being completely gutted by one of its owners—without the permission of the other owner, as was stated in our legal agreement.

"No," Dennison said. Then, in an apparent attempt to smear me, he added another thought. "And that's another thing that's been brought up several times..."

Noyes was on his feet in an instant. "Objection!" he called out. "There's no question pending." Legally speaking, Mike was right on the nose. At no point in this hearing, other than the immediate line of questioning, had the issue of this meeting been brought up by anyone.

Squires decided to pursue another avenue. Did John offer to pay? No. Did Dixie offer to pay? "Absolutely not," was Dennison's answer. (Wrong there, Paul!) Dennison then explained that since it was obvious nothing was going to be accomplished at the meeting, everyone agreed to meet again after a break so John and I could discuss the issue.

True. But remember, during that head-to-head meeting, John and I consulted with Fred Beaver, who told us that what was transpiring was illegal as per our agreement.

Facts Don't Matter 83

Squires then honed in on what happened next. Dennison explained that he had contacted his lawyer at the FCC regarding the FCC license several weeks prior to the meeting, and that he had gathered all of the documents necessary—to force a transfer of the FCC license and eventually the stock—from his various attorneys. He explained that he was growing tired of late payments and that he was forced to contact his attorneys, even though he just wanted to stay retired.

He admitted that he had a conversation with John Kuhens in May, where he apparently told John, "We've got to do something different. I am not going to put any more money back into MediaComm or back into KILJ." He then said that John agreed and told him that, "You'll have to do what you have to do."

What he didn't mention was that John had signed the paperwork necessary for the transfer of the KILJ stocks in May, well prior to the August meeting.

What kind of a president was John being when he said that? As the president of a corporation, do you just tell your creditors, "You'll have to do what you have to do"? His words were essentially implicit consent to try and take back the stocks and to move forward with a plan to seize back the FCC license, which was crucial for the station to continue broadcasting. At the meeting, he explained, he'd brought in all the paperwork for *John* to sign so the license transfer back to the Dennisons could begin.

Now, he said on the stand that he didn't tell John of the plan to transfer the FCC license until at the meeting, that John didn't know. But when John told Paul to do what he had to do, he was essentially giving permission to a creditor to seize assets from a company he was supposed to be protecting. I think it's fair to say that he wasn't an effective president or co-owner based on these actions.

And to think that John had no idea what was coming is ludicrous if what Paul testified to is accurate. John knew from their May meeting that Paul wanted to "do something differently." What did he think that was, exactly, and why on earth didn't he tell me prior to the August meeting?

And as far as that August meeting goes, Paul admitted on the stand that it was illegal when he said, "I called John and Dixie and said, 'We need to meet today.'"

Well, if Paul notified me that we were going to meet, then it's news to me. I was notified by Susie Kuhens that John needed to see me. That was all the warning I got that Paul was planning anything, and as a co-owner of MediaComm I think I should have been paid the respect of being informed that John had met with Paul and agreed that things needed to change. I should have also been given the courtesy of a formal board meeting that followed some rules if I was going to be asked to make a major decision with the corporation.

Paul had a different idea of the meeting. He said that he left after the first portion of the meeting "when it looked like there was nothing going to be accomplished at this meeting," and that he agreed to come back later so that we could have a discussion.

Well, I'll say we had a discussion, alright. We had a discussion with our corporate attorney, who said that the meeting was illegal. To me that would mean the whole proceeding should have been halted. But Dennison said he felt that "once we had thought that things were going okay, that we were going to, you know, be satisfied, is when we, I, brought all of the things that my attorney in Washington, DC, had prepared for John for signatures so that we could get the license transfer started in Washington, DC."

I want to know how Paul thought that things were "going okay," and how exactly he was satisfied at that meeting? Does that mean that he was able to get John to do what he wanted by putting Susie on the board and trying to ignore my legal objections? Does that mean that he was able to convince John to gut the company he was supposed to be president of? Whatever he thought it meant, he acted as though all were okay with the world and had John sign the FCC paperwork.

Squires moved on to after the meeting.

"What was your perception of the status of the radio station?" asked Squires.

Dennison blundered right through the facts, distorting them at every turn, I thought. "Well, Mrs. Burkhart just got up in a huff and said, 'Well, I guess I need to get my things,' and she went up to her office, cleaned it out and left," he explained. Nothing, of course, about Joyce's inappropriate remarks that I got to keep my house or that they had been told about their dairy loss via the mail!

Dennison made it seem as though my leaving the meeting were somehow a concession to his and John's actions. That couldn't have been further from the truth. I left the meeting because I knew it was illegal and because I had been insulted by Joyce Dennison and ignored by John and Susie Kuhens. As the only opposition party to the actions that took place at the meeting, I was outnumbered and being ignored. There was nothing more I could do but leave.

Paul also detailed my return to the station in January and the letter my husband Steve and I had in hand telling him that he was legally obligated to leave the premises.

"Did she ask you to vacate the premises?" asked Squires.

"No," Dennison replied. "Well," he backtracked, "she had a letter from her attorney, which I refused to sign, so then she and her husband left."

I remembered that day well. The arrogance of Dennison when I presented him that letter and nearly $88,956.48 to cure the default plus the current month's payment was now smugly in place as he remembered it for the court.

Questioning continued. Did Kuhens want Dennison to stay at KILJ? Yes. (*Of course, he did*, I thought to myself. *Could you two have been any more obvious about it?*) What was Kuhens's reason? "He wanted a salesperson who could sell," said Dennison.

I laughed inwardly. Finding a salesperson who could sell was the never-ending story at KILJ, no matter who that person was! John Kuhens wanted Paul to stay at the station so that he wouldn't be burdened with the day-to-day operations and responsibilities, or the thousands of dollars in debt obligations he owed. Life was so much simpler for him when he could just be the on-air talent, when he didn't have to deal with a co-owner like me, when he wasn't in charge and therefore responsible for what happened to the station.

Next came a complicated series of questions regarding the financial arrangements. Paul explained the process he'd gone through with the bank, trying to secure the shares of KILJ through declaring a default. He explained that the bank had refused him because the matter was being disputed in court. The person disputing it was me, and I'm glad the bank decided to wait and see what happened.

Dennison also explained that it seemed to him that every time he returned to Iowa from his winter retreats in Arizona, he was having to lend money to MediaComm. On this point, I agree with him to an extent. John was adamant it seemed to pay anyone other than Paul Dennison when it came to handling the accounts receivable. He screwed up so many things related to MediaComm's finances it was hard to keep up.

The injunction hearing and Paul Dennison's testimony dragged on, a grueling process for everyone concerned. At two-thirty, Judge Brown suggested we take a break. No one objected.

Chapter 15

The Injunction Hearing Continues

At about ten to three our recess came to an end—time for round two of the afternoon. I was feeling refreshed, but certainly still anxious, wanting to tell my side of the story. It hadn't surprised me that Dennison was playing fast and loose on the stand. I hadn't considered his word to be any good in a long, long time.

Squires continued questioning Dennison on his operations at the station. "How's it going?" he asked his client. "I'm a little older, so it seems harder work physically, but mentally the reception has been tremendous."

Paul also boasted that under his renewed leadership sales had increased considerably, up to the previous year's levels. "Making the calls, going out and seeing people, taking good care of them," that had been the key to turning things around, he emphasized. Every time we had someone new come on, sales would get a bump. But things were going bad on a national level with radio advertising.

When asked what he'd prefer to be doing, Paul smiled. "I would have been playing golf in Arizona and mowing the yard this summer and playing golf here," he replied. Ah, the idyllic life of a retired man. *If that were true*, I thought, *then why are we here in the first place?* If he wanted he could have gotten his money and stayed retired. He was paid in January of 2004. His actions say that he wanted back into the radio business.

Paul was up on the stand acting as though he were dragged back to the radio station by circumstance. If he wanted so badly to stay retired, he could have left the station when I'd pay him the nearly $88,956.48 in January of 2004. He could have said, "Okay, now you're not in default, I'm going back to Arizona." But he didn't, and I think that's telling of what he really wanted.

Maybe it was his failure in other investment ventures; maybe it was just that he missed the radio station and the attention and control it gave him. I can't be sure what was going through his head, but his actions spoke loud and clear: he wanted back in and he found a way to do it through John and Susie Kuhens.

I thought it was the most ridiculous thing I had ever heard. I felt that if Mt. Pleasant was going to have a radio station then it didn't matter who was going to run it. I was pretty good at keeping my composure, even though it was tempting to go up there and slap Paul Dennison for his testimony, and if I were a man, this whole thing probably wouldn't have happened; we probably would have gone out in the parking lot and worked it out. But I'm not that kind of person, and the only real recourse one has in this kind of dispute is to take it to the courts, which is what I was doing.

Squires moved on and addressed the reasons behind my injunction. "You understand she wants you removed from the station?" Squires asked.

Dennison replied in the affirmative.

"And Mr. Kuhens, from MediaComm?"

Again, Dennison said, "Yes."

Now came the attempted blow against me. "What do you think will happen if that scene of events unfolds?" Squires asked.

Mike was quick on his feet, "Objection!" he declared to the judge. "That's speculation."

Mike's objection made perfect sense. How on earth could Dennison predict what would happen if I had both John and him ousted? There are so many factors, both known and unforeseen, that would make such guesswork impossible—at least for a reasonable person.

The judge considered my attorney's objection for a moment, then spoke. "The witness may offer his opinion and I'll consider it as his opinion. As a trier of fact, I can balance that. Overruled."

I couldn't believe what I was hearing! How could Dennison's conjectures and predictions have any weight against the facts? It made no sense to me, but I had no choice.

Here was a man with a vested interest in how his answer would affect the injunction, and he was allowed to speculate about something that was impossible for him to know. It was in his best interests to make it look as though the station would crumble. But Judge Brown had spoken, so Dennison continued.

"I think Mrs. Burkhart would probably have to sign the radio on because I don't believe there would be anybody there at the station."

This was utter nonsense! Let's face it, John's job wasn't anything complicated. When you think about it, how many college graduates with degrees in broadcasting get started at small, market stations, learn the tricks of the trade and then move on to larger markets? John, I felt, wasn't doing anything anybody else with enough education and broadcast savvy couldn't do. It was a relatively easy job for someone with the know-how.

"Do you think the radio station could continue to operate?" Squires asked.

Paul replied with his obvious, "No."

The next question was very telling. "And what," asked Squires, "would that mean to you?"

"It would mean my life is gone." That's a very big point because it showed that he was drawn to the radio station. It was all he'd ever known. It was a play for sympathy.

Well, if his life would be gone without the station, why on earth had he agreed to sell it in the first place? What's more, none of these questions had anything to do with the main issue: that the Dennisons and the Kuhens had violated the original agreement. As an owner, it certainly wouldn't have been in my best interests to let the radio station be silenced!

Yet, it was a shrewd move. Most people are moved by emotional challenges, and Squires cleverly ended his questioning on how Dennison's life would be destroyed if he didn't have control of KILJ. What's more, I was portrayed as the conniver out to ruin his life!

Squires told the court he had no further questions. Now it was our turn to fire back.

Noyes zeroed in on Paul's $70,000 loan to John. John had borrowed the money from the bank when he first bought into KILJ because he had been short of his required $125,000, even with the money I'd lent him. If you remember, he'd had MediaComm pay back the loan, beginning when he and Mike took their salary reductions.

Well, the loan had been paid back by MediaComm, but John had never paid taxes on the transaction, which he would have had to do because it was an economic benefit. Well, instead of just borrowing enough to cover the taxes, John had borrowed the full $70,000 from Paul. Now he owed the money to Paul. It was asinine. Why would Paul lend money to somebody who already owed him hundreds of thousands of dollars? It was just one more example of the closeness of John and Paul's relationship and how that closeness superseded any loyalty John may have had to MediaComm or his partners.

Did John have to keep his job to make these payments? No, said Dennison. Does he have independent wealth? Again, no. How was John going to pay the money back, then, if he didn't keep his job at the station?

Mike then peeled back a layer of the Dennison/Kuhen relationship. "You know his net worth, don't you?"

"Yes," said Dennison.

This came as no surprise. Obviously, if the loan was made, Dennison would have to know what John was worth. On the other hand, it also demonstrated exactly how close the two were.

Noyes asked if John needed to keep working to make the payments.

Of course. And where was Kuhens working?

KILJ. Where else was he going to work?

Dennison and Kuhens had a long history together. None of this came as a surprise, but in Mike's subtle fashion, he got Paul to reveal just how entwined their mutual interests were.

* * *

Noyes told the judge he had no further questions, so Squires came back for a redirect examination.

"There was some discussion about releasing him (John) from his personal guarantee... What value do you place on that personal guarantee?"

"Nothing," said Dennison.

"Why?" asked Squires.

"Because," replied Paul, "he has nothing."

So, in essence, Paul was admitting that John had no monetary value not associated with the radio station. So, in order for him to recoup his money which by now was in the tens of thousands of dollars, he needed to regain control of the radio station—the only thing of value that John had.

But all of this questioning was getting away from the core meaning of the injunction hearing. I contended, on behalf of MediaComm, that the transfer of the FCC license was illegally done and, therefore, should be voided. That would mean John and Paul would have to leave the station. Unfortunately, Judge Brown was perfectly happy examining only whether MediaComm had defaulted on loans from the Dennisons, because why should procedure, contracts and the law matter to a judge?

The relationship between John and Paul was clearly a deep one. Had Squires made a mistake in revealing that? I certainly hoped so!

Chapter 16

Kuhens Takes the Stand

Finally, Dennison was dismissed and Kuhens was called to the stand. John gave a list of his duties at the station: sign-on announcer, sports director, assisting with news, sales and management of sales, personnel management, scheduling employees and overseeing their job performance.

John was always nervous on the stand. He never did like confrontation or anything that seemed like the providence of adult businesspeople. It seemed like he just wanted it all to be over with. He was his own lawyer, but he put forward no witnesses, made no opening presentation and never took the chance to cross-examine witnesses.

Even on the stand, John was always in Dennison's corner. He was all about the life of the station and how the thing wouldn't survive without him. He looked very solemn, almost scared during his testimony. He isn't one for confrontation, and here he was in court being questioned by an attorney who doesn't care about his best interests or how charming his personality is.

During all my dealings with John, I found that whenever he was confronted with an accusation about his behavior, he just gave in. I never saw him put up a fight when he was directly challenged, and I imagine in his dealings with Paul Dennison, he was the same.

John likes everyone to like him. He gets his jollies from being on the air and going out in the community. He doesn't like being in charge. When he interacted with Paul, Dennison was clearly in charge. Whenever they were around each other, it was clear who was in charge. John always had a good sense of humor and people really liked him. I suppose that when he was at the station by himself with the other employees, he was in charge and people did what he asked; but whenever Paul was around, John was clearly the subordinate.

Oddly enough, the only place John seemed rebellious or out of line was in his relationship with Susie. You see, he and Susie put on the good front, but to me John always seemed like a kid who was trying to get away with things in front of Momma. John seemed to be able to get away with it, too, even right in front of Susie.

This venue doesn't merit going into details, but John and Susie had rough patches that were bad enough to warrant separations, one of which lasted a year. They're still together though, so that says something about their relationship even with all of the rocky patches.

Lest anyone forget, John also told the court that he was an owner of KILJ, even though he was an owner of Media-Comm, which owned KILJ. The distinction may seem small, but it goes to show that John's view of his role was that of custodian over KILJ, not MediaComm, which is the company both he and I were involved in. That didn't seem to matter to him.

Because John was nervous on the stand, he seemed to want to joke to lighten the situation. When Squires asked him where he lived, he said Salem, Iowa. When Squires asked where that is in relation to Mt. Pleasant, John said, "It's a vacation mecca just south of here. No, it's a small town just south of Mt. Pleasant, nine miles."

Of course, Judge Brown, who grew up northwest of Salem, couldn't help but take part in the joking. "I grew up northwest of Salem, so I take that as truth in fact," she said.

Ha-ha, very funny.

Squires asked what Dennison's job was at the station. He was there to do sales. "Anything else?" asked the attorney.

"Well, he covered a ball game last night for us," John replied.

"Did he do a good job?" Squires said.

"Yeah, he's the one that taught me."

This line of questions and answers struck me as both inane and again deeply revealing. To me, it showed the influence

Dennison held over Kuhens since they first met nearly thirty-five years before. Though only ten years separated them in age (Dennison was sixty-one and Kuhens was fifty-one at the time of the injunction), theirs was a strange employer/employee relationship. It almost seemed to me like it was a father guiding his son in the family business. And throughout the decades, even after the sale of KILJ, Dennison was out to protect his surrogate child.

Kuhens further detailed his duties as part owner of the station. He decided which bills should be paid. Since money was always tight, he had to decide the order of importance of every invoice the station (through the corporate owner MediaComm) should pay. John discussed basic items, but had carefully chosen to show the desperate financial shape of the company, I thought.

John was then asked by Squires why he had hired Dennison to take care of advertising as opposed to screening and interviewing potential employees. His response was telling.

"At the time . . . everything was just . . . I was the only one around at the time, so. . ." When times got rough, he ran to the only person he really knew could help him: Paul Dennison. After all, Paul had pretty much given him everything he had—his career.

John gave his version of the events as to how he got involved in MediaComm with Mike Stoffregen. How he took out loans to buy the station. How the stockholders were classified in A and B membership divisions. How he accepted loans from me. How the station operated—then, how the slide downwards to our present situation took place.

When asked what John's plans were to increase our revenue, he replied, "Nothing other than to try and sell more advertising."

Now, this was the president of the company talking about trying to increase revenue and all he could think of was "increase advertising"? It was disgusting how uninterested John was in actually helping MediaComm. I don't know exactly when he gave up on trying. Maybe it was when Mike left and

John was saddled with more responsibility, but whatever the reason, he was a complete failure as president.

And even increasing advertising obviously hadn't worked! Perhaps that was the catalyst that finally sent John in a mad beeline right back to the Dennisons.

"Was there a Plan B?" asked Squires.

"To let the station go back," he replied.

Why not talk to your partner, instead? I thought to myself. *Your Plan B was to just give up the station?* This performance struck me as desperate and rather pathetic. Of all choices he had to make, why not consult with his business associate? It seemed like the most logical decision any corporate owner would make.

No, not John. When asked when the topic first came up for discussion, Kuhens told the court, "Susie and I said that when we took out the $70,000 loan, that that was it, that if that didn't work then we would have to do something else." John could have avoided paying the $70,000 if he'd taken Fred's advice. He could have avoided paying it cash out of hand.

Again, I thought, *why not discuss this with your business partner first in addition to your spouse?* As a person who'd run my own business, it seemed like a much smarter choice. Sure, we all talk about our jobs with our significant others, but when it comes to making the important decisions affecting the business, one should ultimately include his or her business partners.

Now, for the meeting of August 18, 2003. When asked if he recalled the events that day, John replied, "Pretty much, yes."

It was an ironic answer, with just a touch of unintended humor, I thought.

Squires asked John for his version of the events.

"Paul asked for a meeting that day with Dixie and I and said that, you know, something had to be done."

Well, I thought, *how interesting. If Paul had called for the meeting, as he said in his sworn testimony, why had he expressed such difficulty remembering the date?* From the moment that meeting had begun, I really felt it had been a set up between the Dennisons and the Kuhenses. What John said next more or less confirmed in my mind my initial reaction.

"I had Susie come out that morning to join us in the meeting," he went on. "We talked about the fact that there wasn't enough money to make the payments, and I announced my decision to let the station go back to Paul."

This just wasn't true. First, John couldn't just announce his decision to let the station go back to Paul because it wasn't his decision to make. Unfortunately, it seemed no one was paying attention to that fact. But he did give the station back in a roundabout way by putting Susie on the board.

But John's testimony had one other major omission: my offer to make payments.

"Was there any discussion with Mrs. Burkhart at this morning meeting about what to do?"

This ought to be interesting, I thought.

"I don't recall the exact discussion," John replied. "I know she was not in favor of my plan and contended that—you know, that we could make the payment, but I disagreed with what I saw in the book."

Again, where was my offer to make payment from my personal funds? Apparently, John didn't exactly recall that part of the discussion! Why quibble with facts when they might get in the way of your story? For as long as MediaComm had been around, I'd been putting my own money into the operation when it was needed. I'd lent Mike, John and Steve money to buy into the operation, and I'd certainly used it to pay money back to the Dennisons in January, 2004. As I've said before, I did so because I felt that the operation could still be salvaged if not for the virtual sabotage being committed by some of the co-owners.

Next in John's testimony was a discussion of the afternoon meeting of MediaComm's board of directors on August 18, which included John and me. John restated that he wanted to give the station back. Now it was time for the crucial step, putting Susie on the board. "Why did you do that?" asked Squires.

"To get a majority vote of the board," he replied.

Keep in mind, even if such a move had been legal, Susie's presence on the board wouldn't have meant a thing! Remember, any major decision had to be agreed upon by all members of the MediaComm board. I'd say that handing the station over to the Dennisons counted as a major decision.

Besides, the meeting wasn't even held legally. It was called without notice to all stockholders and was done without the proper ten-day notification prior to the meeting that the by-laws called for. Also, the election of board members was supposed to be done at the annual meeting of directors, not some out-of-the-blue meeting that's called without notice or an agenda.

And why did John want Susie? ". . . (S)he was the closest associated person with the radio station and felt she would be a good board member," was Kuhens's reasoning. No, the Dennisons hadn't suggested her. And yes, John thought it was a valid action.

This begs the question: Why did he think she would be a good board member? Did she have experience running a business or even running the radio station? No. She would be a good board member because she'd go along with what John and the Dennisons wanted to do—which is exactly what she did.

Now, the by-laws do allow shareholders to nominate new members to the board, and if the meeting had been put together legally, John might have been able to get Susie onto the board. But anything done during the meeting was illegal because the meeting itself was illegal.

But what John thought would be good for the board and the company, and what we had agreed on were two different elements. Facts were facts, no matter what John thought was, as he put it, "a valid action."

The minutes of that now infamous meeting were introduced as an exhibit. Squires told the judge that these minutes reflected what had happened: Susie was appointed to the board, and that the board then had voted on a transfer ownership agreement to Paul and Joyce Dennison.

"Did you think that the majority of the board of directors had the authority to do that transfer?" Squires asked.

"I felt so, yes," said John.

"Based on what?"

"My interpretation of the powers that I had," John explained.

Again, no time for facts. Interpretation and opinion ruled the day throughout John's testimony. Facts really weren't important.

Now came a question that struck to the heart of why this mess had come to court. "Did Dixie Burkhart say anything at the meeting, either of the meetings, to dissuade you or discourage you from doing the transfer?"

John's answer was short, simple, and unbelievable in my mind. "Not that I recall," he said. Not that you recall? How about the phone call to Fred Beaver? You know the one that told John the whole thing was illegal and wouldn't stand up? I guess my insistence that we make the call didn't count as an objection from me?

Also, he had just testified that I had said we could make the payments and that he disagreed with me. That to me is a clear indication that I was trying to dissuade him from making the move.

Like Dennison, this guy has a very selective memory, I thought.

John then said I had voted "no" to the transfer of KILJ. When asked if I had explained my vote, John replied with another "no."

"Now, Mr. Dennison testified that after this meeting, he came in to start selling advertising. Do you recall that?" asked Squires.

"Yes," John said.

Yup. Definitely selective memory was at work!

* * *

"Mrs. Burkhart alleges that you colluded with the Dennisons to return the station to them for being released from the personal guarantee. Do you understand that?" asked Squires. John replied that yes, he understood.

"Is that true?" asked the attorney.

"No," replied Kuhens.

John explained how he came to this decision independently. He felt the station was falling behind in its financial debt. That was his motivating factor, and the Dennisons had never encouraged him to give up any of his ownership claims or board duties with KILJ.

John explained that he signed the stock transfer agreement with the Dennisons, "Just because the station was falling in arrears to creditors, not only locally, which hurt the worst with our reputation around town, but with ASCAP (American Society of Composers, Authors and Publishers), BMI (Broadcast Music, Inc.), employee insurance, everything."

John didn't mention, though, that those shortfalls could have been fixed by me had he and the Dennisons accepted my money. But that's not important, right? Many businesses fall onto hard times. But if you're committed to a business you find a way to make it work and that sometimes involves sacrifice of a personal nature.

And what about my contention that Paul Dennison be evicted from the station since the transfer of power had been illegally made. "What effect do you think that will have on KILJ operations?"

"Hurt sales," John replied. This, he suggested would lead to more financial problems.

"Do you think the station will survive?" Squires asked.

"No," said John.

While Noyes should have objected this was all speculation, he probably knew better than to jump in. After all, Judge Brown had allowed for Dennison's speculation earlier! Yet, did any of this matter? I'd known Kuhens and Dennison for quite some time now. And one thing I knew for sure, neither of them had a crystal ball that could accurately predict the future.

Yes, Paul and John had been a part of KILJ for years and they were familiar faces. But did that really mean that no one else was capable of doing their jobs or that the station would crumble to the ground? Aren't there other people in the state of Iowa who can work competently on-air? Are there no other people capable of selling advertising?

But John did have one thing he could predict. What would happen if Kuhens were removed as a director of MediaComm, as I wanted.

"I'll quit," John told the court.

Squires clarified the point. "Quit your job?" he asked.

"Yes sir," replied Kuhens.

"How long have you worked for . . . KILJ?"

"Thirty-four years," said John.

It was a brave sentiment, but in reality John didn't have a lot of options. He wasn't going anywhere. I have a feeling that if the station was brought under new management, or if I was brought back in, he would roll with whatever happened. His nature just didn't seem to allow him to make a stand against or for anything, and I doubt that would have changed.

In addition, John stood to benefit hugely from the Dennisons taking the station back, and now that he felt they had, he was comfortable in making his stand. But what if they weren't able to take the station back? What did he stand to lose? Everything. John was the guarantor in the loans MediaComm had taken from both the Dennisons and the bank. He was responsible for paying it all back should something happen to the company. But if the Dennisons took the station back, he would be forgiven most of the loans.

Squires had no more questions.

It was my attorney's turn. "You and your wife. . ." Mike began.

Judge Brown interrupted. "Wait a minute," she said. "I'm still taking notes."

It was a quick moment that gave everyone in the tense courtroom a chance to breathe.

Chapter 17

Kuhens Cross-Examined

Noyes took the floor to cross-examine John. Mike was ready to poke so many holes in John's story that it would resemble the work of an overly zealous Swiss cheese maker.

"You remember that the $70,000 was put in during the fall of 2002?" he asked John.

"That sounds correct, yeah."

I couldn't help but notice that immediately under my lawyer's questioning, John seemed to be taking a hesitant approach with his answers. "That sounds correct," came across to me as someone who was not trying to say, "yes," though it was obvious that's what he meant.

I watched with fascination as Noyes continued.

"You and your wife had already agreed that in the event of a default, you were going to transfer the stock back to the Dennisons, correct?"

Again, John gave a hesitant response. "We decided that there would be an alternative plan—that it would have to be something different than us putting in the money."

Noyes referred back to earlier testimony. He asked if the alternative plan, as discussed earlier in the afternoon by Dennison was to give the stock back to Paul and Joyce.

"That's if it was left up to me," said John. He appeared to me to be very uncomfortable giving answers, sort of like a schoolboy who's been caught in a lie and was now trying to worm his way out of punishment by verbally stepping around his original untruth.

"If there were a third investor brought in or other investors brought in to buy the stock . . . those funds could be used to cure the default and pay the bills."

I found this laughable. If that was an option, why had they held that ambush meeting in August to ramrod their plans past my objections? Why weren't these options discussed with me, the business partner?

Noyes understood this, as well. "Did you discuss that with Dixie?" he asked.

"No."

That simple word hung in the air. It told me that something had happened that Dennison and Kuhens didn't want to get out.

Mike hammered away at John's "Plan B," showing that this backup solution to KILJ's problems was simply an attempt to turn KILJ stock over to the Dennisons, effectively gutting MediaComm. The KILJ stock needed to be back in Paul's hands for the FCC license to transfer.

Next, he focused on John's unethical behavior as a board member. Mike established that in previous dealings, both my signature and John's were required for any checks signed on behalf of MediaComm. We had put this in as a safeguard after the Stoffregen ordeal. It was a standard operating procedure that no one had any problems with, not the bank, not John and not me. That all changed when John informed the bank that only his signature would be authorized for any MediaComm checks. This certainly fell under the clause in our original agreement, stating there had to be unanimous decisions by the board for any major change in policy affecting the station.

"How often has the MediaComm board of directors met, say, in the last five years?" asked Mike.

"I don't recall any official meetings," John replied.

"We know there was one last August," Noyes fired back.

I grinned to myself. Mike knew what he was doing as he took John's story apart, piece-by-piece.

"Yes, I . . ."

Noyes didn't let him finish. "Other than that, have you ever had any board meetings?"

"No, sir."

"Did Mrs. Burkhart ever ask to call a board meeting?"

"No, sir."

What John failed to mention was that he was the one who had requested that we take care of our meetings on an informal basis. He acted as though it was just a decision made by the "company," but we were the company. He didn't want to take responsibility for what happened. As far as he was concerned, all of this had happened *to* him, and not partly because of him.

Noyes had John right where he wanted him. "How did you go about making corporate decisions?" he asked.

John explained that we discussed issues in day-to-day conversation and made decisions based on these informal chats. Then, once every year, we'd file a report on our business decisions to the Iowa Secretary of State's office.

"Did you think you had authority to change the checking account in the way you did?" Mike asked.

"Yes sir, I did."

Mike asked why John thought he had this kind of power.

"Well, basically, just to maintain operation of the station so that we could pay the bills and keep it running in a halfway timely manner," Kuhens said.

Anyone who ever graduated from a Business 101 course knew that this was simply an unsound practice. You don't make decisions without the consent or even counsel of your partners. It was a common theme that John had made decisions, major decisions, without consulting me. For some reason he felt that it was okay because he held the majority voting power as the sole Class A stockholder. But his lack of communication was deeper than just who had the majority voting power.

Communication is imperative in a business relationship, and John's constant habit of making major decisions without consulting me showed that not only did he misunderstand his powers as a board member and president of MediaComm, but he also was not thinking about what was best for the company or his partners. Noyes knew he had John on this point.

He referred Kuhens to a book containing the by-laws of MediaComm. "First of all, on page five, under section five-A, it identifies the powers and duties of the president. Do you see that?"

"Yes," John replied.

"And are you the president of MediaComm?"

Of course he was. John pointed out that he held Class A stock.

Mike waved the book at John. He asked Kuhens if he had ever read the by-laws.

John folded. "No," he admitted, he hadn't read the by-laws.

This is the president of the company and he hasn't even read the by-laws of the corporation? How can you even call yourself the president of a corporation when you don't have a clue as to the agreements the directors have made for how to run it? The by-laws have everything to do with how decisions are made and who makes them. They state clearly when meetings are supposed to be called, who can call the meetings, how much notification is supposed to be given and how much voting power each director has.

In addition, section two of Article Three states that "Nominations must be delivered in writing to the President of the Corporation at least five business days prior to the annual meeting." While it goes on to explain the changes or additional nominations can be made at the annual meeting, the fact is we weren't at an annual meeting in August, 2003. Everything about that meeting was done incorrectly and it shouldn't have even happened. If the corporate attorney for MediaComm, Fred Beaver, believed the meeting to be illegal and non-binding then something had to be wrong.

Mike went in for the kill. If Kuhens had read the by-laws, he told the court, then he would have clearly seen that the actions taken last August were completely illegal. No major changes affecting the station, such as voting one's wife to the board or handing over KILJ lock, stock and barrel to its former owners, could be made unless there was a unanimous agreement by all partners. In this case, that meant John Kuhens and Dixie Burkhart.

It was so obvious. The facts were there on paper for everyone to see. Or, at least that's what I thought. It was decided that we would take a break and reconvene a week later to finish the injunction hearing.

Chapter 18
A Break

At the end of that first day we were exhausted. It was as though we'd all been through an emotional wringer. I will admit, though, it was certainly interesting to watch Dennison and Kuhens give their respective testimonies. It seemed to me a culmination of everything I'd learned about these two men, all packaged up and on display in public. I wondered what the local press might have to say about the trial. Considering it affected the only radio station in town, this skullduggery on display in the public courthouse certainly would make for some juicy reading regardless of which side you favored!

There are two newspapers that cover our town: the local *Mount Pleasant News* and the nearby *Burlington Hawkeye* (remember, Iowa *is* the Hawkeye state!). I expected at the very least to see some interesting stories on the injunction. We seemed to have everything a good trial story would need: money, power and corruption. The only things missing were murder and sex! Those last two would have guaranteed us wall-to-wall coverage, but at the very least I expected to see a few stories.

I certainly didn't expect any news coverage on the injunction from KILJ! No, they operated like nothing unusual was going on, but that was no surprise. They just wanted to keep going and hope that it all went away. In the days after the first injunction hearing, I eagerly scanned the papers, ready to ferret out anything and everything said about our lawsuit.

I didn't find a thing. That was unusual because normally anything of substance gets a mention in the local paper, even my husband getting a hole-in-one at the local golf course.

A day passed and I figured, oh well, they just need time to write it up. Then, another day—and another. Finally, I sank into the realization that we weren't going to get any coverage at all by the local press. It's quite conceivable that our injunction hearing was not out in the open for everyone to see.

* * *

Since we had a week to go before the second day of the injunction, I kept myself busy. I didn't want to think about it or dwell on any part of the case. If you start doing things like that, you immediately begin to second-guess yourself! Did I give my attorney all the evidence? Is the evidence we've submitted good enough to make the case? Just how did Dennison, how did Kuhens come off on the stand? Did Squires make them look good? Did Noyes make them look bad? Or, vice versa?

You can drive yourself crazy with questions like that! I avoided the "woulda-coulda-shoulda" dialog with myself and threw myself into work, into reading, into mindless stuff like watching television. I took walks. I cooked. Anything, everything so I wouldn't think about what may be going on in Judge Brown's mind!

One thing I also didn't do was pester my attorney with questions that week. Believe me, I know that's a strong temptation to call your attorney every five minutes no matter if you're in an injunction hearing like we were, a more complicated case or even trying to beat a speeding ticket!

Mike gave me an excellent piece of advice to consider while we waited for the second part of the hearing. He told me, "Dixie, you never know which way these things can go. It might look like everything is in your favor and you end up on the losing side of the decision. You could look like you have the worst case in the world, but ultimately win. You just never know how these things will turn out. There's just no way to predict it! Even cases that seem open and shut simple can turn out to have complications. It's like investing. When you put money into a business, you could end up rich or you could end up losing everything and then some. It's the same with the legal system. It might all look good on paper, but ultimately the only way to get to the conclusion is to wait it out and hope you presented the best case you possibly could to the judge or jury."

He was right. There was nothing I could do, so I simply waited out a very tense week. At first, I didn't care about the court taking a break. The first part of the injunction hearing had been a long day for everyone. But the second part of the injunction would be very different from the first, and would include stunts and maneuverings that showed how vulnerable the legal system is to collusion and power mongering. Even the courts in a small town like Mt. Pleasant, Iowa.

Chapter 19

The By-laws and Surprise Witnesses

We returned to the courtroom just one week later, on March 10 of 2004. Again, the butterflies tromped nervously in my stomach as I wondered with anticipation if there were to be any unexpected twists or turns in the injunction. Facts were on my side; that was obvious. Any gains John had made for the Dennisons, I felt, had been trumped when Noyes showed him the book of by-laws we originally conceived for the company.

Now, as you recall, John was technically a defendant in the injunction hearing and again later in the trial, but that was in name only. He was really on the stand on behalf of the Dennisons, doing his best to justify the way he gutted MediaComm and allowed Paul and Joyce Dennison to steal what amounted to hundreds of thousands of dollars in equity that we had poured into the company by taking its only real asset: KILJ.

John was called back to the stand. Squires threw some softball questions to the witness and Kuhens answered as you might expect, evading anything that made him, Susie or the Dennisons look foolish. There were some questions on the by-laws of our agreement, but nothing too probing. The butterflies in my stomach beat a hasty retreat. I couldn't help but feel a growing sense of confidence. Then it came time for John to once again face my attorney. Noyes was ready.

"I think last week you said that you hadn't read the by-laws," Mike began. "Did I remember that correctly?" His sarcastic and pointed opening made John look very small.

"Yes sir," John meekly replied.

"Have you read them since last week?" An obvious question—but John's answer, I think, surprised just about everyone in the courtroom.

"No sir, I have not."

I couldn't believe what I was hearing. I never took John to be terribly aggressive and didn't think he was too swift, but not reading the by-laws after being confronted with that fact seemed downright stupid! How could he not have gone over the by-laws when that oversight had hurt him on the stand the week before? It was absurd, ridiculous!

What kind of fool was he? If I were the judge, I told myself, this would be a major mistake and problematic for the MediaComm defense. If John was indeed a co-owner, he had the responsibility, indeed, *the duty* of knowing what we had legally signed in our original agreement. His ignorance of what was now part of the official evidence in the case bolstered my confidence. How could this not sway the judge?

Mike turned to the by-laws. "Exhibit L (the by-laws), do you still have that in front of you?"

John did, of course! Mike referred Kuhens to page three.

"Three?" John said, his voice innocent as a lamb. I wasn't sure if this was an act or if John really was that ignorant of our original agreement.

Noyes looked over the book, and then once again played off John's seeming ignorance of the evidence before them.

"I believe (Squires) asked you about the number of directors," Mike said. "I believe he said Class A gets two directors and Class B gets one. Do you recall that?"

"Yes," John replied. To me, it looked like Mike was setting John up for a major blunder.

"(Squires) didn't read the next sentence, though," Mike pointed out. I felt Kuhens looked very uncomfortable, like he knew exactly what was coming and was attempting to form an answer before the question was out of Noyes's mouth.

"It says, 'The directors shall be elected at each annual meeting of the shareholders,' correct?"

"That's what it says," John replied. I found it very interesting he didn't reply with a more affirmative "yes."

"You didn't do that, did you? You didn't elect directors," Noyes firmly stated. He was cornering John with undisputable facts. "You didn't elect your wife at an annual meeting of shareholders, did you?"

"No sir. We never had an annual shareholder meeting."

Point Noyes. It seemed to me like the two were involved in an intricate form of verbal tango, with Mike clearing leading John through the dance.

"You and Mrs. Burkhart never had regular meetings because you reached agreement on everything, correct?"

"I would say a high percentage of the time, yes." Ah, a "yes" this time. Still, John had to throw in the qualifier before giving that, "Yes." He clearly knew where he stood and was trying to get his way out of him with every desperate move.

"Now, page six you talked about with Mr. Squires," Mike returned. "If you could turn to. . ."

"To?" John cut in. "Excuse me sir, what page?" More innocence, feigned though it was, I thought. That, plus a dollop of stupidity was my feeling. If I were judge, I told myself again, this man couldn't look any worse. And even though he was a defendant and technically on the same side of aisle as me, his incompetence actually played into my hands, I thought. It would make it clear that MediaComm and KILJ shouldn't be put into his hands—that it should be returned to me.

"In Exhibit L, page six, again the by-laws," Mike played John patiently, as if talking to a child. "I believe you think you had the right to change the relationship with the bank, correct?"

"Yes, sir." I liked John's constant use of the word "sir." It really made him look like he was scared, like he knew he was being trapped by the facts. It looked like the facts were triumphing over the underhanded and outright illegal moves!

Mike then asked John to go forward a couple of pages. "Have you read that Article V, paragraph four?" he asked. "That says, 'All checks, drafts or other orders or the payment of money, notes or other evidence of indebtedness issued in the name of the corporation shall be signed by such officer or officers of the corporation and in such a matter as shall be determined by resolution of the Board of Directors."

I silently thanked Fred Beaver for writing such a fair, equitable and *strong* document.

"Were you aware of that in your by-laws?"

"No, sir," was John's reply.

"Okay," Mike said confidently. "So the resolution that we're talking about is the form that you prepared and signed and gave to the bank?"

John said it was, thereby confirming once again that he had ignored the by-laws of the company. Mike had done a remarkable and all too easy job of taking Kuhens apart. It was a simple matter of using the facts!

Having proved John to be something beyond incompetent and foolish, I felt, it would be difficult for any judge to find in favor of the Dennisons because it was clear that MediaComm's interests had been poorly represented, and therefore, the company had been harmed. John's meeting was illegal and his leadership was impeachable to say the least. So how could Judge Brown allow the takeover to go forward? The star witness was vanquished. As John left the stand and silently slunk back to his seat in the gallery, I couldn't help but feel a little triumphant about what had just transpired.

It was Squires's turn. He called Eldon Roth, a local insurance man who had advertised his business on KILJ. Roth told the court he ran The Eldon Roth Insurance Agency and served as salesperson, sales manager and owner. "How long have you been advertising with KILJ?" asked Squires.

"Off and on, since the day they opened their doors here in Mt. Pleasant," was the answer.

"Let's talk about the off and on," said Squires. "When's the last time you were off?"

"I believe it was either in June or July of this year that I wrote a letter requesting to be taken off," Roth said.

That was a mistake. Squires quickly picked up on it to make sure my attorney didn't trip up the witness like he'd done with John.

"Do you mean last year?" corrected Squires.

"Oh, excuse me. I do, yes," replied Roth.

Back on track, Squires continued. "You said you wrote a letter to the station."

Roth gave an affirmative answer. Squires asked him why.

"Basically, just a formal way of telling them I no longer wanted to advertise, that was non-confrontational."

The witness and this line of questioning were beginning to bother me. Why on earth would Squires bring on the stand someone who wanted to *stop* advertising on the station? I felt a hint of butterflies returning to my stomach.

Squires asked Roth how much his agency paid a month in advertising the previous year.

"Probably about $700 a month," was the reply.

"How long did you stay in the off position with KILJ?"

"Actually, I believe it was only about thirty days. I got contacted by Paul..."

"Paul Dennison?"

"Yes."

So *that's* where Squires was leading the charge. Unsure of what turn this would take, I leaned in and listened with anticipation. Roth was being brought on as a sort of character witness, there to explain to the world that KILJ was better off in the hands of the Dennisons. The only problem was, this injunction hearing was about whom the station was better off with, or who was more liked around town. It was about whether the actions that led to the transfer of power from MediaComm to the Dennisons was legal. But the questioning went on, anyway.

Squires asked how this transpired. "He stopped in and said, 'I understand you've recently canceled your contract and wanted to know if there was anything (I can) do to smooth things out...'" was the answer.

The defense attorney confirmed with Roth that "Paul" was indeed his client, Paul Dennison. When Roth did so, the questioning continued.

"What was (Paul's) role at the time?"

"I don't know what his role was," said the witness. "In fact, I knew he was formerly the owner and he was coming back as a businessperson to me."

"Did you think he was representing KILJ when he stopped in?" asked Squires.

Roth said, yes, he did, and that he felt Dennison was definitely trying to get the insurance agency back as an advertiser.

He also said Dennison was a "good salesperson." Ultimately, Roth continued, he decided to return to KILJ. Part of the reason The Roth Insurance Agency had left in the first place was that he hadn't heard from any KILJ sales representative in about two years.

And why did Dennison convince Roth to come back?

"(Dennison) was the first person who took the effort to come and see me."

Okay, now I was beginning to understand. It looked like Squires was trying to build Dennison back in as a good steward of KILJ's interests in the wake of my attorney's cross-examination.

Squires asked if Dennison provided any other services. Yes, said Roth. Paul had offered help in changing the tone of The Roth Insurance Agency's message so the business could utilize its advertising more effectively.

"Are they good suggestions?" asked Squires.

Yes they were, Roth replied.

Squires honed in on his point. "If Mr. Dennison departs the radio station at this point in time for whatever reason, what will happen with your advertising, now?"

Mike jumped to his feet. "Objection," he declared. "Speculation."

Judge Brown looked at my attorney. "We're in equity," she said. "The answer will come into the record subject to the objection."

I didn't understand how that could make sense. After all, the underlying cause of the injunction hearing was the question as to whether or not MediaComm had acted illegally in light of its own by-laws. What on earth did a potential advertising customer have to do with that fact? I didn't like where this was going. Something strange was happening. I felt the butterflies flutter a little harder.

Roth was allowed to continue with his answer. "There's a lot of "ifs" with that and I think if we would lose local control in some way, I would quit advertising."

"What about if the control reverts back to what it was when you quit in July?" asked Squires.

Noyes was back on his feet. "Same objection, your Honor!" he said.

But the answer was nearly the same. "We are in equity," Judge Brown repeated. "The answer will come in subject to the question."

Again Roth continued. "I would probably pull the advertising again," he said. He continued that this would be a normal procedure for any business that paid good money for advertising regularly. "You want to feel as if you're . . . loved or you're wanted or they have a need for you," he said. "I think we've all been in situations where you think nobody cares and so if I don't care, why am I spending the money?"

Squires asked how long Roth had known Paul Dennison.

"Since the day he moved to Mt. Pleasant." Roth pointed out he'd been a teenager when he first came to know Dennison.

Squires seized on this. "What is his reputation in the community?" he asked.

Once again, Mike cut in. "Objection," he said emphatically. "That's not relevant to anything we're here for."

That made sense to me. What did Dennison's standing in Mt. Pleasant, as viewed through Roth's point of view, have to do with my case?

Once more, Judge Brown repeated herself. "We are in equity," she droned. "The answer may come in subject to the record to the objection."

"Paul's reputation has always been as a successful businessperson here in the community," said Roth. "Community involvement, especially, I know, with his involvement with Iowa Wesleyan College and other projects in the past."

This was beyond the pale, I thought. So what if Roth viewed Dennison as an upstanding citizen? I certainly didn't, and I was sure there were other people in town who felt the same way. This had nothing, *absolutely nothing* to do with my case! Why was the judge allowing this kind of testimony into the proceedings? Roth had admitted that he was off and on as an advertiser at the station. He had never been there continuously. And, he was John's account.

The butterflies were back in full force. I had a bad feeling something unexpected was happening. There now existed in my mind, with growing dread, a thought that facts might not matter when the final judgment came down. The entire injunction had been derailed by Judge Brown and her allowance of testimony that had nothing to do with what we were there for. Her response to the objections by my attorney, Mike Noyes, was repeatedly that we were "in equity." Well, in equity means that we are examining what is called a petition in equity, which is what the Dennisons filed in September of 2003. The petition in equity is a notice that you have defaulted on a payment.

But their assertion that we had defaulted was a separate issue than my appeal for an injunction. I was asking that the Dennisons be removed from operations at the station. Judge Brown was examining whether or not there was a default. I felt the two issues should have been handled separately, but Judge Brown continued to focus on the equity issue and ignored the issues related to my request for an injunction.

It didn't get any better as the afternoon progressed. The defense called Robert Meyer, another Mt. Pleasant area businessperson. He was the president of Wayland State Bank, which also advertised on KILJ off and on, but had dropped its commercials with the station. Like Roth, he told the courtroom how Dennison had recently facilitated a new advertising campaign.

"Who initiated that meeting?" asked Squires.

"Oh, probably Paul," said the witness. (*Probably?* I thought to myself. *Who else could it have been?*) "Paul called me and gave me . . . an update, a little bit of what was going on, and said that he thought we needed to be back on the station," Meyer continued. "(He) had some ideas and at that point we met."

Meyer continued. It seemed he and Dennison had a prior advertising relationship before Kuhens, Stoffregen and I bought the station. Since Dennison made his move to reacquire KILJ, he'd struck a deal with Meyer so that his bank would sponsor community activities and services in exchange for advertising and announcements on KILJ. The bank's new motto was "Community-minded just like you," a slogan he said Dennison helped him put together.

"If the outcome (of the lawsuit) is Mr. Dennison leaving the radio station, will that affect the bank's advertising money?" asked Squires.

Again, my attorney objected on grounds of speculation. Again, the objection was noted, but the witness was allowed to answer. Meyers said that inevitably the relationship would change.

As with Roth, Squires questioned the witness about Dennison's reputation in the community.

"Objection," shot Noyes. "Relevance."

Brown was beginning to sound like a clever parrot that was taught to repeat a phrase over and over. "We're in equity," she said for the umpteenth time. "The objection will be noted for the record and the witness may answer subject to the objection."

Why? Why was this considered a reasonable question? Even though we were handling the injunction on the same date, technically, as the petition in equity, it seemed that the injunction side of things was being ignored completely.

"I think his reputation is good," said Meyer.

Now, I'm not sure about you, but I didn't see what Dennison's reputation had to do with any of this. Even if his reputation was perfect, that didn't address any of the issues we were in court to fix, even when you take into account the petition in equity. That question could have been answered through simple checks of the accounting.

It was time for my frustrated attorney to cross-examine the witness. Noyes quickly pounced on a key point in the Meyer-Dennison connection.

"MediaComm is a customer of the (bank), correct?" he asked.

"Yes," was the reply.

"Do they owe you some money?"

Meyer said the company did indeed have a debt to the bank, though he didn't know exactly what the sum was.

Again, it was a long-time acquaintance of Dennison's riding in to make it look as though he were the savior for the bank and that without his leadership and intervention, things would simply fall apart.

One thing was clear from both Meyer's and Roth's testimony: Squires was angling for confirmation that the station was better off in the hands of Dennison, that the town of Mt. Pleasant needed Dennison as a steward of their local landmark and that it was in everyone's best interest to allow him to stay and to transfer the KILJ stock from MediaComm's ownership over to his.

But what wasn't revealed was that both the Wayland State Bank and the Roth Insurance account were John's to service, so any mess-ups were his and were another part of his constant bungling of his responsibilities to MediaComm. Also, before John took it over, Roth had been the account of the long-term sales person who had been laid off for budget reasons. Roth hadn't liked that and in fact he had been on and off with his advertising for years, even while Dennison had been in charge. As for Meyer, he seemed uncomfortable the whole time and was likely there because Paul had been a good customer for years.

It was becoming clear to me at this point that the facts of the case were taking a back seat to something far more subjective: the "greater good" way of thinking. It was starting to look like Judge Brown was bending to the contention by the Plaintiffs that the greater good outweighed the facts in this case. Their character witnesses were building a case that without the Dennison's involvement, Mt. Pleasant would be without a viable radio station; something unacceptable in their eyes. It was all hogwash, but it was beginning to feel like they had the court on their side.

CHAPTER 20

THE AFFIDAVIT

As the second day of the injunction hearing rolled on, a new piece of evidence was added into the hearing and came as a total surprise. It was an affidavit, submitted to the court on behalf of the Dennisons, affirming what Squires was trying to prove: that Paul and Joyce were upstanding people and without their guidance at KILJ, Mt. Pleasant would ultimately lose its radio station and thus an important community resource.

The affidavit came from the attorney who'd represented the Dennisons during the original sale of KILJ to Stoffregen, Kuhens and myself. It was an affidavit from Tom Vilsack, former Mt. Pleasant-based attorney, former mayor of Mt. Pleasant, former State Senator for the Mt. Pleasant area and now writing with the authority of his current office: governor of Iowa.

Vilsack was the sitting governor of Iowa at the time of the injunction, the trial and the appeal that came later. He was also the man responsible for appointing Judge Brown to her post in 2001. That fact had never entered my mind before the affidavit was entered into the record. But with the affidavit, and Judge Brown's penchant for focusing on the needs of the Dennison's and their radio station, it now seemed very relevant.

In the affidavit, Vilsack stated he'd long known the Dennisons, and that they were good, upstanding people. Furthermore, he stated, unless they returned as owners and operators of KILJ, the community would lose its radio station. And without that station, Mt. Pleasant would be cut off from an important resource of news, information and entertainment.

Vilsack stated, "There are several reasons the transaction (meaning the purchase of KILJ from the Dennisons) was structured to include an immediate remedy. First, the nature of the radio business is such that the identity and authority of the station's owners must be certain at all times, both for licensing and advertising purposes. We anticipated that a default by MediaComm could adversely affect the radio station, particularly if the default was accompanied by erratic efforts to keep the station operating. By negotiating and agreeing to an immediate remedy that would permit the Dennisons to resume control of the station, all parties agreed that this remedy was appropriate to maintain the viability of the radio station if an uncured default existed."

Vilsack's contention was that the Dennisons were right in taking back the stock for KILJ because an "uncured default" existed. That's a fancy term for a default on a loan that hasn't been settled. Well, as I've established, I offered to pay the Dennisons out of my own pocket for the money that was owed to them in August of 2003. And, in fact, in January of 2004 I did pay Paul Dennison $88,956.48 to cure the defaults that had occurred before and after that meeting.

You're probably wondering why I would put my personal money further into a business venture that was already experiencing trouble. But I didn't see the situation as being as deeply flawed as I think John wanted to make it seem like it was. John made a point of using MediaComm's money to pay everyone but the Dennisons, and after the trouble we had with Mike Stoffregen, it was going to take some time for us to recover, anyway.

Vilsack stated in his affidavit that a default by MediaComm would adversely affect the radio station, especially if it was "accompanied by erratic efforts to keep the station operating." I suppose he was referring to my efforts at keeping MediaComm alive, namely putting my own money into the station to pay bills. But what's wrong with that? Countless businesses have periods of struggle, and I doubt it's uncommon for the owners to infuse cash into the operation in order to keep it going.

There were times when MediaComm was bringing in more money than others, and like many radio stations around the country, we struggled to bring in advertising dollars. With more of the money going to new media like the Internet, it was becoming increasingly difficult to capture those dollars as we had in the 1990s. But this wasn't a circumstance that called for dire intervention. The station was going to be there and we could have found new ways to generate revenue.

I can't say that I ever felt there was a reason that the radio station couldn't make it to profitability. I still feel that if things were handled differently by Mike and John that the station would have continued as a viable enterprise under our ownership.

When we held the board meeting in August, the money was in MediaComm's coffers to pay the Dennisons. John put the money toward other expenses because I think it was in his best interest to have MediaComm default on the payments to them. As you saw earlier, John was the guarantor on all of MediaComm's debts, and he didn't want to save the company. He wanted to give the station back because he stood to have thousands of dollars in loans forgiven by the Dennisons if he returned the station's shares to them. The money was there for the radio station to cure itself. He made sure the Dennisons didn't get paid, and I felt the litigation would clear all this up.

John was going to be released of thousands of dollars of debt and was still going to be paid an owner's salary, so what motivation did he have to keep working on MediaComm? I was personally invested in the success of the company because it's not as if the Dennisons were going to give me my money back once they took over the station. I had a lot of motivation to hang on to the station for as long as I could.

Because I believed in the station, I continued to put my own money into the enterprise, most notably with the $88,956.48 I paid to Paul Dennison that January. There was no default and Paul was in control illegally with John's blessing.

It was, in short, ridiculous. Like the testimony of previous witnesses, this affidavit stated facts that were irrelevant to the case. Even Noyes would tell me that he conceded to everything the governor said, but that it still had nothing to do with our case. This injunction was about the violation of by-laws, established by MediaComm and approved of many years ago by the Dennison's attorney, John Vilsack, *juris doctorate*!

For crying out loud, I thought. Does the governor not have enough to do running the state? Does he have so much free time that he can provide his two cents in an injunction against a former client? And if he did, why did his affidavit on behalf of the Dennisons have nothing—*nothing!*—to do with the facts at hand?

It was then I realized that the facts of my case simply did not matter. Something smelled bad, very bad. It stank, I thought, of undue influence on the part of the governor's office and a certain prejudice by Judge Brown against my attorney and me. Why had she denied Mike Noyes's objections about relevancy when the Dennisons' character and standing in the community came to question? And why did she deny a jury trial for us in the fall?

I felt sick to my stomach. I knew then that the fix was in for the Dennisons. The illogical overruling of objections, coupled with the governor's letter added up to something. The case wasn't over in a technical sense, but I had a growing feeling that the decision was made before the first witness was called to the stand.

Now, I'm not completely naïve. I know there are political games played in the judicial system and that one hand washes the other in spite of what the law says. We've seen that kind of thing time and again in cases throughout the country, from the smallest traffic court case to judgments by the United States Supreme Court. It's not pretty, but history shows us that these things happen and happen often enough to be part of the system.

But not here, not in rural Iowa, I thought. Sure, fixed trials might take place in big cities, where you expect that kind of thing. But Iowa? America's heartland? Home to *Field of Dreams*? It didn't seem right. It didn't seem possible.

But now I was sure it was happening.

There was one shot left. It was my turn to take the stand and I felt that if I could lay the facts out for everyone to see, then maybe things could be turned around for the better.

Chapter 21

Taking a Stand

I rose from my place at the defense table, confident, yet feeling more than a little apprehensive. After all, I wasn't happy with the way Judge Brown had overruled my attorney on such clear-cut legal points. I knew Mike was right to make the objections he had; any first year law student or regular court-TV viewer would have clearly seenthat the defense attorney's speculative line of questioning was beyond legal reasoning and facts of the case. Still, when you came right down to it, I did have the truth on my side. Bolstered with that knowledge, I put aside all apprehensions and took my place on the witness stand.

I was sworn in, promising to tell the truth, the whole truth, and nothing but the truth (unlike John and Paul, I thought when I finished and sat down). Vernon Squires would have the first crack at me. I knew it wouldn't be easy. He is a good attorney and he was acting as an advocate for his client. I don't hold anything against him; he was doing his job and was always respectful. We went over a brief history of what had transpired, bringing out my version of the facts leading up to that fateful day that previous August.

Yes, I told him, had the rules and by-laws of the company been followed to the letter of the law, MediaComm and KILJ would not be in its current state of affairs. Squires asked why MediaComm had not paid the Dennisons the money they were owed under the stock purchase agreement between August and November of 2003.

I answered, "There were no checks actually issued, but on the August 18th date that the board meeting was held, Mr. Dennison asked me how much money we had and I said that we had $25,000, which would cover two payments, and we also . . . I also thought that we had overpaid property taxes on some more acres than we actually owned. So we had that for the third payment."

I'll explain more about the property tax issue later, but suffice it to say I think we could have come up with the payments owed to the Dennisons in August of 2003. Now, Dennison wanted us to pay for May, June and July, which would have come up to about $33,000.

But as I explained to Noyes, "Mr. Dennison said, 'The day has come and this isn't good enough,' so I considered that to be a refusal of payment on that date." Dennison had made his mind up before that August meeting that he was going to go after the KILJ stock, that's why he and John signed a stock transfer agreement in May, well before the meeting. I don't think there's anything I could have done to stop him, and I wanted the court to know that that was why we had not paid in subsequent months.

"Do you think that somehow MediaComm would have found the money to pay off the Dennisons?" Squires pointedly asked me.

The answer was all too obvious. "I think when push came to shove, I always stepped up to the plate and offered to make payments," I replied. "I offered to put some money in during August when we were short a little bit. Obviously, when we got to the end of the year, I came up with the $88,956.48 to pay (Dennison), so, you know, I would have stepped up to the plate to make sure (he) got his money."

Squires zeroed in on the meeting in August and reminded me that John disagreed with my assessment of the finances at the time.

I answered that I thought it was possible for us to make the payments and said, "Even if we were a little bit short on that (the payments), there were things that John and I had done in the past to alleviate (the situation) if we were short. We would hold our checks or whatever we needed to . . . to make sure (payments were made to the Dennisons). The Dennisons were the priority on the 18th."

I think Squires was trying to prove that the situation was hopeless and that Dennison was right to initiate the default and transfer of stock and license. But I was determined to show that we would have done what we could.

Squires continued, zeroing in on our expenses, including payroll. "You would agree that you already had payroll booked on August 8th of nearly $7,000, correct?"

He was trying to show that the $25,000 we had in our accounts was already partially spoken for, and it was. But Squires asked why payments had not been made previous to January. ". . . Mr. Dennison and John were firmly in control," I said. "It could have been paid. There were a number of ways that the January payment could have been paid. If Mr. Dennison would have left the premises, I would have paid it. If we could, we probably would have had an auction. It could have been paid in that manner. You know, maybe we could have gone out and done some collections."

The auction. One of the most popular events with KILJ listeners was the annual on-air auction. People would put various goods and services up for sale, and we'd announce what was available via the airwaves. Listeners would call in with their bids and the winners would come to the station—often on the same day—to make payment and collect what they had won. Of course, the station got a percentage of what sellers made from the auction, as well. Auctions like this are a very popular feature held annually and even monthly at rural radio stations across the country. It was a quick way for us to make money, always a lucrative operation for the station and—for reasons I never could understand—Dennison and Kuhens decided to cancel it once they'd taken over KILJ in their coup.

I continued. "I'm very, very confident that if we would have gone ahead and had the auction, gotten us over the rough months, that our business would have picked up with me there, Paul there, whoever would have been there."

Squires turned to the illegal appointment of Susie Kuhens to the MediaComm leadership.

"You claimed that Mr. Kuhens breached his fiduciary duties by appointing (his wife) to the board of directors?"

Yes, I replied, knowing the facts were on my side here.

"Did that appointment ever become effective in your mind?"

"No," I stated. Why should it ever have been effective in my mind or anyone else's? After all, it was such a blatant violation of everything we had established when MediaComm was established and came into being! I knew it, my attorney knew it, and we wanted that made clear to the court. And somehow, deep inside, I realized that despite their flagrant breaking of our compact, John Kuhens, Paul Dennison and even Susie Kuhens and Joyce Dennison knew that, too. After all, Dennison had retreated to his home in September of 2003 before returning with a vengeance in December. He thought that we were so far behind that we couldn't make it up. Those had been awkward times from August through December 2003.

When I was finished being questioned by Vernon Squires, my attorney, Mike Noyes cross-examined me and we worked to establish my side of events, most of which had been covered by the questioning by Squires. I felt it was important that we return emphasis to the illegal acts by John Kuhens and Paul Dennison during the August meeting and afterwards.

I wanted to know what had happened to ethical business practices and the importance of being honest with your business partners. If John was so set on giving the station back to the Dennisons, why didn't he approach me first and discuss what our options were? And as for Paul Dennison, why did he refuse to accept payment in August? There were options on the table that neither man explored. I was even willing to sell my portion of the business if the offer was right, but that was never seriously discussed.

What I wanted from the injunction was a return to the status we enjoyed prior to the takeover by Dennison. I was asking that Paul be removed from the premises, along with John, and that MediaComm be put back in charge of the station. That's not to say that we couldn't have come to an arrangement after MediaComm was reinstalled. I wasn't being vindictive against John or Paul, regardless of what they'd done.

I just wanted their illegal actions reversed so that things could be done properly. There was no reason John couldn't put somebody on the board in a proper meeting, and if Paul was determined to foreclose on MediaComm he could have done so through the proper channels. But I think we could have paid him and kept going forward to a better future for MediaComm.

Chapter 22

The Decision

The back and forth testimony was grueling, but finally the injunction hearing/petition in equity came to a close. I felt weary from the process, but also hopeful. Despite everything that went on, with Vilsack's affidavit and the so-called "character" witnesses who showed up on behalf of the Dennisons, I knew that the facts were on my side. John had admitted on the stand that he hadn't read the by-laws, essentially making my case for me. He showed that the move was illegal and that I was right in asking for an injunction to halt any and all actions that arose as a result of the meeting.

It wasn't just my testimony that buffeted my mood; it was also the lengthy paper trail that ultimately proved my case. How could things not turn out well? What's more, John's milquetoast performance on the stand, wilting under direct questioning, plus what I felt was arrogant behavior of Paul Dennison—you tell me, what else could the verdict be?

In an injunction hearing like this there is no jury and the judge decides the case and can decide if final summations will be given in the courtroom or in written form. Ours were to be given in written form through official letters sent by the attorneys for plaintiff and defendant.

Noyes's final brief was short and to the point. In just a few pages he reiterated our stance and addressed the Dennisons's claims to the KILJ stock and the FCC license. With the help of the UCC, or uniform commercial code, he was able to show that MediaComm had been wronged and damaged by the irresponsible actions of John Kuhens and that payment for the January 2004 installment of the stock purchase agreement would have been impossible given that Paul Dennison had effectively taken over the revenue producing powers of MediaComm. Without the radio station in its control and possession, MediaComm was without revenue, and was therefore unable to pay.

The final briefs went back and fourth, my attorneys citing the reasons why I felt I was in the right (facts on my side) versus why the Dennisons felt they were being wronged. Once the letters were received by Judge Brown both Noyes and Squires could provide counter arguments, again via official letters. I received all copies of these briefs. Again, I could only feel that my case was a slam-dunk victory. After all, we had the legal documents which proved the case . . . documents that the Dennisons and Kuhens had signed and followed—until they changed their minds and decided it was perfectly fine to violate the terms of any and all agreements as they saw fit.

March, 2004 turned into April and then May. Still no word from Brown, no decision whatsoever. I vacillated between complete confidence in my case to sometimes wondering if something had gone terribly wrong for me. After all, it seemed all so open and shut. But still, I remained hopeful.

Then, on June 15, I received a call from Noyes's office. His secretary told me that Judge Brown's verdict was in and that I could expect an email very soon with the decision attached. I couldn't tell from her voice whether the news was good or bad. Quickly, I raced to my computer, hitting the "receive" button on my email software time and again until finally the much-anticipated verdict hit my inbox.

I opened the email and looked at the verdict that Judge Brown had issued. Skimming through the initial legalese and summation of the arguments, I eagerly read the section labeled "Finding of Fact."

"The court finds the following," Judge Brown had written. As I read on, my stomach turned into knots. She pointed out that the station went into default as of January 2004—never mind that I was the one paying the Dennisons out of my own pocket. What's more, she ignored the fact that Dennison had accepted my check in January 2004, but had not put the money on the books until much later. And what kind of fool would I have been to keep paying the bills with my personal funds into February, March and beyond? "The undisputed facts are that the only reason the radio station literally gets on the air in morning and continues to have news stories to report or covers local events, such as school sporting activities is because John Kuhens does that work," Judge Brown wrote.

So what? I thought. What did that have to do with our legal agreements? It wasn't like John was the only person who could handle the work—which was an entry-level job he'd been at for what amounted to more than thirty years. But according to her ruling, "Burkhart's involvement with the day-to-day operation of the radio station has been limited to selling advertising." If Kuhens was removed from the station, she added, then KILJ would be in serious trouble, and ultimately, this could lead to the downfall of an important resource for the area. In essence, Judge Brown's decision ruled that in order to keep the radio station broadcasting the plaintiffs must retain control of the station.

And yes, my day-to-day involvement had been selling advertising, but I was also a co-owner and the person who had easily invested the most money into the operation. In fact, the original stock purchase agreement wouldn't have been possible unless I had lent money to all of my co-owners. John, Mike and Steve wouldn't even have been able to buy into the station if it weren't for me. So, I think I was a little more involved than Judge Brown gave me credit for.

As far as removing Dennison from the day-to-day operations of the station, Judge Brown ruled that, "The undisputed record is that Paul Dennison wants to keep KILJ on the air. The only reason that it would be appropriate to keep Dennison away from the actual radio station would be if he was doing something detrimental to the radio station staying on the air and continuing to be part of the Mt. Pleasant community."

To me that was a slap in the face. Dennison had no right to be involved in the day-to-day operations of the radio station because he was there illegally. It didn't matter if he wanted to keep the station on the air. That's like me walking into a car dealership and taking over the accounts receivable and having a judge rule in my favor because I was doing a good job.

Judge Brown did grant my right to a temporary injunction on the transfer of the KILJ stocks to the plaintiffs, i.e., the Dennisons. Before you start thinking that that was a victory for me, though, consider this: In order to have a writ of injunction enforced, I would have had to secure a bond worth one hundred twenty-five percent of the collateral in the case. Since the stock was deemed to be worth $1 million, I would have to come up with a $1.25 million bond. I wasn't going to do that until I was satisfied I had a proper trial for the other issues I'd gone to court for. Consequently, I didn't secure the bond and the stock was foreclosed on, resulting in an auction, where the Dennisons were the only bidders.

Another reason I didn't come up with the bond was that I felt confident that I would be vindicated in the trial to take place later in the year. I felt as though there was no need to come up with the $1.25 million if the station would just be returned to me later in the year.

If you're thinking that Paul Dennison had to come up with a million dollars to "buy" the radio station then you're wrong. Since he was the lender in the sale of the enterprise, he would have been buying the station back from himself. There were other interested parties when the radio station went up for sale, but the sight of the place was probably enough to scare off any potential investors. It was around that time that John Kuhens had accidentally run into one of the guide wires that supported the radio tower, knocking the tower down. The radio station was essentially broadcasting from a wire until the tower went back up.

I personally believe that the Dennisons didn't make any effort to improve the situation while the station was up for sale. What motivation did they have to do so? If they were the only bidders, they'd get the radio station back like they wanted all along.

During the entire injunction, Judge Brown focused on the wellbeing of KILJ, never mind the fact that MediaComm was the defendant in the case and that MediaComm's by-laws were the ones broken by the president of the company: John Kuhens, the very man she said was vital to the survival of

KILJ. The guy doing the most damage was the one named as the savior of the radio station. Well, that's great for the radio station to survive, but what about the corporation that owned the radio station? It had been hijacked and gutted of its most valuable asset in KILJ, and Judge Brown simply ignored that fact and the law and said that Dennison could resume ownership of the KILJ stock unless MediaComm could present the bond to the escrow agent to secure the injunction.

Well, I don't have to tell you that we didn't have that kind of money in MediaComm's accounts. And in my view it was not necessary to put the bond up if the courts did their job in the fall. I wanted to go to trial and settle this thing and I wasn't going to pay the Dennison's a penny until order was restored within the corporation.

Because we didn't come up with the money, the station was allowed to go up for auction, and the only bidders were the Dennisons, but more on that later.

Judge Brown said that Kuhens and Dennison were acting in the best interest of KILJ and that unless they did something to harm KILJ, then she couldn't order an injunction. Of course Dennison and Kuhens wouldn't do anything to harm KILJ— that was their baby. They'd been involved with the station for thirty years. But they didn't have a problem harming Media-Comm, which would only adversely affect me, since John could keep his job at the radio station and have his $70,000 loan from the Dennisons forgiven with the transfer of KILJ stock back to them. It was like a catch-22. I had to prove they wanted to harm the station in order to have them ordered out, when harming the station would only have hurt *them*. Somehow in Judge Brown's mind, the reality that John Kuhens had something to gain from gutting MediaComm and restoring KILJ's stock to the Dennisons was lost.

MediaComm was forgotten in the rush to keep KILJ operating.

End of story.

From the marrow of my bones to the tips of my toes, I felt numb all over. Facts, as it turned out, did not matter. What did matter was the importance of the radio station as a community entity, and that apparently could only happen with John behind the mike. No one else, it would appear by Judge Brown's decision, could do that job and hence the case I had was negligible. Thus Dennison and Kuhens—for the moment—could do as they pleased.

How could this have happened? I felt like an enormous weight had fallen on me, sort of like those cartoons where an anvil falls on the head of the coyote when he's chasing the roadrunner—except this wasn't funny. This had to be a joke, a strange and utterly ridiculous joke. Surely the real verdict would come next with Judge Brown finding in my favor.

But it was not a joke. The verdict lay before me, as real and as legal as anything I'd ever read. As real and as legal as the documents I'd signed with the Dennisons and Kuhens in what seemed like a million lifetimes ago.

Up was down, down was up. White was black and black was white. And facts didn't matter.

* * *

As far as the actual injunction hearing goes, Noyes had done an excellent job of proving that there had been a signed legal agreement, that I had held up my end of the bargain, and that the Dennisons and the Kuhenses had openly and brazenly violated the terms of our contract. I felt Squires hadn't proved a thing, other than that John was a radio announcer and Dennison previously owned the station.

Yes, Paul Dennison was successful at selling advertising, and yes, John occupied most of the on-air time at KILJ. But to say that they could never be replaced and that KILJ would cease to exist without them is ridiculous. Advertising salesmen and on-air talent are replaced at stations all the time, and without a complete collapse of the station. To say that I couldn't have found anyone who could perform the duties those two were performing is ludicrous.

Yet, there had been clues, I realized, that the injunction would go against me. Judge Brown had given me some insight into how the case was going during the two days of the injunction hearing. Remember how she overruled my attorney's objections? Noyes's objections were based on solid legal ground, yet I felt Judge Brown was completely unfair in her overruling of the objections. It was, it now occurred to me, as if she didn't care about what the facts of our contracts and agreements had been. She was, it now seemed to me, never interested in hearing my side of the story.

"Dixie," my husband said to me, "you've been screwed."

He was right. I had put my faith in the legal system to right the wrongs and somehow, someway this process had failed me miserably. But why? I just couldn't put my finger on it.

As the days passed I continued to mull over the case. Time and again, I looked over the evidence, at the transcripts and all the legal papers filed on my behalf. The contracts were laid out bare—you just couldn't dispute the facts within them, not in a court of law, or so I thought. What had happened? What could have possibly gone wrong?

Then it hit me. I didn't want to think that this could be true, but it hit me very hard. What had decided the case, I thought, could be summed up in a single word: politics.

Keep in mind, there was that affidavit Governor Vilsack had sent to the court on Dennison's behalf. Remember that Vilsack had been Dennison's attorney so many years ago, and now, having risen through the ranks of Iowa politics, had achieved the most powerful position in the state. He was no longer mayor or state senator: he was the governor with the ability to veto anything he saw as wrong and sign into law anything he thought was right. Remember what I thought when I first heard about the affidavit the governor had written to the court—that I was curious about how the governor's desk was so uncluttered that he had the time to get involved in what amounted to a violation of a business agreement between two parties? A terrible realization hit me: I was outgunned by someone with better connections than me. Paul Dennison was better connected and had called on his former attorney to wade into our little squabble and tilt the table in his favor.

So I couldn't help but think that there was an obvious reason my facts—no matter how strong—simply didn't matter.

You have to wonder what the motivation for the ruling was. I don't know what happened or if anything happened at all. It just struck me as being contrary to common sense and the law.

I felt sick, angry and cheated. What happened to me was a terrible miscarriage of justice. I'm not a whiner and never have been my whole life. I've had to live through some hard times, like the death of my first husband, and other difficulties and traumas that life inevitably throws at me, you and everyone else in the world.

But the unfairness of the decision, the seemingly deliberate ignoring of facts and hard-core legalities just didn't settle with me. Facts didn't matter, or—as, as my husband had so bluntly put it—I'd been screwed.

Chapter 23

Regrouping in a Mud Storm

Though Judge Brown's decision on the injunction seemed like a cold slap, I realized there was no point in whining or moaning about it. I did all the right things—put forth my case, presented evidence and was given a decision. It's the way the system works. One side gives their presentation, the other side shows their point of view, and attorneys cross-exam before giving a final summary of their respective clients' cases before the court. Judge or jury consider these aspects, then make a binding decision based on the presentations.

Although the results weren't what I was expecting (to say the least), I did have my day—my first day—in court. The judicial process had spoken. I still believed in the court system and that facts did indeed matter when all was said and done. Rather than mourn, I organized. I realized that the healthiest thing I could do for myself was to put my disappointment in the verdict behind me. Rather, I would concentrate my energies to the upcoming fall hearing, where I remained convinced justice would be served.

I had a plan to implement should I be allowed back at the station, including a consultant that would examine our operation and give recommendations. I also had someone in mind to take over the on-air duties that John was doing.

Dennison knew what I wanted to do, but he wasn't going to let realities of radio operation get in his way. John was his boy and easy to control; the man I wanted to bring in wouldn't have been. So Dennison did what he did best: lie through this teeth about him. Of course, that would come later, during the trial. On the stand, Dennison would say that my prospective on-air talent was a drug addict and was a troublemaker. It was absurd and was in keeping with a pattern Paul had of badmouthing anyone who got in his way.

He would continue to badmouth me around town, saying that I had stolen from the station. When I spoke to Noyes about it he said it was probably because I had been able to get the money out of MediaComm's accounts that was owed me from the Stoffregen loan. Dennison never could get it through his head that I was a creditor like anyone else.

I don't know what I did to Paul Dennison that made him so vengeful. Maybe it was that I was going against his protégé in John Kuhens. If only I had known his true character when I first got involved with the radio station a few years before. Instead, I was now mired in a battle of personalities and unethical behavior. Well, this, too, would pass, I kept telling myself. I was ready to move on to the next phase: our case against the Dennisons.

Again, Judge Brown was chosen to hear the case in what would be a bench trial. Despite the results of the injunction, neither my lawyer nor I had any real concerns over facing Dennison and Kuhens in the courtroom again under Judge Brown's authority. Maybe I was naïve, but I still maintained that we had proof on our side that unethical business practices and illegal actions—backed up by documented facts—would still prevail at the end of the day.

Once more we put together our case, getting all our ducks in a row. Papers, evidence, briefs and so forth. We had the routine down. While I was still feeling a little burned after the decision Judge Brown gave on the injunction, I still believed that the facts were on my side . . . and that the facts *did* matter. I was ready to face off against Dennison and Kuhens once again.

Chapter 24

The Trial Begins

With these many thoughts swirling through my head, I confidentially mounted the stairs to enter the courthouse. There was a light breeze in the air and the sun shown brightly, warming on the skin. Good omens, I suppose. Such a difference from underhanded meetings plotted and carried out in the dank atmosphere of a rundown basement office.

Noyes, my attorney once again, was equally confident. Keep in mind, he had told me that anything could happen in any court proceeding—you couldn't always count on everything to go your way. It's like that old saying goes, there are one hundred ways to blow your case in court and if you can come up with the first twenty-five then you are a legal genius. He had also told me that those that go by the rules usually win.

It didn't matter, not at that moment. When we entered the courtroom, with the Dennisons and the Kuhenses at bay, I knew I was ready to take on all the things they were ready to throw at me.

When Dennison took the stand he was questioned by his attorney, Vernon Squires, first and his lies were obvious from the start. He seemed to want to misdirect Judge Brown, making it look like I'd had little financial involvement with the station, and furthermore, my participation had led to the troubles KILJ was having.

When asked by Vernon Squires how the sale of the radio station had come about, Squires said that he had been "bugged for a long time by Mike Stoffregen that he was interested in getting into the radio business, and I hired a financial person to see" if the sale was possible.

When asked who he sold the radio station to, Dennison said that it was to "a company called MediaComm, but it was basically Mike Stoffregen and John Kuhens, and then I believe that Ms. Burkhart was brought in as a silent partner."

I was being characterized as a silent partner, which I was. But Dennison wanted to make it seem as though I had zero involvement. What he didn't mention was that I was the only reason Stoffregen and Kuhens had been able to fulfill their investment responsibilities in the first place and that I was now the largest shareholder in MediaComm.

Dennison also explained how he had come to work for KILJ selling advertising in late 2003, and how he had originally worked under the Time Brokerage Agreement the FCC provides as a framework, and that after that agreement became "controversial" as he called it, he and Kuhens came up with a management contract.

The contract was structured so that KILJ, under the authority of MediaComm, was paying Mount Pleasant Management, LLC to run the radio station and sell advertising. Well, Mount Pleasant Management, LLC was Dennison.

And the reason the Time Brokerage Agreement became controversial was because the meeting was illegal! Go figure. People got nervous about an illegal meeting that gutted a company against the wishes of the board. Can't figure that one out.

Anyways, Dennison said he had agreed to the management agreement because "I felt (it) very, very, very necessary that I stay there and sell advertising or the radio station wasn't going to continue to be on the air, and since I was the one that really had the most to lose, I needed to be there . . ."

Dennison's logic was baffling to me. He said that he felt as though the radio station wouldn't be there without him. But if he had just left the station after I paid him the $88,956.48 in January of 2004, I would have come back into the station and resumed selling advertising. There would have been management there, and the station would have continued to go on the air each day.

And how the heck did he think that he was the one with the most to lose? He had a lot to gain, and should MediaComm fail to pay him he could take the station back and have all of the money we'd paid him over the years, plus the station back.

I had the most to lose in this deal. I was at risk of losing the only real revenue-generating asset my company owned, and if I lost that then I would lose my entire investment of several hundred thousand dollars. I would say that qualifies as having more to lose than Dennison.

I'm sure he was trying to make it seem that if the radio station folded then he wouldn't be able to get any of the money he'd sold the station for. But that was never a real possibility and he knew it.

Dennison was also asked whether I'd been involved in the station in 2004 and whether or not I'd made any efforts to do so. Dennison answered, "No," to both questions. He didn't elaborate, of course, or mention that I would not return to the station until he left. That must have slipped his mind.

Dennison explained that after MediaComm refused to post bond for the KILJ stock, how he had it transferred back to his ownership and notified the FCC of that transfer, making it all official. Of course, he wasn't done knocking MediaComm for the job we'd done at the station. When Squires asked him about the amount he had bid for the station during the "sale," earlier that year, he railed against us for letting "everything go" at the station.

As I explained before, Dennison couldn't just take the station back. Because the court had ordered MediaComm to come up with a bond to cover the KILJ stock after the injunction, and since we didn't, the station could go up for auction. The Dennisons were the only ones to bid on the station, and apparently Paul thought it was because the station was in such a state of disrepair.

"Well, because of their financial problems the past several years," he said, "they've basically let everything go, from equipment to office furniture. For example, it's hard to find a chair for people to sit on because they're all broken. The computer equipment that runs the radio station should have been replaced. I think it's seven or eight years old now. It should have been replaced three or four years ago. The equipment that runs the remote control that runs the AM radio station won't work, and that's basically against FCC rules. It's against the law, so we got an order in for the new equipment to control the AM, the remote amplifier, everything, so it just goes on and on, expenses that we've had."

If you'd listened to Paul Dennison on the stand you would have gotten the impression that the station was falling to pieces and that any minute now, the building would collapse into a sinkhole because of the neglect bestowed upon the station by MediaComm. We had roofed, painted, replaced flooring, painted some more, wallpapered and made other repairs during our ownership. It was farcical listening to him describe the situation. Heck, if the state of the station was that bad, and if Paul and Joyce Dennison were having to spend so much on repairs, then why didn't he just accept my personal funds in August of 2003? Why did he go through all that trouble of having John place Susie on the board and contacting the FCC and getting the paperwork together to take over a decrepit station?

Paul could have accepted the money I offered in August 2003 as he had done with the January 2004 payment. He even said during his testimony that he had wished someone else would have bought the station. He said he wished that because, "then I could have retired again." Well, he could have stayed retired if he hadn't taken part in the illegal August meeting and if he'd accepted a personal check from me.

And then the attacks got personal. You see, part of the reason for the trial was that Dennison was suing MediaComm to recover the attorney's fees he'd had to pay during the buildup to the injunction and the hearing itself.

"Now, are you still seeking to recover those attorney's fees?" asked Squires.

"Yes, I am," answered Dennison.

"From whom?"

"From whomever is responsible. I suppose Mrs. Burkhart, who is now elongating this situation."

"And why is it you think you should recover your attorney fees from Mrs. Burkhart?"

"Well, I think she's the one that's caused this situation."

What?! I caused this situation? But he wasn't done yet.

When asked what I had done to cause the situation, meaning the lawsuits, Dennison said, "Drug her feet in every situation. Hasn't recognized the fact that her company was broke, and also that she and John were not capable of running the company."

I'll admit John was not capable of running the company. That's why Judge Brown removed him as president of Media-Comm after the trial. But there was nothing to indicate that I wasn't capable of running the company. I had never been given a real chance. After Mike Stoffregen robbed the company blind, John took over and essentially lay down so the Dennisons could walk right back in.

I felt at the time of the trial, and I still do today, that if I had been able to get John and Paul out of KILJ, I could have found people to come in and make the radio station work with the plan I had in place. Paul didn't think that at all. He told Squires that, "Without my work, they wouldn't be on the air today."

Again, this played into the notion that there was no one in Iowa who could run KILJ. Apparently, it was a skill set unique to John Kuhens and Paul Dennison. I suppose there wasn't a single person in the state who could run a small town radio station. Strange.

After discussing the state of the building some more, Dennison said something that I think is telling. Squires asked Dennison, "First of all, what has motivated you since May of 2003 to try to get the radio station back, to get it back and to go out and start selling advertising?"

Dennison said, "You know, I really haven't tried to get the radio station back. I have tried to get paid what's due me. We had a contract agreement. My life was set. All I wanted was to be paid."

Dennison had a right to be paid and he was. That's why I gave him so much of my own money, to cure the default. I wanted to make sure that he got paid. But to pretend he didn't want the station back and to use the contract to support his argument was hypocritical.

It seems everyone wants to use a contract to support their claims, but no one wants to live by the ones that are going to inconvenience them. If Dennison was so concerned about contracts then why didn't he worry when the contract that John Kuhens signed with me was violated?

The only way that Dennison was able to get the FCC license and KILJ stock transferred to him was because of a violated contract. But that didn't seem to bother him. It was only when he perceived a negative impact toward him that he started getting upset about contracts. Dennison was a snake in the grass and he would do anything to get what he wanted, contract or no.

And when Squires mentioned my assertion that Dennison wanted the station back and that John helped him because he would be forgiven loans, Dennison got upset.

"That's . . . that is just ridiculous," he said. "Absolutely not. Why would I want to go back to work when I had my life set?" Funny, during the injunction he said the station was his whole life.

Dennison's argument couldn't even stand up under his own testimony. Squires asked him about my assertion that John was motivated to give the station back because of the massive loans he'd guaranteed and couldn't pay back.

"And is Mr. Kuhens now released from his guarantee to your understanding?" asked Squires.

"Yes," said Dennison, "I think he is."

"And why is that?"

"Because we have the radio station, the stock back."

Well? Did he have a motivation or not to give the stock back to the Dennisons? I'd say so. He went from owing them hundreds of thousands of dollars as part of MediaComm to owing then just over $60,000 from the personal loan that he'd gotten from them in 2002. Now, I don't think it's a stretch to say that John had some motivation to flout the contract he'd signed.

But it gets worse. Here's the kicker. When Squires asked Dennison if he knew of John's intentions to put Susie on the Board of Directors in order to vote for the stock and license transfer, Dennison said, "No, it was a complete surprise to me that it was going to occur."

I find it hard to believe that John and Paul had no discussions about the FCC license and the possibility of making it happen by putting someone new on the board. They'd known each other for years and had worked closely together for much of that time.

In short, Dennison's testimony under questioning from his lawyer was a joke. He couldn't even keep his own assertions straight and the idea that he somehow really wished he was retired, and that he had to come back to the station to save the day from the grossly incompetent people running it was ridiculous. The only problem was, the judge had believed it during the injunction and there was a chance she would again.

CHAPTER 25

DENNISON CONFRONTED

It was Mike Noyes's turn to cross-examine Dennison and he came out firing, focusing on the possible actions MediaComm could have taken to pay Dennison his money following the January 2004 payment of $88,956.48 that had brought us current.

Noyes tried pinning Dennison on his cancellation of the very successful on-air auctions, the promotion he had started years before. As I said earlier, it had always been a financial boon for KILJ and was a much-loved element by our listening audience. Killing the auction was a stupid move on his part, albeit a very calculated attempt to get a "troubled" radio entity back into his greedy hands.

"The auction was a big help in cash flow, correct?" asked Noyes.

"When we first started it years ago, yes," Dennison admitted. Then, trying to maintain his line of attack, he switched gears. "In reviewing (KILJ's) financials of the past several years, it was not the big impact item that it used to be."

Again, this was a lie on Dennison's part. Sure, it wasn't a "big impact" item, but that was weasel wording the fact that our auction did indeed make a significant contribution to the station cash flow. It always had, and would have continued to be a boon for the station had Dennison not decided to halt the cash cow.

Noyes was ready for this. "You were aware, though, after you reviewed those financials that in February of (2003) they received approximately $23,000 of cash because of the auction, correct?"

"Yes," Dennison said. So if that was the case, then why would he cancel it? That $23,000 dollars, or something similar to it, would have provided two months' worth of payments to him. But, as sales manager in 2004 under the management agreement, he cancelled it. Why would a sales manager turn down almost guaranteed money?

Facts. Cold hard facts. I wondered to myself how Dennison would worm his way out of that. When he responded that yes, he was aware that KILJ made $23,000 (no small sum, to be sure) from the 2003 auction, Noyes fired back.

"Had you had the auction in February of 2004, wouldn't they (the station) have received cash?"

Of course we would have, I thought. That's how it always worked.

Dennison was ready with a defense of half-truths and financial fabrication. "Probably," he told Noyes and the court, "but they received cash from regular advertising that I sold, and they received one hundred percent of it and not fifty percent of it." If that was the case, why hadn't he and John allotted money to pay him the January 2004 payment? After all, they were in control of the station now.

Where was he going with this? I wondered.

"But when did they receive that?" asked Noyes.

"Same time they would have received it for the billing in January," replied Dennison. Of course, he was referring to the January bills that he claimed we couldn't pay. The facts didn't matter; Dennison pressed on.

"They (KILJ) received it in February for the billing in February. They received it in March so there was no . . ."

He hesitated, and then finished the thought. ". . . no difference."

Noyes was ready. "Well, there is one difference, isn't there, sir?" my attorney asked, injecting some heavy sarcasm into his words. "Had they had the auction in February, they would have received the money in February."

"No, not necessarily," replied Dennison. "Several of those people (who made successful bids) did not come and pick up their certificates for weeks."

"But, you're familiar with the fact that in February of (2003) they actually received $23,000 cash?" asked Noyes.

"That's correct," Dennison said. I thought for sure Noyes had nailed Dennison on this point. If we had a history of getting the money we needed as a result of the auction, a steady fact that happened year after year, then why on earth would he have canceled the event? Being in charge of KILJ meant he had a fiduciary duty to pay the bills, including the money he owed himself. Sure, it was a gamble that we would raise the money we needed via the auction, but again, as the history of the event showed, that certainly was one of the safest bets we as a business could possibly make.

"I think," said Dennison, trying to dance around the fact, "if you will look at the cash receipts comparing the two months for the two years, they'll be the same, so I don't . . ."

He composed himself for a moment, and then continued. "It did not affect the amount of cash that MediaComm had a bit."

What Dennison was trying, unsuccessfully, to assert was that MediaComm made the same amount in February from his advertising as it would have from the auction. That the auction's absence had no effect on the amount of money we would have made. But he couldn't have known how much we would make. And besides, if he was operating under the pretext of doing what was right for the station, then why didn't he do both the auction and advertising sales? That's what would have been best.

But the real problem with holding the auction and working hard at sales was that the auction would have helped MediaComm, whereas the advertising sales Dennison was doing served only to help his case that he was the pillar on which KILJ stood. His game was obvious and it just would not stand up under scrutiny.

Another lie, I thought. So did Noyes, who put a KILJ balance sheet before the witness.

"Now," said Noyes, "that's a profit and loss statement." My attorney explained that it showed the February revenues from our last auction. "It shows auction sales of $23,373.25, correct?"

"Uh-huh," Dennison replied. *Such contempt!* I thought to myself.

"That's what we've been talking about?" asked my attorney.

"Yes," replied Dennison.

"Okay," said Noyes, ready to nail home his point. "And that is cash in the door, correct?"

"Correct."

"Okay. So you would anticipate if you had an auction in '04 that you would receive maybe not the same amount, but an amount of cash?"

Evidently this question, with its yes-or-no nature, was not good enough for Dennison. All Noyes was asking was whether or not the auction would have earned any money.

"No, we would not have received any more cash," Dennison said. "You have to look at the two totals . . ."

Dennison was answering the wrong question. He was trying to show that his sales job had been so good that the total cash earned in 2004 under his watch had been more than that earned in 2003 with sales and the auction combined. And he was right, he had earned the station a lot of money since coming back. But that wasn't what Noyes was asking. He wanted to know whether or not the auction would have earned any money for the station. And that, Dennison couldn't deny, no matter how many times he tried to skirt the question.

It was a fact that, as any reasonable person could see, truly mattered. The auction would have raised money for us and helped us cure the default in February 2004. But Dennison just couldn't admit it. When Noyes asked if the auction would have raised at least $11,000, the amount owed each month, Dennison balked at the idea, saying that we couldn't have.

But Noyes used Dennison's own notice of default to hang him. He showed that the notice was issued on January 27, 2004. That means we had the entire month of February to cure the default. The auction would have done that for us. But Dennison didn't hold the auction, and he didn't leave the station when I paid him for the last months of 2003. So, he was to blame for my refusal to pay him after that.

Again, my attorney pounced on Dennison regarding my attempts to use my own personal funds to pay off the money woes of the station in January of 2004.

"As of January, you'd already received payments for October and November (2003), hadn't you?" asked Noyes. "You'd received $88,956.48, correct?"

"Yes," was the reply.

In fact, that money covered the payments of May through December of 2003.

"Okay," said Noyes, as he set out the lay of the land. "So, the fact that Mrs. Burkhart paid herself didn't affect your ability to receive the $88,956.48, did it?"

"But that doesn't have anything to do with the January payment," retorted Dennison.

"Okay," Noyes replied. "But as of January 7, you'd been paid everything, right?"

This again was a fact that couldn't be ignored. Dennison, however, wasn't going to believe anything he didn't want to and that ethic of his extended to the courtroom witness stand. He had taken the $88,956.48 check, refused to go home and had not put the money on the books until August 2004.

"That, again," he replied rather dryly, "is a difference of opinion between you and MediaComm and myself."

"Well, you took the check and cashed it, didn't you?" asked Noyes.

"I think I told you that before. Yes, I did, counselor." Dennison was upset at being challenged. But he couldn't deny what he had done. He had taken my $88,956.48.

He agreed to a contract that allowed us thirty days to cure any default, in this case the January payment, and now it had come back to bite him. Paul was done on the stand. I felt Noyes had done a solid job of getting down to the details and showing that despite MediaComm's difficulties, we were still allowed our legal rights under the contract. What John and Paul had done was illegal. There was not default and Paul would not leave.

Chapter 26

More Lies

Now came time for John to take the stand. In a strange way, I thought this might be a little entertaining. John, as I've pointed out, is a weak man who depends on Dennison in their strange daddy/child relationship. Singled out on the witness stand, without Dennison to protect him, I wondered how he would handle the pressure. Would he hang in there or would he wilt like a dandelion given a jolt of weed killer?

Remember, John was a defendant in all of this. He wasn't considered a friend to Vernon Squires and Paul Dennison for the purposes of the law. If they had to run over him to win their case they would, but they didn't have to worry too much about him causing them problems.

Squires questioned John first. He referred John to May of 2003.

"Who owned MediaComm (at that time)?" Squires asked.

"That would be myself and Dixie Burkhart and Jeff Broeg (a Class C stockholder)," John replied.

"What was your total investment in MediaComm?"

"Stock-wise, $125,000."

Squires kept things at an even keel. "Did you have any other investments in MediaComm?" he asked Kuhens.

"I had put some other funds into it, yes," my former partner replied.

"What kinds of funds or how much?"

John took his timeline back to the time that Mike Stoffregen had embezzled from the company. "It was determined that I had benefited from some dealings, so I returned those monies to the company, which totaled, over the years, close to $100,000. There was a repayment of $19,000 for excessive salaries that was termed, and then another $25,000 put in towards a $70,000 total. . ."

He was referring, of course, to the tax scam that Stoffregen had pulled and John had meekly followed.

"It was a salary deduction, and the company paid it, so the interest brought them back up to $70,000 and I put that final $70,000 into the company."

And, I thought, into your pocket.

"It sounds like the money you put into the company beyond your initial investment is not really equity," said Squires.

Of course not, John told him.

"So your equity is $125,000?"

"Yes sir."

I liked that "yes sir." How so John Kuhens that was, playing the meek, mild mannered milquetoast.

"Again, as of May 2003," asked Squires, "who ran Media-Comm?"

"I did and I guess . . ." John paused, then recovered. "I did."

"And who helped?" asked Squires.

"Dixie Burkhart was there on a day to day basis," John replied.

A day-to-day basis. That's good, I thought. I was a partner and a member of the board and he knew it. Clearly John had learned a thing or two about weasel wording from his mentor.

"What were the responsibilities of each of you?" Squires wanted to know.

"I was on the side as announcer," John replied. "I did at that time, was carrying quite a bit of responsibility for news, and also did a portion of the sales work."

Mr. KILJ, I thought. *Always had been, always would be.*

"Who did most of the sales work?" asked Squires.

"That was left up to Mrs. Burkhart."

"Left up to Mrs. Burkhart." He made it sound like I had only a tangential involvement, like the sales work was just a piece of scrap left over for me because I wasn't doing anything else. Didn't these people realize that my financial involvement was just as important as their work at the station? MediaComm wouldn't have existed without my investments and work.

"Who was responsible for paying creditors?"

"Dixie took up that chore."

Again, making it seem like I was not a partner in the business. I wasn't surprised by any of this.

Squires then asked if we had discussed who needed to be paid with the money that MediaComm generated through KILJ.

"Yeah, we had conversations about what bills to pay and who was hollering the loudest."

John made it seem as though we were on the same page as to who should have been paid. It was always my contention that the Dennisons had first priority when it came time to pay bills. I knew they could force a default if we didn't take care of them. That's why I tried to offer Paul Dennison my personal funds in August of 2003. If you'll remember, John used MediaComm funds to pay other creditors that year while I was gone from the station. He should have paid the Dennisons.

Squires asked Kuhens if there was anything we could have done differently to take care of our creditors. And just as he had at the injunction, he answered, "The only thing I know is to sell more advertising."

Squires moved on to the months before the August 2003 meeting and asked John whether we had been able to "take that step (selling more advertising) to an adequate level as of May 2003?"

John said, "No." He also said, "No" when Squires asked him about June, July, August and September.

John didn't seem to remember that we had enough money in MediaComm's coffers to pay Dennison for the months leading up the August meeting. And he neglected to mention that I had offered my own money to cover any shortfall we had. But like Dennison, John was capable of selective memory. He sat on the stand looking nervous and anything but the jovial voice of KILJ he wanted so desperately to be again.

Squires moved on to the meeting itself.

"Now, (Burkhart) has made a number of allegations of misconduct that she attributes to you, and I want to talk about each of them a little bit. The first of which I think is when you attempted to appoint your wife to the MediaComm board on

August 18, 2003, and do you recall that meeting when you attempted to do that?"

"Yes, sir."

"Why did you appoint your wife to the board?"

"To avoid a deadlock."

"What do you mean by that?"

"Because I knew Dixie wasn't in agreement with what I wanted to so, so I felt that appointing Susie to the board would break the deadlock, and so we could proceed."

John never did put up a fight when confronted with his illegal behavior, but Squires was wrong on a couple of points. First, my assertions about John were not allegations, they were facts and everyone knew it. Unfortunately, the inside of a courtroom is often a place where facts go to die. Secondly, John didn't attempt to put Susie on the board, he did it. And the consequences were devastating to MediaComm.

Apparently though, John didn't believe that what he had done was harmful to MediaComm.

Squires asked John, "When you attempted to appoint your wife to the board of directors, were you trying to harm MediaComm?"

"No, sir," said John.

"Were you trying to harm the radio station?"

"No, sir."

"Even though you knew that if you were able to do that, she would vote to return the stock to the Dennisons?"

"Yes, sir."

Now, here Squires tried to head Noyes off at the pass by bringing up the obvious question: "How is it that that would not harm MediaComm?"

"Well," John said, "I felt that MediaComm and the radio station were failing, so to avoid any more failing, I thought that putting an end to it would be the appropriate thing to do."

It was dumbfounding. First, John asserted that giving away the only revenue-generating asset that MediaComm had would not harm the company. How is that possible? That would be like Coca-Cola giving away the rights to produce Coke and the board of directors saying that it didn't intend to harm the company.

Also, if your company was in trouble, would your first move be to give away the only thing that made you any money? If McDonald's had a bad quarter, do you think they would transfer all of their assets to Burger King? It would be idiocy, and it was when John appointed Susie to the board and gave away KILJ.

The odd thing about John's testimony was that right after saying the move wouldn't harm MediaComm, he turned right around and said that the radio station was the entity that would benefit from the move when Squires asked who benefited from "putting an end to (MediaComm's) ownership."

When asked why, John replied, "It would stay on the air, hopefully be a more viable business and serve the community better."

What? I thought the president of MediaComm was supposed to be looking out for MediaComm as a whole, not just one of its assets. And shouldn't he have been more concerned with making MediaComm more of a viable company by making KILJ more viable and allowing it to serve the community better? Why did he have to do that through a giveaway of the company's major asset?

Squires then asked why John had signed the stock transfer agreement in an attempt to let the stock go back to the Dennisons.

"Because I felt that was the best thing to happen to the radio station, was to go back to them." Again, John's loyalties were to the things he held dearest in his life: the radio station and Paul Dennison.

"Did the fact that you had a personal guarantee of the debt which would have been extinguished by the Stock Transfer Agreement, did that influence you?"

"No, sir." Right. Being relieved of thousands and thousands of dollars in personal loans had no bearing on him at all. Ask yourself whether you would have done what John did if it meant that you would be excused from paying back hundreds of thousands of dollars and I think you'll know what I thought of John's answer to the question.

But John didn't stop there.

Squires asked, "Had you and Mr. Dennison or Mrs. Dennison negotiated relieving you of the personal guarantee?"

"No."

"Was that something in the forefront of your mind?"

"No."

I'm not sure how John could say that being the guarantor for a million dollars in loans wasn't at the forefront of his mind. It would have been on my mind every day if I had been in his shoes.

Finally, they reached the topic of Dennison and his takeover of the radio station.

"What terms or duties did you want Mr. Dennison to assume?" asked Squires.

"What he had been doing, that is sales," replied John. Another lie, I told myself, and an obvious one.

"Did he control the radio station?"

"No," said Kuhens. Again, it was obvious that John was lying. I flashed back to that backhanded basement meeting where John told me he couldn't handle the pressure of running the station anymore. Of course this wouldn't come up under Squires' questioning.

"When you hired Mr. Dennison, were you trying to harm MediaComm?"

"No," said John.

Then, I asked myself, why did you try to gut the company? I wished I could face him in a room, one on one, and ask John Kuhens these questions directly, myself. I wondered if I would have gotten a straight answer. Certainly he wasn't going to tell the truth on the stand. Facts, to him, were only what he and Dennison had agreed upon, not what were the legal arrangements with his business partner.

Squires then got to the heart of the matter. "Were you trying to harm KILJ?"

"No sir." John was Mr. KILJ. Why would he try to harm the station he loved, right?

"What authority did you think you had to hire or you possessed that would allow you to hire Mr. Dennison?" Squires asked.

"As president of MediaComm and manager of. . ." John stopped, then corrected himself. "The owner of the station."

"And it looks like you signed Exhibit 1 as president of KILJ?" asked Squires.

"Yes, sir," he replied.

"Do you think you needed to consult with anyone else before taking this decision?" Squires asked.

"No sir," John said again.

"You didn't need to consult Mrs. Burkhart?" Clearly Squires was trying to cement what he wanted Judge Brown to believe were the facts of the deal, truth be damned.

"I felt it would be a fruitless venture," John replied.

"A fruitless venture." *Good word choices*, I thought. Yet, of course, they had nothing to do with our agreement, our legally binding pact. John could not make major decisions unless I was consulted. Fruitless venture or not, he was bound to consult with me.

Squires forged ahead. "How would you describe Mr. Dennison's performance of his duties under Exhibit 1?" he asked.

"Just what I expected," John replied. *Of course*, I thought cynically. *John's testimony would have been almost funny, it seemed, if he wasn't so pathetic.* I couldn't help but feel that somewhere along the line he'd been coached into exactly what to say and how to say it under Squires' questioning.

Squires wanted to know what John had expected. John's reply was short, sweet and explained nothing.

"Good."

Squires asked if Dennison was the only person in the Mt. Pleasant area who could perform the duties of running KILJ.

"There was no one else," John replied. "Not to my knowledge," he said.

Of course, not to your knowledge, I thought. *You'd always depended on Dennison and you always would.* I shook my head. John Kuhens just wasn't bright enough to look past the tiny world he and Dennison had created for themselves.

Totally unbelievable, it's just a matter of time until it's off the air.

"When you hired Mr. Dennison to increase the revenues in January of 2004, MediaComm did not make the January payment under the Stock Purchase Agreement to the Dennisons?"

"Yes, sir."

"Why not?"

"We did not have enough funds," he replied.

Of course John didn't have the funds. He paid everyone except for Dennison whenever he had money available. That makes me think he really wanted to give it back to the Dennisons all along.

"Who made the decision not to make the January payment?" asked Squires.

"Me," Kuhens replied. I felt like I was watching some strange human puppet show, John providing the answers with Dennison pulling invisible strings somewhere behind a curtain.

"What bills were more important to pay than that bill (to the Dennisons)?" asked Squires.

"We had numerous," John replied. "First of all, the staff salaries, to keep them working. Next would be the electricity. Next would be telephone and then the various music licenses that we subscribe to, the copy machine lease, because if we don't keep that fairly current, they won't come and service it, and we depend very heavily on that to bring in some income off a daily news sheet and various others."

"Were you aware," Squires asked, "that by not making the payment and not curing the default, the Dennisons would have to get the stock back?"

"Yes, sir," John replied.

Of course.

"You accepted that as a consequence?" Squires continued.

"Yes, sir."

"Why?"

John's reply again seemed like it was something Dennison was telling him to say at that moment. "I didn't see any future for MediaComm," Kuhens said.

So what? He still was legally bound to our agreement. His opinion was fine and dandy, but according to all terms, John was supposed to work with me on any major decisions affecting the radio station and the corporation. If anything qualified as a major decision, what Squires was honing in on was exactly that thing.

"Did the Dennisons influence your decision not to pay (them) in January?" Squires asked.

"No," said John. Again, he simply ignored the facts and plowed on with what Dennison decided the facts were.

"Did they (the Dennisons) discuss it with you?"

"No," said John. Another lie.

"Did they influence your decision not to cure the default?"

"No."

"Did they discuss it with you?"

"No, sir."

It was hard to keep my composure during this line of questioning. If John had been the one in charge at the time, why was Dennison able to stay and why didn't my payment of $88,956.48 go on the books until August? John was so blatantly lying on the stand, I could hardly believe it. *He always was dumb*, I thought to myself, *but I never realized just how dishonest he could be.*

Squires continued. "Did Dixie Burkhart call you up and talk about it?"

"No, sir," said John.

Of course I hadn't. Dennison was the person I was dealing with at that point in time, not John. John was just a puppet.

I couldn't wait for Noyes to do his cross-examination. John would certainly be a sad sight to watch, but in a rather strange way, I really looked forward to it.

* * *

After a lunch recess, Squires went back to questioning Kuhens.

"Mr. Kuhens," he said, "before we broke for lunch, we were talking about some of the things that Ms. Burkhart claims you've done wrong on behalf of MediaComm."

Squires again wanted to establish who was in control of the station.

"There was testimony this morning about how KILJ with the Dennisons now owning it is not paying rent for the radio station building that is being bought on contract by Media-Comm. Did you hear that?"

"Yes," John replied.

"You are," Squires continued, "the president of Media-Comm?"

"Yes," John said. *A president*, I thought, *who didn't want to run his own company*.

"Why are you not requiring rent to be paid?" asked Squires.

"Basically," said John, "because of the repairs that are being made on it (the station building). We decided that not to go any further with that to just . . . you know, when . . . if we . . ."

I found his sudden stuttering interesting. Was he going off script? Had he forgotten his lines? Finally, John recovered and spit out what he really wanted to say.

"After the repairs were made," he said, "the needed repairs, why, then we would negotiate what was going to happen after that."

"You understand," said Squires, "that the company that had the authority to make repairs is Dennison, Inc.?"

"Yes," said John.

"Whereas, the company using the radio station is KILJ, Inc.?"

"Yes."

"And how can you justify that KILJ doesn't pay rent?" asked Squires.

"Basically," John replied, "because I feel that, you know, (that Dennison, Inc.) it's Paul and Joyce, the same company. . ."

"Do you dispute that the repairs needed doing?" asked Squires.

"No, I can't do that," replied Kuhens.

Squires moved forward. "What was the condition of the radio station as of January 2004?" he asked.

"We had some leaks around the windows," John replied. "The snow didn't come in, but if you got a rain, why it would leak several places in the front office and onto the telephones."

"Any other aspects of the radio station or the property that were in disrepair?" Squires asked.

"Well, they . . ." John hesitated, then found the words he wanted. "You know, it's an older building and twenty-five, twenty-six years old, so it's showing signs of aging."

"What does MediaComm plan to do with the real estate contract?"

John's answer nearly made me laugh.

"That remains to be seen yet."

Sure, I told myself, *right, John*. He knew exactly what would happen; even though I technically was still an owner of MediaComm, I wasn't consulted on this, and it would come as no surprise to me if Paul and Joyce Dennison had already made John's decision for him.

John was still acting as though he had some say in the process, as though he were still the president of a corporation and when the court proceedings were over he would consult his people and decide what to do with the building. But John had no such power. He was just saying whatever sounded good for the Dennisons. He should have been charging rent for the building so that MediaComm had some form of income. He should have been looking out for his business partner and the company.

Facts didn't matter on the stand, that was for sure.

"Have the Dennisons begun any forfeiture proceedings?" Squires asked.

"No," said John. *Of course not*, I told myself. *Why should they?*

"There's been discussion about the fact that before the Dennisons bought the KILJ stock in August the money in the MediaComm bank accounts was zeroed out and the money moved over to KILJ," Squires said, switching topics just a bit. John confirmed this.

"Were you aware that that was happening?" Squires inquired. Again, John replied in the affirmative.

"Who made that decision?" Squires wanted to know. I could have answered that one myself. It was almost like a game at this point, seeing if I could anticipate John's answers before he uttered them.

"Basically," Kuhens replied, "(we) just (were) keeping that money in there because we had a payroll coming up and bills to pay, so (we) just left it there."

Had there always been a "bright line between MediaComm accounts and KILJ accounts?" Squires wanted to know.

"It's . . ." Kuhens paused. "I didn't set the thing up," he backtracked. "It's back in the original days of Fred Beaver and Mike (Stoffregen). They set it up so that the money would go—run through MediaComm, and I think it's an accounting and tax purpose that it's done for."

"Because MediaComm doesn't independently generate any money, does it?" Squires wanted to know.

"Not anymore, no," replied John.

It can't after you've gutted the company, I thought.

"It all comes from KILJ?" asked Squires. John told him that this was true.

"Other than the real estate that MediaComm is buying on contract, does MediaComm have any assets?" Squires asked.

"No, sir."

"Do you expect that you will get your equity investment out of MediaComm ever?"

"No, sir."

"If there had been a way for you to accomplish that, would you have?"

"Yes, sir."

Of course there had been a way, I told myself. If John and Susie Kuhens and Paul and Joyce Dennison had behaved ethically and honestly, none of this would be happening. MediaComm's story would be very different, a business that offered something to the public rather than wasting taxpayer money in a courtroom.

The next question rankled me. "If there had been a way for Dixie Burkhart to get her equity investment out of Media-Comm, would you have hindered that?" asked Squires. I leaned forward in my chair, curious to the bone wouldn't and you didn't. You just wanted everything to how John would answer this one.

"No," he told the court. "(I) would have helped all I could."

No, John, I thought, *you go away and let the Dennisons run their machinations. That*, I told myself, *is why we were facing off in court in the first place.*

"Have you hindered it?" asked Squires. I already knew the answer John would give.

"I don't feel so, no," Kuhens replied.

The whole thing made me sick. John's pack of lies didn't come as a surprise to me, but still, the idea of what drove him to this point really angered me. If only he had behaved honestly. If only the Dennisons had done what they agreed to do in the first place. I had kept my part of the bargain; why hadn't they done the same? Of course, that was a question that couldn't be answered, not in this courtroom or in board meetings. *The real reasons were hatched behind closed doors*, I thought, *with Dennison doing the talking and John nodding his head like a good little puppy dog.*

Chapter 27

Noyes Fires Back and I Take the Stand

Once Squires was done interviewing John, it was Mike Noyes's turn to respond. And his questioning detailed a systematic pattern of neglect and poor decisions on John's part. It was amazing just how brazen John had been in moving the company's assets to the Dennisons and using MediaComm for payment when he needed money for both personal loans and payments to an attorney.

"You owe Mr. Dennison $70,000," Mike said, referring to the personal loan the Dennisons had made to John to cover the loan he'd taken from the bank to help buy KILJ. "You are paying him how?"

"From my personal account," John responded.

"From your paycheck?"

"Yes. And my wife's."

"If you didn't have a job, you would have difficulty in making payments, correct?" Mike was establishing just how indebted to Paul Dennison John really was. Without him, he wouldn't have had the $70,000 to pay back. And without him he wouldn't have had a job with which to pay it back. It was obvious that his intent was saving his own skin, not telling the truth.

"Yes, I would," answered John.

Next, Noyes moved on to John's failure to collect rent on the building, showing just how callous John had been in his duties to the company.

"Now, we talked about rent. Did you ever discuss with Mr. Dennison the payment of rent?"

"No, sir."

"Actually, you received a letter from me demanding that you do that, didn't you?"

"Yes, I did."

"Did you ignore that letter?"

"Pretty much."

It was shocking how unaffected John was in all of this. He just didn't care anymore what happened to me, his business partner. It wasn't as if I had shown him any great malice over the years. In fact, I had used my personal funds to try and make sure that a company he was heavily invested in was successful. And somehow it had come to him ignoring the possibility of making MediaComm *any* money. It was as if he was determined to not only restore the radio station to Paul, but also to make sure MediaComm was finished once and for all so that he wouldn't be proven wrong when he said the company was hopeless.

Mike then asked, "How can MediaComm make its payments to Dennison if it doesn't have rent coming in?"

"It can't," John said, exactly the way he wanted it.

What may have been more blatant a violation than the lack of rent collection was John's use of MediaComm dollars to cover his legal expenses in a case in which he was not being named as a defendant in his capacity as MediaComm president. John had an attorney from Des Moines on board before we actually went to trial. He had parted ways with the attorney before getting to court, but had still paid him $10,000 of MediaComm funds for his work.

"You never asked the other shareholders if it was okay?" Mike asked.

"No, I did not."

"You never asked the other director if it was okay?"

"No, I did not."

It was just one more thing in a long list of offenses John had committed against the company. He was done testifying shortly after that, and it was soon my turn to take the stand.

Defending MediaComm

I took the stand believing that I was the only one in the courtroom who was telling the truth. It was upsetting to watch Paul and John up on the stand, talking as though they were somehow saving the town's radio station from destruction at the hands of MediaComm. It was terrible.

Mike made sure to emphasize that the August meeting was illegal. He also pointed out that I was a full member of the board of directors and had been from the very beginning of MediaComm.

"When you voted in August of 2003 at the directors' meeting, did you vote as a director?"

"Yes."

"At all times did you think that MediaComm could make payments to Mr. Dennison?"

"I thought there were various options," I answered, "and yes, one way or another, those payments would be made."

"Had you been running the station in January through now of 2004, would the Dennisons have been paid?"

"Yes." I answered without a doubt in my mind.

Mike then helped establish that Paul Dennison's involvement at the radio station was partly to blame for him not being paid during the first months of 2004.

"Do you feel that not having the auction in February contributed to not paying the Dennisons?"

I returned to my gut for the answer. "I think what contributed to not paying the Dennisons was that John and Paul were in charge," I replied smartly and with a hint of sarcasm.

"That's why you decided not to put any more additional money (into the station)?" Noyes said.

Again, my answer was all too obvious and came right from the gut. "If Paul did not leave after he was paid the . . . $88,956.48 and would not leave, why would I believe he's going to leave if I paid him in the January payment, the February payment, March payment, and so on and so forth?"

Why not, indeed? Had I been foolish enough to continue making the payments from my personal funds on behalf of the station, it would only validate what John, Paul, Susie and Joyce had done. They would be taking my money, using it to run the station—which included their salaries—and laughing all the way to the bank. No one in his or her right mind would have agreed to such a business arrangement. Not even the judge.

"Did you ask (Dennison) to leave?" asked Mike.

Yes, I explained when I had asked Dennison to sign a receipt saying that he would leave the premises. It was then that Dennison had refused to leave and that is when I made up my mind that he wouldn't be getting any more of my money.

"In fact," Mike asked me, "you asked me to send a letter to Mr. Squires (about this), didn't you?"

"Yes."

"And in that letter it says that the check is being delivered?"

Yes, I told the court. We had established that I had made payment of $88,956.48 in January 2004. Dennison refused to sign a release saying he would leave the building after accepting the payment, which means he stayed there illegally even after I cleared any default. The payment covered all payments over the last half of 2003. Dennison refused to leave. The issue was legal, not personal, and was now out there in court for everyone to hear. The facts, backed by a paper trail, were impossible to dispute.

Mike underscored the point. "Through that letter, you did ask him to leave, didn't you?"

"Yes," I told him. Dennison didn't look at me. Neither did John. I was cool, confident. The facts were on my side and they knew it. They hadn't been able to face me at the station, and now they could not look at me under the scrutiny of the legal system.

My case was clear-cut to me. I had the facts. But I wasn't done yet. I had to answer to Vernon Squires.

Squires attacked my lack of evidence in my theory that John and Paul had conspired to take the radio station back.

"Do you have any indication that, or any evidence that Mr. and Mrs. Dennison encouraged Mr. Kuhens to appoint Susie Kuhens to the Board of Directors?" he asked me directly.

Well, of course I didn't. All I had to go on was a gut feeling, based on the long relationship between John and Paul, coupled with the shady manner in which the meeting had been called and the way it was run. And on top of that was the paperwork showing that John had agreed to a stock transfer in May 2003. But gut feelings don't facts make, so I had to answer the question honestly.

"I don't know that, no," I replied.

"Do you have any evidence that you can point us to that Paul or Joyce Dennison told Mr. Kuhens what bills to pay on behalf of MediaComm in January 2004?" was the next question. And again, all I had to go on was my gut. Obviously, I had to give the honest answer.

"No."

"Do you have any evidence that they encouraged Mr. Kuhens not to pay the installments owing under the Stock Purchase Agreement?"

Again, I did not.

"No."

Facts are facts, and without that smoking gun, I couldn't prove a thing. If anything, Squires was proving I was honest here. I wasn't making wild accusations, going crazy on the witness stand, or lying through my teeth. Yet, in my heart, I knew (and believed that Squires and his clients knew) that something very strange had gone on behind the scenes—and I wasn't the party pulling the strings.

"And would you agree," Squires asked, "by that point in time that you and Mr. Kuhens were basically deadlocked about the future of MediaComm?"

Now there was a question with plenty of evidence to back up my answer. I gave a resounding, "Yes" in response.

We quickly got to the fact that John still owed me money from the loan I gave him early on in the deal so he could meet his financial obligations.

"And you understand," asked Squires, "that if MedaComm goes belly up, Mr. Kuhens doesn't get that equity back, (and) the stock isn't worth anything if MediaComm (fails), is it?"

"The loan that he has with me is not secured by his stock," I said. "It's secured by KILJ and MediaComm." Keep in mind, that's the original protection Fred Beaver wrote into our business deal should we run into problems down the road.

"That wasn't my question," replied Squires. "He owes you money because he had to borrow money from you to buy (KILJ)?"

"He did," I said.

Judge Brown looked at John. "Mr. Kuhens, do you have any questions for Mrs. Burkhart?" she asked him.

"No, your Honor," he replied meekly. Of course he did not have any questions. What did he have going for him at this point?

Noyes asked a few questions on redirect, and then Squires rose again to continue his assault on my case.

Squires took the floor. There was a brief silence as he and I studied each other. It was like two adversaries in a chess match. Each of us was looking for an opening, trying to make an advance and remove enough pieces to weaken the opponent's defense. I knew that as an attorney Squires was an old hand at this, oozing confidence from every pore.

But I was ready for this. He knew and I knew what our respective roles were in the courtroom drama about to unfold. And we both also knew I wasn't going to be an easy witness for him to destroy. Not with the facts in my corner.

We quickly established that my January payment to Dennison, the money he accepted, was out of my personal funds. This was, in essence, not "MediaComm money."

"Now, as I understand your testimony today," Squires said, "you believe that if you had been in control of the radio station beginning in January 2004, you could have generated enough money so that the Dennisons would have been continuously paid the monthly installments?"

"Yes, I do," I told him.

"Is that accurate?"

I refused to be cowed down. "That is accurate," I replied, throwing Squires's exact words back at him.

He then talked about our sales figures previous to that fateful day. "During that time period," he went on, "you did not generate enough money to pay the Dennisons, correct?"

I could see quite clearly where he was going with this. Squires was trying to show the court that under my leadership KILJ was losing money. Well, that had nothing to do with the case before the court. The argument, quite simply, was that Dennison had been illegally given control of the station and continued to flout the law in the face of all binding agreements. I was ready for Squires.

"There are a couple of things here," I replied coolly. I wasn't about to give him the straight "yes" or "no" answer this man was looking for. I refused to allow that opening.

"Number one," I continued, "if you remember, I keep going back to (the) board meeting in August where Mr. Dennison had refused the payment.... If he would have agreed to those payments in August, we would have paid May and June. July would have been immediately due, but I think we would have worked through that. If we wouldn't have, I would have put more money in there."

Squires returned to the advertising issue. After establishing that MediaComm had generated little income through advertisements, he asked if the payment I made in January came from the corporate funds.

"No, it did not," I told him. "We paid other obligations once. I did take out my obligation, the $26,000. John had, I think, a $5,000 bill he had put on his credit card for the (radio) tower. He was repaid that ... and we were paying down the payables. We were paying other MediaComm obligations, because we knew Mr. Dennison would not take the money. I guess we were waiting for it to come to a head so we could get it resolved," I concluded.

Again, Squires came back to advertising during the period around the August 2003 meeting. "There was not enough sales revenue to start a fund for the Dennisons, correct?"

"We didn't do that," I told him.

"Because then," he continued, "you had to contribute all of your personal money to bring the bill current?"

"Yes, that's correct," I told him. What's more, there was nothing illegal about that. Payment is payment, no matter what the source of the money. If any businessperson wants to pour an entire bank account into his or her corporation, that's entirely acceptable. Companies throughout the world do it every day.

But Squires seemed to think this was a sign of weakness on my behalf. "So despite having the opportunity in the second half of 2003 to generate more sales revenue than expenses, there was no money left at the end of the day, was there?" he asked.

I easily deflected his insinuation. "That wasn't the way it was handled, no," I told him. I refused to let him intimidate me or get sidetracked from the strong foundation I had brought to the courtroom: the facts.

He thought for a moment, then tried coming at me from another angle. "Now as I understood your testimony, the reason you did not cure the January default is because Mr. Dennison stayed at the radio station after you paid the $88,956.48?" he asked.

"That's correct," I replied.

"And you thought he should have left?" Squires asked.

He was singing the same song, but trying a new tune. I didn't buy it. "Well," I sang back, "he'd been paid." There was no default and with John's blessing he wouldn't leave.

Stung by the facts, Squires again tried to rephrase his attack. He asked if my actions were based on my "requirement or demand . . . predicated on a belief" that John could not put Dennison into power without my consent.

It was all so silly and so pointless. Squires was trying to make my adherence to the facts of our agreement seem like something I conjured up out of thin air. He wanted to make me look foolish in front of the court. Why else use words like "requirement or demand"? Why insist my arguments were "predicated on a belief"? I knew he had a job to do, but I thought he was doing it rather poorly.

I again pointed out that John could make no major changes without my approval. Putting Susie on the board and handing control of the company and KILJ to Dennison were obvious violations of our by-laws. I had not, did not nor ever would have consented to such an agreement.

"Well, that's where I'm heading with this," Squires said. (*Obviously*, I thought.) "Is it your position then that Mr. Kuhens did not have the authority to hire Mr. Dennison under this agreement?"

"That's correct," I told him.

"That as president of KILJ, Mr. Kuhens could not hire somebody to generate sales for KILJ?" Squires fired back. He was using anything he could to trip me up. Again, I wouldn't let him get away from the original by-laws.

"Not in this capacity," I told him straightforward.

Squires attempted to show that I knew Dennison had been selling advertising for the station after the coup and had increased the sales figures. That, of course, had nothing to do with the matter before the court.

"Two things there," I replied. "Number one, (Dennison) had no right to be there, so it really is irrelevant how much he sold. Number two, I think the economy is such that we would have been going up anyways regardless of who was doing the sales."

I was glad that I had been able to refocus the question onto the central issue of the whole trial; the question that it seemed everyone in the courtroom except for my attorney and myself had forgotten: that everything after the August meeting was null and void. Dennison had no right to be at the radio station, and it wouldn't have mattered if he'd made ten million dollars for it.

The improving economy was another indisputable fact. Advertising sales for radio stations throughout the country had increased during this period. And Dennison was no miracle worker.

Realizing that there would be no headway he could make in this argument, Squires backed off and tried a new tactic. "Do you have any reason or any evidence, I guess, for us that Mr. Kuhens signed this letter agreement or hired Mr. Dennison believing that he did not have the authority to do so?"

I was ready for this one. And this time, the gun was smoking hot. And to his unintended credit, Squires had given the opportunity to me by asking if I had "any reason" to believe John acted illegally.

"I think John felt that he did have the authority to do it," I told Squires, "because he had had the day-to-day authority. I think he didn't read far enough in our agreement to say if he's going to substantially change the condition of the company that he needed my approval."

Keep in mind, John had openly admitted on the stand that he had *not* read the by-laws of our agreement before the first injunction hearing. And, given a week between the first and second hearing dates, John also told the court he didn't take a *second* chance to read the by-laws before giving testimony.

"I think (John) probably did think he had the right to do that," I said.

Squires again tried to prove a point.

"So he believed he had authority to hire Mr. Dennison?"

"I think John thought he did," I said, basically repeating myself.

"Okay," said Squires.

Inside I felt great, assured and with a sense of complete victory. Squires had done his best to make me look foolish and naïve to the court, a business novice who didn't know how to play the game. I shot back at the offense with the facts, something Squires apparently hadn't counted on. If that's the best he could do, I thought, then he doesn't have much of a case against me.

"That's all I have, your Honor," he told Judge Brown.

I couldn't have put it any better myself.

Following questioning by both Squires and Noyes, Judge Brown decided to ask me some questions of her own.

"Ms. Burkhart," she said, "could you outline for me, specifically, how you or what your opinion is as to how MediaComm has been harmed or damaged from Mr. Kuhens's actions?"

The answer seemed all too obvious. "Because of Mr. Kuhens's actions, MediaComm has lost it all," I told her. "Every bit of its assets and still has debts."

CHAPTER 28

THE TRIAL ENDS AND WAIT BEGINS

That's how it went for about three hours or so. The testimony was quick and—as far as I could tell—rather pointless. The trial was over and I was worried about how things had gone. Judge Brown was insistent from the get-go that this was a simple issue of foreclosure on the station and not more involved with the heavy issues of what transpired between the Dennisons, the Kuhens and me.

I had had a bad feeling in the pit of my stomach before this trial began. Of course, I still believed in the legal system as a way to amend wrongs and still believed that facts *did* matter. Yet there were clues from the start that I wasn't going to get a fair shake. I'd seen this in the testimony that John and Paul gave; now, thinking back, I realized the whole—amazingly *short*—trial was merely a charade.

For one thing, this being what Brown felt was a simple foreclosure issue, by law there was no jury involved. But in the decision, Brown would say there were too many issues to deal with. Simple foreclosure equity issue, only? I don't think so. Ultimately, this meant, the decision would be based on Brown's opinion alone. That meant no consideration from a group of people—a jury pool—without preconceived notions. Granted, I had agreed that Brown could serve as our judge for this trial, but now I regretted that decision. Both Noyes and I thought this could stand a chance as a jury trial; without that option, our chances were rather limited. Having a bench trial was the only way Judge Brown could get the decision she wanted.

Furthermore, by selectively choosing what issues she was going to deal with—and by saying this was a simple matter of default—Brown was selectively picking and choosing what could affect her decision. She held all the cards, so to speak, in this regard. You never know how those kinds of decisions are made, yet still . . . it just seemed to me, in retrospect, I should have suspected something more was going on. Keep in mind, regardless of what had previously transpired at the injunction hearing this past spring, I truly believed that the legal system operated in an ethical manner without any kind of influence peddling or authorities in power casting a blind eye to one party or litigant while winking and nodding at the opposition in what could be a judgment made long before the trial had begun. But that certainly wasn't happening in my case. After all, this was rural Iowa! Sure, the movies and television always show these kinds of things, replete with fat, pompous judges and conniving attorneys cutting backroom deals. But that kind of thing didn't happen in Mt. Pleasant courtrooms, did it? I was convinced that this was impossible. Corruption was for other venues; the legal system I was involved with was unimpeachable.

What a lesson I learned, and learned it in the hardest way possible. Judge Brown's focus kept both the spring injunction and the fall trial on one thing and one thing only: what would be the ultimate outcome on KILJ? Hence, the ignoring of the legal issues and ethical transgressions when it came to the agreements between Dennison, John and me. There were so many layers to these events, so much aiding, abetting, colluding and misdeeds. Keep in mind all the flagrant violations of our corporate agreements, the kind of stuff they warn students against doing when they are enrolled in Business Management 101. It was all so basic that I'm sure any jury would have seen what I was after: basic fairness and adherence to the law.

It bothered me, to say the least, that Judge Brown was not even taking into account the lawsuit really boiled down to MediaComm's interests versus the Dennison's interests. Dennison's contention throughout the injunction and the trial, as well as via the gossip he spread through town was that without him, there would be no KILJ and thus no local radio in Mt. Pleasant. The town would be losing a valuable community resource if the Dennisons weren't in charge and if no one else but John Kuhens ruled over the local airwaves.

I was infuriated that Judge Brown was putting emphasis on the health and well being of KILJ when the trial was about by-laws that were broken under the management of Media-Comm. This trial had nothing to do with KILJ, other than the fact that the stock in KILJ had been given away illegally by John Kuhens because he didn't want to manage the company, and because it was easier to give the stock back to the Dennisons. This was a case of a corporation, in MediaComm, that had been wronged by one of its directors. John Kuhens acted illegally when he appointed his wife to the board, and that was the only way the stock was returned to the Dennisons. If that hadn't happened, I could've found a way to pay the Dennisons for the default and avoided this whole mess in the first place.

Judge Brown's stance and actions were inappropriate and misguided. As you've seen, I put all my time and effort, and a considerable amount of my personal finances into keeping KILJ running. Keep in mind, I originally invested in Media-Comm and KILJ because I was insistent on developing my money through a local business. I've been a proud member of this community for nearly my entire life and that was my bottom line. I knew how important the station was to our area and I wanted to do my best. And seeing how things operated behind the scenes, it wasn't difficult to conclude that the basic formula for the station could be run and maintained by anyone with basic talents and experience in broadcasting. It's not like KILJ was a major station out of New York or Chicago, or the center of an important broadcast syndication service. We were what we were: a small niche market station that served a specific market within a limited area. We offered music, local and regional news and other services that people genuinely enjoyed. We were a vital resource, and it would have been completely idiotic of me to have pretended KILJ was anything else, or try to change that format.

Yet, my involvement had shown to me that the office politics and social/psychological dynamics behind the scenes at KILJ were a force to behold. An internal culture existed that did not want any kind of change, nor was any kind of questioning encouraged. Things were done certain ways because they were *always* done certain ways. Never mind that these methods were based on a rather convoluted sense of reality and ethics twisted more tightly or intricately than a balloon sculpture created by a crafty circus clown.

Keep in mind, throughout the year and the course of the two court procedures, both Paul and Joyce had been badmouthing me all over town and had even accused me of stealing from the station. Dennison was not shy about this either, as you'll remember, loudly telling patrons in our local diner that I was crazy. Also, at the trial, he had badmouthed the man I had hoped would replace John as the on-air talent at the station. Meanwhile, Joyce was heard on several occasions telling people that either I was crazy or just bitter because I had lost money on my investments and was taking out my problems on the Dennisons, the Kuhens and KILJ.

All of this was absolutely untrue, a pack of lies spread around like the manure it was. While I didn't let any of it get to me, I wasn't going to let this kind of thing go unchallenged. I consulted attorneys about possibly filing a defamation of character suit against the Dennisons. I wasn't the first one they'd attacked in public with no basis in fact, and I gave serious thought to calling them on their untruths. Wouldn't that have made for an interesting trial?

But in the end, I decided it just wasn't worth my time to go after this pair for their unbridled character assassination. Sure, it was hurtful to have people say such terrible things about me. But taking this kind of bile to the legal system was at best a risky venture. It would have to require enormous proof on my part, including gathering witnesses and testimony that could take years to compile. What's more, the whole suit had the potential to spiral downward into a "he said/she said" spat in front of a judge. These kinds of lawsuits could go on for years, chewing up enormous time and energy, while running up a significant tab for attorneys and the court system. And for what end? A defamation of character suit is so hard to prove, which is why such cases rarely go to court unless circumstances are extraordinarily overwhelming. In the end, I realized that unless I wanted to part with a good deal of money to chase a rabbit down a hole, there really wasn't any point in pursuing this kind of lawsuit.

Chapter 29

The Bomb Drops

The September trial took just a few hours, but we wouldn't have the ruling for at least three months. Roughly speaking, Judge Brown's decision wouldn't come until February. We got through the holidays with still no decision, and it felt like a dark cloud hanging over the joy that normally comes with the season. A week went by and then we were into the new year. And still, no decision. What was taking so long?

In mid-January, I heard news that Susie Kuhens decided to take an early retirement from her job as clerk of court.

* * *

It dawned a clear and cold February morning, a crisp clean Iowa morning. Every day for a month I had anticipated hearing something and every day I was disappointed. Today seemed like it would be no different.

Then came the phone call. As with the injunction decision, the judge's ruling was sent to my attorney who then forwarded it on to me via email.

As before, the words unfolded before me on the computer screen with a growing sense of disbelief that quickly turned into rage. Essentially, Judge Brown's decision stated that without the Dennisons there would be no KILJ and therefore they would continue to hold onto the station. In essence, they had won because Judge Brown believed MediaComm should have paid Dennison the January 2004 payment, even though he wouldn't leave. While I still owned my MediaComm stock, these holdings were now worthless. MediaComm was completely gutted and KILJ handed back to the Dennisons.

Judge Brown ruled that the Dennisons were not entitled to recover attorney's fees from me because I was not a "third party" that had interfered with the contract between them and MediaComm. I was part of MediaComm and was therefore not liable. That was only part of the trial, though. The rest hinged on whether Kuhens acted according to the by-laws, and Judge Brown even admitted in her ruling that he had not!

She stated, "First of all it is important to note that Kuhens, of course, has never denied any of the allegations contained in the pleadings as he has never filed an answer. The court is mindful of the fact that cases should be resolved on their merits, not legal technicalities. Even though the court would be well within its authority to deem everything alleged by Burkhart admitted because of Kuhens' failure to file an answer, the court will instead address the merits of the claims."

Do you believe that?! Judge Brown as much as admitted that if the case had been determined on the strict observance of the law, then Kuhens' failure to respond to the charges against him in the negative would have been an automatic confirmation of my charges against him. In other words, I would have won the case. But Judge Brown decided to go further and address the "merits," of the claims.

She ruled that Kuhens' actions had to be judged under what's called the "business judgment rule," which is Iowa Code Section 490.830. This rule is the standard "by which the actions of corporate directors are measured," according to Brown. Consequently, Kuhens was not liable because, "The purpose of this rule is to limit the second-guessing of business decisions that have been made by those who the corporation has chosen to make such decisions. In essence, when a director acts in good faith, the decision is reasonably prudent and the director believes the action to be in the corporation's best interest, there is no liability."

But how can Brown say that Kuhens acted in good faith when he admitted on the stand that he hadn't read the by-laws of the corporation that he was president of? That to me sounds like he wasn't acting in good faith because his job as president was to protect MediaComm's interests, not the Dennisons' interests. I don't think that his decision to transfer the KILJ stock back to the Dennisons was a prudent decision, so how is it protected under the business judgment rule?

But Judge Brown ruled that it was not unreasonable for Kuhens to "throw in the towel," because as she put it, "The undisputed record is that during 2002 and 2003, MediaComm was having severe financial difficulties. These financial difficulties resulted in the corporation being unable to meet its contractual obligation to (the Dennisons). Even while Kuhens and Burkhart were both working at the radio station, the radio station was not making enough money to pay all of its obligations each and every month. The record is also undisputed that Kuhens was working more than full time to keep the radio station on the air. As a result, the reason the radio station was not making money must have been because of the inadequacy of Kuhens' and Burkhart's abilities to operate and successfully manage such an operation."

Judge Brown was basically saying that because we were struggling to maintain our financial duties, Kuhens was allowed to ignore the rules of the contract, put Susie on the board and transfer the KILJ stock back to the Dennisons. He was allowed to break the laws of the corporation because he had tried hard and failed? Judge Brown's ruling completely ignored the law, and it had essentially gutted MediaComm, rendering my stock useless.

The only real good that came from the ruling was that Kuhens was removed as president and director of MediaComm because he had ignored his fiduciary duties to MediaComm by not charging rent to KILJ for the building and the antenna in the months following the transfer of the stock to the Dennisons. Also, he allowed $22,000 of MediaComm money to be given away with the transfer of the stock, even though the money should have been used in MediaComm's best interest, which was maintaining their remaining assets: the building and the antenna. In addition, I guess it didn't matter that John had given away, or allowed Dennison to steal, the more than $500,000 of equity on MediaComm's books. The equity came from ownership of the radio station and John had allowed that to go away.

Judge Brown stated, "The record indicates that there had been a determination that $1,300 a month in rent could be charged for the real estate involved. The current monthly obligation on the real estate contract is $1,000. With those figures in mind, MediaComm could continue to own this real estate indefinitely and make a 'go' of it. This would be easier if the needed improvements had been made to the building with the resources that were available to MediaComm, to counteract tenant claims that the property is inadequate. The court concludes that Kuhens, in June, July and August, 2004, had an obligation to make decisions that were reasonably prudent concerning the real estate. It is almost as if Kuhens forgot that this real estate contract existed. He, in essence, had given up on his effort to maintain the radio station."

I don't know how many times Judge Brown could say that MediaComm was harmed by Kuhens and still not award the verdict to us. After the injunction, the KILJ stock was released from escrow by the bank because MediaComm didn't put up the $1.25 million bond. Well, the Dennisons were the only bidders and they got all of the stock back. Following that, the FCC license transfer was completed. MediaComm was left with just the building and the antenna, and the Dennisons were claiming those were in terrible shape.

I just couldn't understand how the verdict had gone so wrong. The law was on my side, the facts were on my side; the only thing that wasn't on my side was the flawed legal system that allowed a judge to ignore the facts and the law and render a verdict in a case that clearly had larger implications.

But Judge Brown dismissed the crux of my case outright, saying, "The court cannot find that Burkhart has established that Kuhens violated the business judgment rule in his efforts to return the KILJ stock back to the Dennisons voluntarily. In doing so, the court acknowledges that Kuhens improperly held board meetings, attempted to improperly appoint another member of the board, and without corporate authorization removed Burkhart as a signatory from various bank accounts. These actions, in and of themselves, did not harm Media-

Comm and its financial standing. They were merely motivated by Kuhens's thought that the ship was sinking and he wanted to get off of it."

How could she say that the illegal meeting didn't affect MediaComm's financial standing? The illegal meeting was where MediaComm's financial standing was forever ruined. Because of John's actions at the August 2003 meeting, Media-Comm was left with nothing but a building, a building that housed its former money-making asset: KILJ. Everything came from that meeting. Without it, MediaComm would have still been in control of KILJ, we could have paid Dennison his money using what we had in our accounts plus the money we'd overpaid on property taxes, then found a way to cover the rest if we had to.

And when February rolled around, we could have held the auction and had money for more monthly payments. Judge Brown made a decision during the trial, and maybe even during the injunction hearing: MediaComm was beyond saving. She had decided that MediaComm's rights to due process were superseded by the needs of community asset in the form of KILJ. To her, MediaComm was a failing shell of a company that would drag KILJ down with it. How tragic that would have been. What about MediaComm? What about saving that? That's the company I invested in. That's the one that needed saving.

Judge Brown went on to provide further evidence that John was acting in a way detrimental to MediaComm when she ordered him to repay $10,000 in legal fees that he had had MediaComm pay to an attorney from Des Moines on his behalf. John had paid an attorney $10,000 prior to the injunction to help in his defense. If you'll remember, he was also named as a defendant when the Dennisons sued MediaComm. Well, John's lawyer never went as far as the injunction if you'll remember, and John wasn't being sued as the director of Media-Comm, which would have allowed him to use company funds to pay the legal fees. So he had no right to use MediaComm money for the attorney.

"Clearly, the corporation had absolutely no responsibility to pay those fees," Brown wrote, "nor did Kuhens do anything to obtain appropriate corporate authority to pay those fees. This money is owed back to the corporation."

Not only did Judge Brown order Kuhens to pay back the $10,000 he'd stolen, she ordered the Dennisons to make restitution in the amount of $22,000; the amount stolen from MediaComm's accounts when the Dennisons took over in 2003.

Judge Brown also berated Kuhens for not maintaining the radio station building and for not charging rent to KILJ for its use, since MediaComm still owned the building. She said in her decision, "It is almost as if Kuhens forgot that this real estate contract existed. He, in essence, had given up on his effort to maintain the radio station. As a result, he was doing nothing to enhance MediaComm's corporate existence."

The end result for Kuhens was that he was removed as director of MediaComm. Judge Brown also ruled that the Dennisons could not be a part of the board of MediaComm for at least five years, and she ordered that MediaComm should have a shareholder meeting within thirty days to elect new members to the board of directors.

But while those were victories for MediaComm, the biggest issue, and the main reason I had come to court in the first place—having the foreclosure sale of KILJ rescinded and returning control of the radio station to MediaComm—was shot down by Judge Brown. She ruled, "The court does not consider rescinding the foreclosure sale as a viable option. Wrongs that have been committed in this case were committed by Kuhens, not the plaintiffs. Rescinding the foreclosure sale would punish the plaintiffs. Also, given the current status of MediaComm and its apparent inability to operate the radio station, returning MediaComm to control of the radio station would not be in MediaComm's best interests."

First, we'll address her assertion that the wrongs done in this case were by Kuhens and not Dennison. If Dennison went along with an illegal meeting in order to regain control of the station, doesn't that mean he did something wrong? I think so, and the facts are on my side.

Next, she ruled that it wouldn't be in MediaComm's best interest to be returned to control of the station because of its "inability" to operate the station. Well, if the director of the company was guilty of fiduciary irresponsibility and the radio station was the only real revenue generating asset, then wasn't it *imperative* that MediaComm be returned control of the station. It was the only way that MediaComm could recover from the illegal actions of both Mike Stoffregen, John Kuhens and Paul Dennison.

And how did Judge Brown know that we were incapable of operating the radio station? John may have been, but she didn't give MediaComm the chance to recover from a director she herself admitted was incompetent and "self-dealing." It was a farce and it was wrong.

Was the verdict made long before the trial had begun?

Remember when my attorney said, "I think we can get things back to the way they were before?" Well, things were back to the way they were before . . . before I made a good faith investment in the company. I was effectively ousted and Dennison was back in place, with his good lackey John safely ensconced behind the microphone and ever happy in his dead-end job. I had heard on the street about a year prior that Dennison was saying that he had to get back into the radio station and work for another ten years, then sell the station. I had dismissed it at the time, but he had told me things weren't as they appeared. He told me it had not been a good time for investment. Had Paul and Joyce been desperate and come up with a plan that had ended up working? I do remember Paul saying at one point, "You have to do enough to keep yourself out of jail."

What had happened? *Dixie*, I told myself, *the fix was in*. Dennison wielded enough power through his old contacts that led right up to the governor's office. Why had Governor Vilsack written that affidavit stating that Dennison should have continued ownership of KILJ because only under Paul's leadership could the station continue? The information in the affidavit was not factual. Would Judge Brown have ignored that letter if it had been written by any Joe Blow coming off the street as opposed to our governor (and, I might add, a brief presidential candidate).

Of course not. It seemed to me that this was an obvious case of influence peddling. If Judge Brown wanted to stay on the bench and get ahead in her career, would it make sense to cross the governor's word? Facts had been openly ignored, facts did not matter one iota. What ultimately mattered was clout, pure and simple. Dennison had it. I didn't. And now, despite all the details, all the violated contracts, all the broken deals and unethical behavior, I was the loser in this case.

My attorney was dismayed as well. "If only they had given you *something*, Dixie," he told me. "Then I could accept this verdict. But they didn't. You didn't get a thing." Yes Paul and John were required to make restitution; the Dennisons $22,000 and John $10,000, but what about the more than $500,000 John had allowed the Dennisons to steal? In return, John received an owner's salary and thousands of dollars in loans forgiven. How self-serving of both. Damn the law when you have the governor doing political influence peddling for you. Facts don't matter.

Judge Brown had abused her powers of judicial discretion. She ruled based on the wrong set of laws and had made her ruling without any real evidence to support it. She said that MediaComm was failing and that we had failed to keep up with payments do the Dennisons. But there was no default after the January 2004 payment, which made Paul Dennison's claim of a default erroneous. Judge Brown should not have even considered a default in her ruling.

Also, because it was a bench trial, she had the opportunity to set aside any aspects of the case she didn't like. One of those aspects was the illegal actions taken by John Kuhens in his transfer of power to Paul Dennison. Judge Brown said she believed that none of the illegal actions harmed MediaComm financially since Paul Dennison came in and made good money for KILJ doing sales. But it did harm the company because it led to him taking KILJ away from MediaComm.

The injunction had failed me; the trial had failed me. I had to right this thing and was sure the legal system would see that mistakes had been made—that in the end, someone of authority would agree with me: facts *do* matter.

If all sorts of violations had been made with no default and the Dennisons still prevailed, what does that say?

My next stop had to be the Iowa Supreme Court. Surely they would listen.

Chapter 30

One Step Forward, One Step Back

The next step was to the state appeals court, which is a division of the State Supreme Court. It's where most appeals from the lower courts are heard. Mike Noyes told me upfront that taking my case to the Iowa Supreme Court level would be a long and arduous task that involved a myriad of paperwork. Essentially, I was taking the case to a high-level appeals court, which serves as a division of the Iowa Supreme Court. If they agreed to take my case, then perhaps, at last, I would get some justice. Rarely are appeals requests denied.

It made sense; after all, we already had the bulk of the casework done. Noyes saw it this way:

- Dennison and Kuhens had to make restitution. The bottom line was that John had failed in his fiduciary responsibilities;
- He had no right to give away $550,000 in business equity to Dennison;
- According to the rules and by-laws we had established in our initial contract, all major decisions had to be approved by the board of directors, something which obviously had not been done throughout the turmoil of returning KILJ to the Dennisons;
- Ultimately, John gave away all assets of MediaComm, which he had no right to do.

I felt Judge Brown's decision failed on so many different levels. She certainly had not taken any of the facts of the case into the final ruling. Had the facts mattered, had the contracts mattered, had the ethics mattered, had the financial obligations mattered, then I wouldn't have to look to a high court to solve the issue. What's more, it struck me that having an affidavit from the governor arguing that Dennison should have his way regardless of signed agreements smacked of influence peddling. According to *The American Heritage Dictionary*, influence peddling is, "The practice of using one's influence with persons in authority to obtain favors or preferential treatment for another. . ." Well, this certainly seemed like a clear-cut case of that! Why would a governor get involved in something so mundane as a radio station business deal gone sour? What could he possibly have to gain in doing that? I was clueless, but perhaps Dennison wasn't showing all his cards when it came to his connections with the governor. It was something I just couldn't prove. On the other hand, I wasn't naïve. If Judge Brown wanted to get ahead in the legal system and further her career on the bench, it stood to reason that disagreeing with a sitting governor on a case wouldn't help her cause. Politics and clout, pure and simple, seemed to be at play here. The content of Governor Vilsack's letter had nothing to do with the facts of my case, as laid out by my attorney and all of our legal exhibits. There was a strange disconnect here; facts, it seemed, did not matter when a governor stuck his finger into the proverbial pot.

And so we pushed onward. Keep in mind, the legal process had begun in May of 2003. We were now in 2006. Finally, in June, Mike Noyes was allowed to make my case before the Iowa Appeals Court.

It was a strange event. Only Noyes and Squires were there, with me as just a witness. It was almost surreal to me; after all this time and energy and arduous work, we now were going as high as we could in the state. There was no new evidence; just the facts as presented at the two previous trials. Noyes counted with an appeal to reason. We had the facts, plain and simple. Facts, cold hard facts. Where could we possibly go wrong? Surely the appeals court would see the errors of Judge Brown's decision and let us make a case to the Iowa Supreme Court. The case was heard by a panel of three judges. I felt somewhat hopeful, as the leading judge asking questions seemed to understand the aiding, abetting and collusion issues.

* * *

While waiting for the verdict to come back from the appeals court, Paul Dennison filed suit against MediaComm requesting that the building that housed the radio station be turned over to him. Dennison was insistent that there were numerous repairs needed to the building and even though John hadn't been charging Dennison rent, he wanted more.

Well, we ended up back in court where Paul made his claims. He'd gone on a spending spree in 2004 to make the external part of the KILJ building match his house, and now he was pleading that the building was in shambles. It was absolutely ridiculous and it was just another thing to go to court over in the MediaComm debacle.

I wasn't sure what to do at this point. I had withdrawn from public life in Mt. Pleasant for a couple of years to concentrate on the injunction and the trial. The lawsuits consumed too much of my time, and I was afraid to commit to anything for fear that I would have to drop it if I was returned as owner of the station upon appeal or in the original trial.

The quiet life was fine for me, there's a lot to be said for the simple things and for stepping back, but it was hard to explain the situation to my friends and family. It was just too complicated and I also didn't want to have the lawsuits consume conversations with my siblings and kids like it had consumed me. My husband had kept up with things and he was irate over the way things had gone at the injunction and the trial. Did I really want to go through another battle with the Dennisons over the building?

I spoke to Mike Noyes and told him that I wasn't willing to go through more of a fight. I had wanted to wait until the decision came back from the appeal, and I suggested to Dennison that we could wait for the appeal decision and then work something out. He didn't want any part of that and so I was forced to make a decision.

One of the reasons that John was removed as director was because he was not charging rent. If we had charged rent we could make the payments. Mike Noyes asked me if I wanted the building and I said, "No." It just wasn't worth the hassle.

They would have made sure that we spent every dollar on attorney's fees. Paul Dennison was prepared to bring in experts to testify that the building was in disrepair. It didn't appear that we would get help from the courts, either. Our recent experiences had told us that.

I told Mike that I didn't want the fight. We were charging rent to KILJ at this point, but the payments were essentially the same as what we were paying on the mortgage payments, so we decided to cede ownership of the building to Paul Dennison. It was one more victory for him in the legal system and on top of that, it seemed he was winning the battle for public opinion.

I never got into a public talking match with Paul, but that didn't stop him from telling anyone and everyone that I was a loon and that I was running the station into the ground. He was able to spin the situation to make it look as though he was going to save KILJ from the bad ownership that was in charge of it.

Because Paul won in court, his arguments in the public were given some weight. I didn't really bother trying to go out and defend myself publicly. I felt that even though contracts are often problematic, that there is a proper forum for deciding who is right in a dispute of this kind, and that forum is the legal system.

Chapter 31

Three Strikes, You're Out

Unfortunately for me, the legal system wasn't to be on my side, even in the appeals process. I'm sure you can guess what happened next. After sweating out another waiting period, hanging on to what the decision might be, the appeals court upheld Judge Brown's ruling. Their logic was that Media-Comm should have made the January payment because the company had not made the payment as required, the station was in disarray and they saw no problems in what Kuhens had done in handing over the station to Dennison.

Facts didn't matter.

The court ruled that Kuhens' decision to not cure the default in January, 2004 was made in good faith; that his decision to pay people other than the Dennisons was allowable because he needed to pay those other bills to keep the radio station viable, since it was MediaComm's only real, revenue generating asset. But if Kuhens had paid the Dennisons and cured the default, we could have found ways to pay the other bills. The ruling goes on to say, "In concluding that Kuhens acted in good faith"—that's laughable—"with respect to the January 2004 default, we have considered the fact that KILJ generated enough revenue in February 2004 to fund the January loan payment within the thirty days specified in the notice of the right to cure . . . However, the company's long-term prospects were bleak. As Kuhens stated, the company had been failing for some time and 'putting an end to it would be the appropriate thing to do.'

Essentially, the court decided that MediaComm wasn't worth saving. Everyone admitted that John had acted contrary to the best interests of MediaComm when he transferred the stock, they just felt that it was inevitable that MediaComm was going to fail and so they said that his betrayal of the company's interests were justified, or as they put it, "in good faith." Well, I certainly didn't feel as though they were in good faith at all.

Everyone was essentially letting John off the hook and leaving MediaComm to die because it was already in trouble and because KILJ would not have survived, in their view, without the guidance of the Dennisons and Kuhens.

Also, my contention that Kuhens was motivated by his desire to get out of the loan obligations he had and to get away from the responsibility of running MediaComm was called "immaterial" by the appeals court. As they put it, "The fact that the Dennisons knew Kuhens's financial condition and elected not to pursue that remedy is immaterial. Given the terms of the guaranty agreement, they could have changed their minds at any time. Indeed, the contemporaneous loan agreement stated the Dennisons would first enforce their security interest by disposing of the collateral and would hold Kuhens liable if a stock sale proved 'insufficient to cover the outstanding contract balance.'" Here's where it gets good: "As it turned out, the Dennisons bid $1.1 million for the stock, which was the 'aggregate consideration' for the KILJ shares under the stock purchase agreement and the total owing under the loan agreement."

So, the amount the Kuhenses bid—and they were the only bid by the way—just so happened to coincide with the amount remaining in the stock purchase agreement and the total under the loan agreement. Right.

I felt defeated, demoralized and absolutely numb. What had I done wrong? I had all the signed agreements, evidence of illegal activities and given honest testimony. Dennison and John, on the other hand, didn't back up their claims with our business contracts and—as you'll remember—John claimed not to have even read the contracts in the first place. Both men had clearly perjured themselves on the stand. Dennison had gone around town claiming I was a bitter woman because I lost money. And keep in mind, he had told a would-be returning employee not to worry about the pending court case since he had already won it—telling her this a few months before he and I even set foot in the courthouse for the trial.

Something here smelled very bad. Facts did not matter. And there was nothing I could do about it.

Dixie, I told myself, it's time to let it go. I had been soundly defeated.

Chapter 32

Restitution and Theft

My last act in the MediaComm saga took place in the fall of 2006, months after the appeals court had upheld Judge Brown's ruling. I had to meet John Kuhens to recoup the $10,000 the judge ordered he pay in restitution; the money he'd stolen to pay his attorney early in the legal process. That money had to be paid to MediaComm, not to me, and it was agreed that he would turn in his MediaComm stock in lieu of a cash payment. The Dennisons were also ordered to pay restitution to MediaComm. They were ordered to pay $22,000.

John also still owed me money from the personal loan I'd given him to buy into KILJ in the first place. He had stopped making payments in the middle of the legal process, but had picked up payments after a letter reminding Dennison that KILJ would be making the payments for John should he not come through with the payments on time.

The $22,000 that the Dennisons owed was the money they stole from the MediaComm accounts when they took over.

John and I agreed to meet at the offices of a local accountant. He was going to bring the check for the Dennisons and also the money he owed to me on the personal loan. We were also supposed to sign paperwork prepared by our attorneys that would end the whole mess for good. As part of the agreement, Paul Dennison had included a provision stating that I could not bring any further legal action against the Dennisons after they'd paid restitution for the money taken from the MediaComm accounts upon his takeover of the station. I had agreed to sign the paperwork as long as John paid me for the personal loan to him that KILJ had guaranteed.

On the day of my meeting with John, I arrived on the street where the offices were a little early. The offices are only a couple of blocks from the courthouse and something told me to pull into the courthouse parking lot. I don't know why to this day I did this, but I went to the clerk of court's office, the one Susie Kuhens had occupied for so long before her retirement.

Because all of the court agreements with Mike were public information, I could look at them right at the courthouse. I looked over the documents and what I found was alarming. Mike's salary from his new job was being garnished to help repay some of the thousands of dollars he owed to MediaComm. The last I had heard of his payments was a $2,500 check from years before.

Well, it turns out that his pay had been garnished over the years since that first payment, but the money wasn't to be put into MediaComm's accounts. Instead, John Kuhens was taking the money for himself. It was one final insult in a years-long battle with the Dennisons and the Kuhenses. The garnishment had been going on since I left in 2004. The garnishment records are there for everyone to see, and Susie Kuhens's signature was on many of the documents in the settlement from her former role as clerk of court. So, not only was her husband taking the money, but it seems she probably knew something about it.

From the time I left the station until the time we had the wrap up, John had been garnishing Mike's wages and the money had never seen the MediaComm accounts.

When I found out that John had been taking the money, I didn't know what to do. My attorney was out of town and would not be at the meeting, but I was able to reach him on my cell phone. I asked him whether I should confront John with this new information and he said yes. I also asked him about the section of the documents I was to sign that stated I could not take any further legal action against the Dennisons or Kuhens. I didn't want to be kept from suing Kuhens over the money. My attorney advised that I scratch that section out and not sign any document that said I couldn't sue John because of his theft of the monies garnished from Mike's pay.

I went to the meeting with John, where I found he had a check from the Dennisons for their ordered restitution, a check from himself to cover the personal loan to me. I had paperwork for him to sign accepting his stock in MediaComm in lieu of the money he stole to pay his attorneys. But he didn't know that I knew about his theft of the funds from Mike's garnished wages.

I confronted John about the missing funds. He didn't deny what he had done and was mostly in silence. John didn't do confrontation very well. He sat silently for a long time and then said, "So, what are you doing to do?" I didn't know how to respond. I said, "I don't know," and that I was going to have to think about it. I was still trying to take in what I had found out. After a long silence, John said, "How about I pay half of it?" I collected the checks he'd brought and told him to meet me the next day at the same time and place.

When John showed up for our next meeting he had less than we'd agreed on, but not by much. It was something probably taught him by Paul; you bring enough less than the agreed upon amount, but still enough to make the deal attractive so that people won't want to walk away at the last minute. We also signed the paperwork saying there would be no more lawsuits, since I had been paid what John owed me for the personal loan.

And where did John get the thousands of dollars he owed? It was a check written out to me from Susie Kuhens's Edward Jones money market account. It was just unbelievable. I just don't see how she couldn't have known. I took the money and signed the paperwork and was done with it. I just didn't want to do anymore.

John, like the puppy dog he was, followed me out to my car and wanted to chat as though nothing had happened. It was just unbelievable. The whole thing was just unbelievable. I didn't want anything more to do with the whole situation.

Chapter 33

Now and the Future

So now it was over. What had I gotten out of this long struggle with the legal system? Well, I felt the whole things was really an insult to common sense, let alone the law. In every ruling we got, I felt like we'd been wronged and the system failed. I really felt that the appeals court had understood everything, but chose to rubber stamp with their decisions, deciding that ultimately the facts really didn't matter.

I really felt like so many different people had violated me. Paul and Joyce Dennison and John and Susie Kuhens had started out to steal the station from MediaComm, and sure enough, they'd gotten away with it. I felt the "Honorable" Judge Mary Ann Brown had ignored her legal obligations by denying me a jury trial, ignoring violations of contracts and the universal business code and code of Iowa, obvious examples of business fraud and where the answers truly were to be found: our corporation documents. She also abused her judicial discretion and the Iowa Code of Judicial Conduct.

The code says in part, "A judge should respect and comply with the law and should act at all times in a manner that promotes public confidence in the integrity and impartiality of the judiciary."

Judge Brown certainly did not respect and comply with the law. She allowed political influence peddling in her courtroom by allowing Tom Vilsack's affidavit to be used as evidence during the injunction hearing and she ignored the illegal actions of Paul and Joyce Dennison in their collusion with John Kuhens. It was a clear violation of her duties as a judge.

We all know things can and do go wrong in businesses, and you go to the court systems to straighten it out. I don't hold any hostility or animosity toward the Dennisons or the Kuhenses. By the time we got to trial I already knew what they were. Also, I know there are always winners and losers and not all will be happy. But my experience with the legal process had been something wholly other, a nightmare of epic proportions that left me feeling thwarted, cheated and violated at every turn.

My rights were also violated by Governor Vilsack when he submitted his affidavit to the case. It was a completely inappropriate move on his part to get involved with the case as a sitting governor even though Dennison had been a previous client of his. Plus, keep in mind, the information in the governor's affidavit was flat out wrong. According to his letter, Governor Vilsack said we'd put very little down to buy the station when MediaComm was formed. Remember, we put down $500,000 right at the top. I don't know about you, but where I come from half a million dollars is not considered a small amount of money! Plus, there was no default; I'd made every good faith effort to pay off the debt. When Paul and Joyce Dennison forged ahead to take control, John was in complete agreement with them. He had everything to gain financially, plus he no longer had the responsibilities that he never wanted in the first place. This group got KILJ back just the way they wanted it to be; exactly as it operated prior to our deal in 1991.

But what the Dennisons got back is a tarnished product. They are very much like someone driving around in a fancy new car. It seems impressive from the side of the street, but when you find out it was stolen, the luster is lost. KILJ was stolen and now the luster is gone.

Looking back, I had hoped every time that every procedure I went through would make things right. I was sure things would come to their senses and be corrected, but in the end facts just didn't amount to anything. I could only feel that somehow the case had been decided long before it ever came to trial. Despite having excellent counsel, I never had a chance. We all went through motions and procedures and it really didn't matter what was done. In my opinion, with Dennison and Kuhens tied at hip and in perfect lockstep, coupled with the inappropriate actions of the governor and his influence on Judge Brown and the Iowa Supreme court, I was trapped in the middle of a perfect legal storm.

Believe me, none of this was sour grapes. I was aware of the risks that were involved with financial investments from the get-go. But ultimately, I was thoroughly disappointed in how the court system operated. I think we have a good judicial system, but one should not be so naïve as to believe there is not corruption in the system. We do kind of think out in the rural areas we are isolated from things that go on in big cities. The truth of the matter is we're just as bad. What happened is a good indication of that. And the facts don't always matter, especially if there is influence peddling. Once you put corruption factor in there, facts go right out the window. When judges are allowed to pick and choose what they address, when they make decisions on opinion, not law, I think this is a real problem.

We can easily become a lawless nation when laws become meaningless. What happened to me should be a wake-up call. If my case is the precedent, anyone with any type of legal contract in the state of Iowa should be on notice. As I so unhappily discovered, when unexpected and underhanded means enter the picture, the laws don't matter at all. They absolutely don't matter and we're all in very deep trouble.

In the end, what can we do? It is my opinion that we need to pay more attention to judges as they come up for elections. I will be first to admit this is something I was lax on. Unless you have reason to be disillusioned with the legal system or you keep up with what the system is doing—I just about glaze over when I see all the judges for retention on election ballots. But when you're not paying attention to what judges do, they're pretty much set for life . I understand that there are winners and losers in every case and the judge will say there will always be someone unhappy. But I wrongly assumed that if you follow the laws, you will come out on top. But every time we got a ruling I had hoped we would get some justice. I felt like the system had absolutely failed me.

* * *

Overall, my involvement with MediaComm and KILJ has cost me close to $374,000. I spent $150,000 on the initial buy-in, I took MediaComm stock in favor of Steve paying me back the $25,000 I'd lent him when he came to the station and I took $10,000 in stock in lieu of payment after one of the Class C stockholders at the station decided to leave after a falling out with John. My legal bills total approximately $100,000 and I spent $88,956.48 of my own money in paying the Dennisons to cure the default in January of 2004.

I still own MediaComm. I am the sole MediaComm stockholder. John gave up his shares in lieu of paying the $10,000 restitution ordered by the court, but that's like owning snow in a blizzard. MediaComm no longer even owns the building that KILJ is housed in. At one point it did, but a couple of years after the original trial, as we awaited the decision from the appeals court, I decided to let the building go back to the Dennisons.

If I had to do it again, I suppose I would probably do most of it the same. I did my due diligence before buying into MediaComm and had the proposal vetted by people I respect. I couldn't have foreseen the corruption of my business partners and the court system I went to, to help rectify the situation. I feel like the investment I made in the local community was worth the effort. I tried to do something for Mt. Pleasant and for myself, but it turned out badly.

We had a lot of problems at the radio station during my tenure at MediaComm. Mike Stoffregen embezzled money and we had, perhaps, too many chiefs and not enough Indians, as the expression goes. We were paying multiple partners with ownership salaries and also ran up against the ever-decreasing market share that radio stations held in the advertising world. But it still could have worked if not for the desire of John Kuhens to return ownership to the Dennisons and the failure of the courts to recognize that intent.

I can't close MediaComm as a corporation because it still owes the bank $36,000 of a $130,000 loan borrowed to buy out Steve Staebell. The loan was sold to a company based in Omaha, Nebraska, States Resource Corporation. The company is now going after John Kuhens for the remainder of the money because he was a guarantor of the loan. He has put up the FCC license as collateral on the loan, but that went to the Dennisons when they were gifted KILJ. Oddly enough, John has secured legal representation in the dispute. He had gone without representation and had essentially lain down during the trial.

Because I expected to be reinstated as owner of KILJ during the trial and subsequent appeal, I haven't performed much work in the insurance business I started years ago. I have found more success as a consultant to larger companies.

Though my husband and I took a serious financial hit during my years with MediaComm and the subsequent battle with the Dennisons, we are still living as we were in the house that I bought with my first husband. I still live in Mt. Pleasant, but now most of my investments are in national companies that offer more stability.

Life, as I happily discovered, goes on, regardless of how people treat you. I do my best to live responsibly and with joy. Of course, when I do my investing today, I don't do it locally and may never do so again.

Oddly enough, I ran into Paul Dennison while we were waiting for the decision from the trial. I was with Steve and two of my grandchildren at Fun City, an amusement center for kids in Burlington that has a bowling alley. Dennison was a few lanes down with his grandchildren. He acted as though I didn't exist. Dennison ignored us throughout the entire proceedings except to badmouth me. And that was fine by me.

The whole situation was a strange way to eliminate some of my naiveté about the courts and the ways that law and fact can be ignored if it is in someone's best interests to do so. The fact that it was deemed impossible for KILJ to operate without John Kuhens and the Dennisons, and the idea that procedures can be ignored at the highest levels of a corporation is almost impossible to believe.

Maybe I was foolish to think that a court in Iowa would somehow be immune from the kind of lies and deception that you would expect to see in a "big city" courtroom.

If you look at the KILJ Website, there's a section on the station's history. You'll find information on format changes through the years, along with the interesting factoid that the station was acquired in 1977 by Paul and Joyce Dennison. Nothing, of course, about what ensued when they tried to sell the station. Of course, this is no surprise to me. The only mention you'll find of John Kuhens is that he has a radio show on the station. And that's just the way he wants it, I suppose. Of course, as soon as the Dennisons took over, they flipped the AM/FM format back to the way it was before in 1991, prior to our purchase of the station.

I haven't been to the station since January of 2004 when I delivered the personal check to Paul Dennison and asked him to leave. Since that time I haven't seen John and Paul very frequently. In fact, I only see them by accident, like when I saw John and Susie at the local country club when we were all playing golf.

Facts don't matter to some people. To them, the only real test for whether they should do something is if it will benefit them. I put my own money into MediaComm on several occasions in an attempt to save it from foreclosure. I poured what I had, in good faith, into the operation, with the belief that the other people who went into business with me might do the same. I trusted people with the running of the business and assumed they would protect the interests of an operation they were also heavily invested in. But for some reason they found it acceptable to steal funds, in the case of Mike Stoffregen, or to simply ignore the best interests of the company in deference to the best interests of the former owners of the company's largest asset. John Kuhens ignored what was best for the company he was president of, MediaComm, so that he could put things back the way they were, the way they were comfortable.

The courts may not have supported my assertions, but I think the facts are straightforward enough to survive the legal mistakes of the Iowa court system. I've learned from my mistakes and I've moved on; and I can say that I did what I did with a clear conscience and pure intent. The same can't be said of the people who destroyed MediaComm.

The facts don't matter to some people. But to me, they always have and always will.

APPENDIX

BY-LAWS OF MEDIACOMM, INC.

BY-LAWS
OF
MEDIACOMM, INC.

ARTICLE I
Offices

The registered office of MediaComm, Inc. (Corporation) shall be located at 1317 East Monroe, Mt. Pleasant, Iowa. A new registered office may be established upon passage of a resolution by the Board of Directors and filing of the document required under the Iowa Business Corporations Act. The Registered Office shall be located in the State of Iowa. The Corporation may establish additional offices within or without the State of Iowa and the Corporation's principal place of business may be different from the Corporation's registered office.

ARTICLE II
Shareholders

1. Annual Meeting. The annual meeting of the shareholders shall be held on the date established by the Board of Directors. Directors shall be elected at the Annual Meeting and any other business may be transacted at such meeting, if otherwise properly presented.

2. Special Meetings. Special meetings of the shareholders may be called by the Board of Directors or by holders of not less than 10% of all shares, regardless of class, entitled to vote. Non-voting shareholders shall be given notice and allowed to attend such meetings.

3. Notice and Place. Written notice stating the place, date, hour and the object of the Shareholder meeting shall be given to each shareholder not less than 10 nor more than 60 days before the date of the meeting. The notice shall be delivered by mail or personally at the direction of the President of the Corporation. Notice of any meeting may be waived if such waiver is executed in a manner which satisfies the Iowa Business Corporations Act. The Board of Directors may designate any place, either within or without the State of Iowa as the meeting place.

4. Closing the Transfer Books. The Board of Directors may direct that the stock transfer books be closed for a stated period not to exceed sixty days for purposes of identifying shareholders entitled to receive notice, to vote, to receive dividends or other distributions, or for any other purpose where the identity of shareholders must be determined. The Board may fix in advance a record date for identifying and determining shareholders, in lieu of Closing the Stock transfer books. Any record date shall not be more than sixty days and in the case of

meetings less than 10 days, prior to the date upon which the particular event will occur which requires such identification. The date upon which a meeting notice is delivered or the date upon which dividends or distributions are declared shall be the record date, if the stock transfer books are not closed and no record date has been fixed by the Board of Directors.

5. Voting List. The President or some other agent having charge of the stock transfer books shall make a complete list of the shareholders entitled to vote at least 10 days prior to any shareholder meeting. The list shall contain the address of each shareholder, the class and number of shares held by such shareholder and the number of votes which such shareholders entitled to cast at such meeting. The list shall be maintained at the Corporation's principal place of business for a period of 10 days prior to the shareholder meeting and shall be made available to any shareholder for inspection during normal business hours throughout the 10 day period and at the shareholder meeting. The stock transfer books shall be used to determine shareholders entitled to inspect the shareholder list.

6. Quorum. Shareholders entitled to cast a majority of the votes on any matter who are represented in person or by proxy shall constitute a quorum at any meeting for purposes of taking any action other than to elect directors. Shareholders entitled to cast a majority of the votes attributable to Class A or Class B Common Stock of the Corporation respectively who are represented in person or by proxy shall constitute a quorum for purposes of electing directors. A majority of the votes cast at any meeting by shareholders represented in person or by proxy at such meeting where a quorum is present shall be sufficient to take action on any corporate matter requiring a shareholder vote, except for actions which require more than a majority vote under law, the Articles of Incorporation or these by-laws and except in case of the election of Directors. In the case where more than a majority vote is required the votes cast at any meeting in which a quorum is present must be sufficient to satisfy the voting requirement related to such action. In the case of the election of directors, Shareholders of Class A and Class B common stock respectively may elect the number of directors which they are otherwise entitled to elect at any meeting in which a quorum of such Shareholders are present as provided in this Section 6. A majority vote cast by shareholders represented in person or by proxy at any meeting shall be sufficient to adjourn such meeting regardless of whether a quorum is present.

7. Proxies. A Shareholder may vote by proxy executed in writing by the Shareholder or a duly authorized attorney-in-fact. No proxy shall be valid after eleven months from the date of execution, unless otherwise specifically provided in the proxies. Proxies shall be filed with the President of the Corporation before or at the meeting in which votes will be cast by such proxy. Any proxy must otherwise satisfy the requirements of the Iowa Business Corporation Act, as amended,

which relate to such proxies.

8. <u>Voting of Shares</u>. Shareholders of Class A and Class B common stock shall be entitled to cast two and one vote respectively with respect to each share of such stock held by them, except as otherwise provided in the Articles of Incorporation or in these Bylaws. Class A and Class B shares of Common Stock acquired by the Corporation shall be deemed authorized but unissued shares and no votes shall be cast with respect to such Shares. Shares held by any person, other than an individual, may be voted by any duly authorized officer, partner, agent, trustee, receiver, administrator, executor, guardian, conservator or other legal representative of such person. A shareholder who has pledged any or all of his/her Shares shall be entitled to vote such Shares until such Shares have been transferred to the pledgee and all other legal requirements related to such transfer imposed by any law or regulation, or agreement, including those imposed by the FCC, have been satisfied. Thereafter, the pledgee shall be entitled to vote such shares. Voting may be by voice unless the presiding officer shall order or any shareholder demands that the vote be by ballot.

9. <u>Informal Action</u>. Any corporate action requiring a shareholder vote may be taken without a meeting by written consent of the shareholders, provided that all requirements under the Iowa Business Corporation Act, as amended, have been satisfied which govern informal action by written Shareholder consent.

Article III
<u>Directors</u>

1. <u>General Powers</u>. Except as expressly stated in the Articles of Incorporation or these By laws, the Board of Directors shall have all the powers granted to it or which can be granted to it under the Iowa Business Corporation Act, as amended. The Board of Directors shall otherwise be responsible for directing the affairs of the Corporation.

2. <u>Number Term and Election</u>. The number of directors shall be 3. Shareholders holding Class A and Class B Shares of Common Stock shall be entitled to elect 2 directors and 1 director respectively. The directors shall be elected at each annual meeting of the Shareholders. Directors shall serve a term of one year or until a successor is elected at the next Annual meeting, whichever occurs first. Each Shareholder of Class A Common Stock shall be entitled to nominate a separate individual to fill each of the 2 seats on the Board of Directors which the Class A shareholders are otherwise entitled to fill. Each Class B Shareholder shall be entitled to nominate 1 individual for the seat on the Board of Directors which the Class B Shareholders are otherwise entitled to fill. Nominations must be delivered in writing to the President of the Corporation at least 5 business days prior to the Annual Meeting. Any Shareholder may change his/her

nomination(s) or make an additional nomination(s), provided that such change or addition is made in person at the Annual Meeting and the number of nominations ultimately made by such Shareholder otherwise satisfies the requirements of this Section 2. The election of directors shall be conducted separately by the Class A and Class B Common Stock Shareholders. Class A and Class B common stock shareholders shall only be entitled to vote for those nominees which have been nominated by the Class A and Class B Common Stock shareholders, respectively. Each seat on the Board of Directors shall be filled by the nominee for such seat which receives a majority of the votes cast either in person or by proxy by the Class A or Class B Common Stock Shareholders, as the case may be, who are otherwise entitled to vote for such nominee. The number of votes which each shareholder is entitled to cast shall be determined in accordance with the Articles of Incorporation and Article II of these By laws. The Board of Directors may by resolution adopt supplemental rules needed to carry out the requirements of this Section 2, regarding the nomination and election of directors.

3. Changing the Number of Directors. The number of Directors which shall serve on the Board of Directors may be changed at any meeting of the Shareholders which is called and convened in accordance with Article II of these Bylaws. The votes cast in favor of such change shall represent at least two-thirds of all the Votes Cast by the Shareholders either in person or by proxy at the meeting. Not withstanding, any change in the number of Directors which is adopted by the Shareholders shall otherwise be in accordance with the Articles of Incorporation.

4. Regular Meetings. A regular meeting of the Board of Directors shall be held without notice, immediately after and at the same place as the Annual meeting of the Shareholders. The Board of Directors may provide for additional regular meetings by a resolution setting the time and place for holding such regular meetings and no additional notice need be given.

5. Special Meetings. Special meetings of the Board of Directors may be called by the President or any director. The person calling the special meeting shall fix the time and place of such meeting.

6. Notice. Notice of any special meeting or any regular meeting, if required, shall be in writing and shall specify the time, place and date for the meeting. The Notice shall be given at least two days prior to the meeting if delivered personally or at least 5 days in advance if delivered by mail. The notice shall be deemed delivered when deposited in the United States mails. The Attendance of a director at any meeting shall constitute a waiver of Notice of such meeting, except where the director attends to expressly object that the meeting was not lawfully called or convened. A written waiver of notice signed either before or after the meeting shall be deemed equivalent to giving notice.

7. Place. Meetings may be held at any place within or without the state of Iowa. Meetings may also be conducted by telephone or similar communications equipment, provided that all participants in the meeting can hear each other. Participation in any meeting whether held in person or by telephone shall constitute presence in person at such meeting.

8. Quorum and Manner of Acting. A majority of the directors shall constitute a quorum for purposes of transacting business. The act of the majority of directors present at any meeting where a quorum is present shall be the act of the Board of Directors, except as expressly required otherwise by law, the Articles of Incorporation, these By-laws or by a lawful agreement of the Shareholders.

9. Informal Action. Any action required or permitted to be taken by the Board of Directors may be taken without a meeting, if written consents are obtained from all the directors. The written consents shall specify the action to be taken and shall otherwise satisfy any requirements related to such consents which are imposed by law.

10. Vacancies. An vacancies on the Board of Directors may be filled by the affirmative vote of a majority of the remaining directors. Any director so elected shall serve the remaining term of the director being replaced.

11. Removal and Resignation. A director may be removed from the Board of Directors at any special meeting of the shareholders, if a majority of the votes cast by the Class A or Class B shareholders, as the case may be, who as a class originally elected such director are in favor of such removal. Any director may resign by giving written notice to the President.

12. Compensation. The Board of Directors shall have authority to establish by resolution compensation for any director and may additionally by resolution pay reasonable expenses incurred to attend any meeting of the Board of Directors or incurred in connection with any other business of the Corporation.

13. Committees. The Board of Directors, by resolution, may designate one or more committees each of which may exercise the powers conferred to such committee by the Board of Directors, subject to the requirements of Iowa law.

ARTICLE IV
Officers

1. Officers. The officers of the corporation shall consist of the President, the Executive Vice President and Secretary and any other officers elected or appointed by the Board of Directors.

2. **Election and Term.** The Board of Directors shall elect all officers and shall establish the term of each officer which shall not exceed three years. The election of officers may be conducted at a regular meeting of the Board of Directors. Vacancies may be filled or new offices created and filled at any regular meeting of the Board of Directors. Each officer shall hold office until his/her successor has been duly elected and qualified or until his/her death, resignation or removal, whichever occurs first. The election or appointment of an officer or agent shall not of itself create contract rights.

3. **Removal and Resignation.** Any officer may be removed by the Board of Directors whenever the Board of Directors believes that such removal is in the best interests of the Corporation. Any such removal shall be without prejudice to any contract rights of the person removed. Any officer may resign by delivering written notice to any director or any other officer. The resignation of any officer shall be without prejudice to any contract rights of the Corporation or the person resigning.

4. **Vacancies.** A vacancy in any office shall be filled by the Board of Directors for the unexpired portion of the term assigned to such office.

5. **Powers and Duties.**
    A. **President.** The President shall be the principal executive officer of the Corporation and shall supervise and control all of the business and affairs of the Corporation, subject to the general direction of the Board of Directors. The President shall preside at all meetings of the shareholders and the Board of Directors. The President may sign certificates for shares of the Corporation, deeds, mortgages, bonds, contracts or other instruments, agreements or documents which the Board of Directors has authorized to be executed. The President shall be additionally responsible for: (i) keeping minutes of all meetings of the Shareholders or the Board of Directors; (ii) arranging to give notices required by law, the Articles of Incorporation, these by laws or any agreement; (iii) maintaining and authenticating the records of the Corporation (iv) keeping accurate records of the name and address of each shareholder of the Corporation; (v) having custody and accounting for all funds and securities of the Corporation; (vi) depositing all monies in the name of the Corporation in such banks or other depositories selected in accordance with these by laws and (vii) paying or receiving monies due to or from Corporation and others on a timely basis. The President shall perform all other duties incident to the office of President or assigned to him/her by the Board of Directors.

    B. **Executive Vice President and Secretary.** (Referred to herein as the Executive Vice President) The Executive Vice President shall perform the duties of the President when the President is absent or if the President refuses or is unable to act. The Executive Vice President may sign certificates for shares of the Corporation, deeds, mortgages, bonds, contracts and other documents, agreements or instruments which the Board of Directors has authorized to be executed. The Executive Vice President shall perform any other duties assigned to him/her by the Board of Directors or the President.

   C.   Other Officers. The Board of Directors may authorize and appoint one or more additional Vice Presidents, and one or more assistant secretaries. Any officer so authorized and appointed shall have the duties assigned to such office by the Board of Directors, the President or the Executive Vice President.

6. Compensation and Employment Contracts. The Board of Directors shall set the Compensation paid to each officer. An employment contract may be entered with any officer under the terms and conditions approved by the Board of Directors. The salary of the President, the Executive Vice President and certain other individuals and any related employment contracts shall be subject further to the provisions of Section 1, Article VI of these By-laws. No officer shall be prevented from receiving such salary by reason of the fact that he is also a director of the Corporation.

7. Bonds and Insurance. The Board of Directors may require officers and employees to give adequate bonds where such officers or employees are responsible for the custody of funds or property of the Corporation. The cost of such bonds shall be paid by the Corporation.

ARTICLE V
Business Transactions

1. Contracts. The Board of Directors may authorize any officer to enter any contract or execute any instrument in the name and on behalf of the Corporation. Any such authority may be general or confined to specific instances.

2. Loans. No loans shall be contracted on behalf of the Corporation and no evidence of indebtedness shall be issued in its name unless authorized by resolution of the Board of Directors. Such authority may be general or confined to specific instances.

3. Deeds and Mortgages. All deeds and mortgages made by the Corporation shall be executed by the President or Executive Vice President and attested by an officer upon authorization of the Board of Directors. Any such authority may be general or confined to specific instances.

4. Checks, Drafts and Other Instruments. All checks, drafts or other orders or the payment of money, notes or other evidence of indebtedness issued in the name of the Corporation, shall be signed by such officer or officers of the Corporation and in such a manner as shall be determined by resolution of the Board of Directors.

5. Deposits. All funds of the Corporation not otherwise employed shall be deposited to the credit of the Corporation in such banks or other depositories as the Board of Directors may select.

ARTICLE VI
Special Business Transactions

Each of the following actions shall require the approval of at least 3 of the directors then sitting on the Board of Directors:

1. Executive Compensation Plans. The adoption of any Executive Compensation Plan. An Executive Compensation Plan shall be any arrangement between the Corporation and any officer or employee who owns more than 5% of the total shares, regardless of class, in the Corporation, then issued and outstanding, and meets all of the following conditions: (i) the arrangement represents an increase in benefits or compensation which exceeds any increase in benefits or compensation which will be or has been offered to all other officers or employees; and (ii) the increase in compensation or benefits does or could represent an increase of more than 10% of the lowest level of compensation or benefits which such officer or employee has received within the 12 month period immediately preceding the date upon which the arrangement will be implemented. Executive compensation plans shall include any stock or cash bonus plan, any stock option plan or any other similar incentive plan designed to provide key executives with incentives to enhance the performance of the Corporation.

2. Sale of Assets. Any recommendation under section 490.1202 of the Code of Iowa related to a sale of substantially all of the Corporation's assets. For purposes of applying this Section 2, the sale or disposition of substantially all of the stock of an Affiliated Corporation shall be deemed to fall within such Section 490.1202. An affiliated corporation shall be any corporation in which the Corporation together with other Affiliated Corporations own more than 80% of all shares then issued and outstanding in the other corporation.

3. Merger. (i) the adoption of any plan of merger required under Section 490.1101 of the Code of Iowa; (ii) the approval of any share exchange required under Section 490.1102 of the Code of Iowa and (iii) any recommendation to the shareholders regarding such a plan or exchange as required under Section

490.1103 of the Code of Iowa.

4. <u>Issuance of New Shares</u>. Any authorization to issue new shares in the Corporation, regardless of Class, pursuant to Section 490.621 of the Code of Iowa.

ARTICLE VII
Shares and Certificates

1. <u>Certificates</u>. Certificates representing shares of the Corporation shall be in such form as may be determined by the Board of Directors. Certificates shall be signed by the President, the Executive Vice President or any other officer authorized to sign certificates by the Board of Directors. Signatures on the certificates may be facsimiles. All certificates for shares shall be consecutively numbered and the name of the person to whom the certificates are issued shall be entered on the books of the Corporation. All certificates surrendered to the Corporation for transfer shall be canceled and no new certificates shall be issued until the former certificates for a like number of shares shall have been surrendered and canceled. Notwithstanding, new certificates may be issued to replace lost, destroyed or mutilated certificates upon such terms and indemnity to the Corporation as the Board of Directors may prescribe.

2. <u>Legends</u>. Each certificate of shares of any class shall contain all appropriate legends which are required under law, the Articles of Incorporation, these by-laws, any agreement among the shareholders and/or the Corporation or any agreement between a Shareholder and some other person which has been recognized by the Corporation. Each certificate shall without limitation include the following legend which shall be set forth conspicuously on either the front or the back of the certificate:

> The corporation is authorized to issue Class A, Class B and Class C shares of Common Stock under its Articles of Incorporation. Each Class of such Common Stock has different voting rights and different rights regarding the election of directors to the Corporation's Board of Directors. The Corporation will furnish to the person named on this Certificate information defining the rights attributable to each Class of Common Stock without charge upon the written request of such person. The sale or assignment of these shares is also subject to the requirements of 47 USC 310(d) of the United States Code. This section among other things requires the holder of these shares to obtain FCC approval under certain circumstances before any such assignment or sale can be consummated.

3. *Transfer of Shares*. The Board of Directors may authorize the Corporation to enter an agreement with any or all of the Shareholders restricting or regulating the transfer of any or all shares of the Corporation. The Board of Directors shall additionally honor any agreement between or among the Shareholders related to restrictions on transferability of shares in the Corporation. Any transfer of shares in the Corporation shall only be made on the books of the Corporation by the holder of record thereof; by his/her legal representative, who shall furnish proper evidence of authority to transfer; or by an attorney-in-fact authorized by a Power of Attorney to make such transfer provided that such Power of Attorney has previously been filed with the President of the Corporation. No transfer shall be recognized by the Corporation or otherwise be valid or enforceable by the transferor or transferee until all of the following conditions have been satisfied: (i) the certificate for such shares has been canceled and a new certificate has been issued containing all of the legends required by Section 2 of this Article VII; (ii) the transferee and transferor demonstrate to the satisfaction of the Corporation that any and all restrictions on transfer have been satisfied or that such restrictions can not be enforced pursuant to an appropriate court order obtained by the transferee or transferor; (iii) all other rights of the Shareholders, other than the transferor, imposed by law, the Articles of Incorporation these by-laws or by agreement have been satisfied; (iv) The transferee has agreed to enter and has executed all agreements, if any, which the transferor has previously entered regarding restrictions on transfer of the acquired shares and (v) the transferor and transferee demonstrate to the satisfaction of the Corporation and its legal counsel that all requirements under 47 USC 310(d) of the United States Code, including all necessary approvals by the FCC, have been satisfied. Except as otherwise provided by law, the person in whose name shares stand on the books of the Corporation shall be deemed the owner thereof for all purposes regarding the Corporation.

4. *Issuance of New Shares*. The Board of Directors may authorize the issuance of new shares of any class of stock authorized under the Articles of Incorporation which have not been issued, provided that the requirements of Section 4 of Article VI of these By-laws have been satisfied. The Board of Directors shall honor any preemptive rights which existing shareholders may have under the Articles of Incorporation regarding such shares and shall additionally honor any lawful agreements which have been entered among the Corporation and/or one or more Shareholders. The Board of Directors shall not authorize the issuance of any new shares in the Corporation until: (i) the transferee agrees to enter the same agreement, if any, which has been entered among the Corporation and/or all or part of the Corporation's existing Shareholders regarding restrictions on the transferability of the Corporation's stock by such Shareholders, and (ii) the Board of Directors determines that the consideration be paid for such shares is adequate and (iii) all approvals from the FCC have been obtained.

5. **Acquisition of Shares by the Corporation.** The Corporation may acquire its own shares of stock, regardless of class, upon approval by the Board of Directors and subject further to any agreements between the Corporation and any of its Shareholders. Any shares acquired by the Corporation shall be deemed to be authorized and unissued shares and not Treasury shares. Any shares so acquired may be reissued in the future, subject to any requirements related to authorized and unissued shares imposed by law, the Articles of Incorporation, these by-laws and any lawful agreement.

ARTICLE VIII
Fiscal Year

The fiscal year of the Corporation shall be fixed by resolution of the Board of Directors.

ARTICLE IX
Seal

The Corporation shall not have a corporate seal.

ARTICLE X
Voting of Stock in Other Corporations

The Board of Directors by Majority Vote shall vote Shares and take any other actions with respect to the stock of another corporation owned by the Corporation. The Board of Directors may authorize by resolution any officer or director to vote shares, attend meetings, execute proxies, waive notice, execute informal consents and take any other actions on behalf of the Corporation which otherwise relate to the stock or ownership rights of such stock of another corporation which the Corporation owns and may additionally authorize or elect such officers or directors to serve on the Board of Directors of such other corporation. The power granted to such officers or directors pursuant to the foregoing sentence may either be general or confined to specific instances and such officers and/or directors may take any actions consistent with such authorization without any further authority.

ARTICLE XI
Indemnification

1. **Authorization to Indemnify.** The Corporation shall indemnify and hold harmless each director, officer, employee or agent of the corporation and any individual representing the corporation as provided in Section 2 of this Article XI to the maximum extent required or permitted by Iowa law and this Article XI. Notwithstanding, no indemnification shall be made by the Corporation in the event that

such director, officer, employee, agent or individual: (i) breached his/her duty of loyalty to the Corporation or its Shareholders; (ii) committed acts or omitted to take actions not in good faith or which involved intentional misconduct or knowing violation of the law; (iii) derives improper personal benefit from a transaction between the Corporation and another; (iv) is liable under Section 490.833 of the Code of Iowa or any other provision of the Iowa Code which amends or replaces such Section 490.833 after the adoption of these By-laws or (v) is expressly prohibited from being indemnified by the Corporation under the laws of the State of Iowa.

2. <u>Scope of Indemnification</u>. The Corporation shall indemnify any individual who is otherwise entitled to indemnification under Section 1 of this Article IX against all Liability or reasonable Expenses incurred in connection with any Proceeding which such individual is a Party in his Official Capacity with the Corporation or in his capacity as a director, officer, partner trustee, employee or agent of a foreign or domestic corporation, partnership, joint venture, trust, employee benefit plan or other enterprise, if such individual is serving in such capacity at the request of the Corporation. The terms Liability, Expenses, Proceeding, Party and Official Capacity shall have the same meaning for purposes of this Article XI as the meaning assigned to each of these terms in Section 490.850 of the Code of Iowa or any provision which amends or replaces such Section after these By-laws are adopted.

3. <u>Indemnification Procedure</u>. Indemnification shall be authorized in each specific case after a determination has been made that indemnification is permissible in the circumstances because the director, officer, employee or agent has met the standard of conduct imposed by Section 1 of this Article XI or under law, as the case may be. The determination shall be made as follows:

   (a) by a majority vote of a quorum of the Board of Directors, provided that no director shall vote who is a Party to the Proceedings for which indemnification is being sought.

   (b) If a quorum cannot be obtained in "A," by a majority vote of a committee duly designated by the Board of Directors, consisting of two or more directors who are not a Party to the Proceedings for which indemnification is being sought.

   (c) If a quorum cannot be selected in "(A)" or a committee designated in "(B)", by special legal counsel selected by a majority vote of the Board of Directors; and

   (d) Under any circumstances, by a majority vote of the shares held by Shareholders who are not a Party to the Proceeding for which indemnification is being sought.

4. <u>Payment</u>. Upon authorization, the Corporation shall pay all amounts which the individual is entitled to receive under Section 2 of this Article XI. The determination related to the reasonableness of expenses shall be made by the same individual(s) who authorized indemnification under Section 3 of this Article XI, except where authorized by legal counsel in which case such determination shall be made a committee of directors consisting of those directors who are not a Party to the Proceeding for which indemnification is sought. The Corporation may pay for or reimburse in advance reasonable Expenses incurred by any individual if: (i) the individual otherwise satisfies all the requirements of Subsection (1) and (2) of Section 490.853 of the Code of Iowa; (ii) indemnification is otherwise authorized under Section 3 of this Article XI and (iii) such expenses are determined to be reasonable under this Section 4.

5. <u>Insurance</u>. The Corporation may purchase and maintain a policy on behalf of an individual who is or was a director, officer, employee or agent of the Corporation or who is or was serving as a director, officer, employee, partner, trustee or agent of another foreign or domestic corporation, partnership, joint venture, trust, employee benefit plan or other enterprise at the request of the Corporation. Policy shall mean insurance against liability asserted against or incurred by the individual while serving in any of the capacities described in the foregoing sentence, whether or not the Corporation would have the power to indemnify such individual against the same liability under this Article XI.

ARTICLE XII
Amendments

These By-laws may be altered, amended or repealed and new By-laws may be adopted at any meeting of the Board of Directors at which a quorum is present; by a majority vote of the directors present at such meeting. Notwithstanding anything to the contrary in this Article XII, Sections 2 and 3 of Article III, any section in Article VI and this Article XII may only be altered, amended or repealed by a vote of the Shareholders at any meeting duly called and convened pursuant to Article II, provided further that the votes in favor of such amendment, alternation or repeal and the adoption of any new Bylaw replacing any of the foregoing sections in this sentence shall represent at least two-thirds of all votes cast either in person or by proxy at such meeting.

STOCK TRANSFER AGREEMENT
(MAY 20, 2003)

STOCK TRANSFER AGREEMENT

Stock Transfer Agreement, made and entered into this 20th day of May, 2003, by and between MediaComm, Inc., an Iowa corporation ("MediaComm") and Joyce F. Dennison and Paul L. Dennison (the "Dennisons"):

WITNESSETH:

WHEREAS, on July 19, 1991, a Stock Purchase Agreement was executed providing for the sale of all of the stock in KILJ, Inc., an Iowa corporation, by the Dennisons to MediaComm; and

WHEREAS, KILJ, Inc., is an Iowa corporation and holds licenses issued by the Federal Communications Commission ("FCC") for the operation of AM Broadcast Station KILJ and FM Broadcast Station KILJ-FM, Mt. Pleasant, Iowa; and

WHEREAS, FCC consent was obtained to the sale of the Dennisons' stock, constituting 100 percent of the issued and outstanding stock of KILJ, Inc., to MediaComm, and such transaction was subsequently closed and consummated; and

WHEREAS, the consideration for the sale of the stock was approximately $1,010,000.00, payable in installments over a period of 18 years pursuant to a Loan Agreement which was executed pursuant to the aforesaid Stock Purchase Agreement; and

WHEREAS, there remains a substantial balance yet to be paid by MediaComm pursuant to the aforesaid Loan Agreement; and

WHEREAS, MediaComm desires to be relieved of its obligations under the Loan Agreement and in consideration thereof to transfer all of the stock which it holds in KILJ, Inc., to the Dennisons; and

-2-

WHEREAS, the Dennisons are willing to accept the conveyance of such stock and in consideration thereof to relieve MediaComm of all of its obligations under the aforesaid Loan Agreement; and

WHEREAS, such transaction requires the prior consent of the FCC;

NOW, THEREFORE, for and in consideration of the mutual promises and covenants hereinafter set forth, it is agreed as follows:

1. **Application for FCC Consent**: Within five (5) days of the date of this Agreement, the parties hereto will file an application with the FCC, asking the FCC to approve the conveyance by MediaComm to the Dennisons of one hundred (100) shares of common stock of KILJ, Inc., constituting one hundred (100) percent of the issued and outstanding shares of stock in that corporation. Fifty (50) shares shall be conveyed to Paul L. Dennison and the remaining fifty (50) shares shall be conveyed to Joyce F. Dennison. The parties will vigorously prosecute the application and do all things reasonably necessary and/or appropriate to obtain a grant thereof.

2. **Consideration for Transfer of Stock**: The consideration for the above-described stock transfer shall consist of the dissolution, cancellation and termination of the Stock Purchase Agreement dated July 19, 1991, between the Dennisons, MediaComm and certain other parties, and the Loan Agreement executed pursuant to the July 19, 1991, Stock Purchase Agreement.

3. **Closing Following FCC Consent**: Within ten (10) days after the date when the FCC grants its consent to the transaction contemplated by this Agreement, a closing will be held at the law office of Pat Brau in Mt. Pleasant, Iowa. At the closing MediaComm will execute a valid conveyance of fifty (50) shares of stock in KILJ, Inc., to Paul L. Dennison and another valid

conveyance of fifty (50) shares to Joyce F. Dennison, so that the Dennisons will own 100% of the issued and outstanding stock of KILJ, Inc. The Dennisons, in turn, will execute whatever documents are necessary and/or appropriate to fully release MediaComm of any and all of its obligations under the Stock Purchase Agreement of July 19, 1991, and any other agreements executed pursuant thereto including, but not limited to, the Loan Agreement, so that MediaComm shall have no further obligation of any kind whatsoever under the agreement. To the extent that John Kuhens has had any obligation under said agreements, whether as a guarantor or otherwise, he shall also be fully relieved of all such obligations. To the extent that the certificates are being held in escrow by the U.S. Bank Corporation, the parties will execute whatever instructions are necessary and/or appropriate to secure release of the stock certificates to the Dennisons.

4. **Notices**: Any notice required by this Agreement shall be sent by electronic means or Federal Express or equivalent overnight delivery service, addressed as follows:

If to the Dennisons:
Paul L. Dennison
Joyce F. Dennison
2417 Lisa Lane
Mt. Pleasant, IA 52641
Fax: (319) 385-1595

If to MediaComm:
MediaComm, Inc.
c/o John Kuhens
281 Radio Road
Mt. Pleasant, IA 52641
Fax: 9/4- 385-1517

5. **Iowa Contract**: This Agreement is an Iowa contract and shall be construed and interpreted in accordance with the laws of that state (other than laws relating to conflicts of laws).

-4-

WHEREFORE, the premises considered, the parties have set their hands and seals and/or the hands and seals of their authorized representatives on the day and year above written.

JOYCE F. DENNISON

By: *(signature)*

PAUL L. DENNISON

By: *(signature)*

MEDIACOMM, Inc.

By: *(signature)*
Title: *(signature)*

TIME BROKERAGE AGREEMENT
(AUGUST 21, 2003)

TIME BROKERAGE AGREEMENT

Time Brokerage Agreement, made and entered into this 21st day of August, 2003, by and between KILJ, Inc., an Iowa corporation, the licensee of AM Broadcast Station KILJ (FCC Facility #34605), and FM Broadcast Station KILJ-FM (FCC Facility #34604), Mt. Pleasant, Iowa ("Owner."), and Paul Dennison, an individual and resident of Mt. Pleasant, Iowa.

WITNESSETH:

WHEREAS, Owner is the holder of licenses issued by the Federal Communications Commission ("FCC") for the operation of AM Broadcast Station KILJ and FM Broadcast Station KILJ-FM, Mt. Pleasant, Iowa (the "Stations"); and

WHEREAS, Broker desires to avail itself of a portion of the Stations' broadcast time, and Owner desires to make such time available to the Broker on the terms and conditions hereinafter set forth;

NOW, THEREFORE, for and in consideration of the mutual covenants herein contained, the parties hereto have agreed and do agree as follows:

1. Sale of Broadcast Time:

Owner hereby sells to Broker and Broker purchases all of the available broadcast time of the Stations, subject only to Owner's rights to pre-empt time to fulfill its FCC obligations, as set forth in paragraph 10, infra. The price for such time shall be a sum of money, payable monthly, equal to the actual costs of operation of the Stations during the month to which such payment applies, including the costs of electricity, utilities, equipment maintenance, rents, and any other expenses reasonably incurred or required to be incurred in order to keep the Stations operating in the public interest.

2. Payments to Owner and Owner's Obligations:

Broker hereby agrees to pay Owner for broadcast of the programs hereunder the amounts specified in paragraph 1, supra, and Owner agrees to accept the obligations imposed upon Owner in such paragraph. Payments for programs are due and payable in arrears on the first business day of each month for the actual costs of operation during the previous month. Any payments made by Broker directly to vendors or service providers, e.g., utility companies, contract engineers, landlords, etc., in order to keep the stations on the air, shall be deducted from Broker's payments.

3. Broker's Remedies:

The parties to this Agreement recognize that Broker's rights under this Agreement are unique, and that mere money damages may be insufficient to adequately compensate the Broker in the event the Owner breaches this Agreement. Therefore, in the event of a breach of this Agreement by the Owner, Broker shall have the right to either (a) sue the Owner for specific performance of this Agreement (in the event that Broker elects to sue for specific performance, the defense that Broker has an adequate remedy at law is hereby expressly waived and shall not be asserted by the Owner); or (b) bring an action to recover the actual damages suffered by the Broker as a result of the breach.

4. Term:

The term of this Agreement shall commence on December 21, 2003, and continue so long as there remains in effect a valid agreement for the Broker and his wife to acquire the ownership of all of the stock of KILJ, Inc.

5. Programs:

Broker shall furnish or cause to be furnished the artistic personnel and material for the programs as provided by this Agreement and all programs shall be in good taste and in accordance with FCC requirements. All programs shall be prepared and presented in conformity with the regulations prescribed in Attachment II hereto.

6. Handling of Mail:

Except to the extent required to assure compliance with FCC requirements governing maintenance of the Stations' public inspection files, Owner shall not be required to receive or handle mail, cables, telegraph or telephone calls in connection with the programs broadcast under this Agreement unless Owner at the request of Broker has agreed in writing to do so. Owner shall, however, be advised promptly by Broker of any public or FCC complaint or inquiry concerning such programming, and Owner shall be given the originals of any letters from the public, including complaints, concerning such programming for inclusion in the Stations' public records files as required by the FCC.

7. Programming and Operations Standards:

Broker agrees to abide by the standards set forth in Attachment II in its programming and operations. Broker further agrees that if, in the sole judgment of Owner or its Stations' general manager(s), Broker does not comply with said standards, Owner may suspend or cancel any program not in compliance.

8. Responsibility for Employees and Expenses:

Broker shall employ and be responsible for the salaries, taxes, insurance and related costs for all personnel used in the production of its programming. Owner shall employ and be responsible for the salaries, taxes and insurance and all other costs of its own personnel necessary to fulfill its obligations under the FCC's policies and to transmit the programming provided by

Broker. Broker shall pay for all telephone calls associated with program production and listener responses, for all fees to ASCAP, BMI and for any other copyright fees attributable to its programming broadcast on the Stations. To that end, Broker will obtain its own ASCAP and BMI licenses and hold Owner harmless from any liability thereunder.

9. Operation of Stations:

Notwithstanding anything to the contrary in this Agreement, Owner shall have full authority and power over the operation of the Stations during the period of this Agreement. Owner shall retain control in its absolute discretion over the policies, programming and operations of the Stations, including, without limitation, the right to decide whether to accept or reject any programming or advertisements, the right to pre-empt any programs in order to broadcast a program deemed to be by Owner to be of greater national, regional, or local interest, and the right to take any other actions necessary for compliance with the laws of the United States, the State of Iowa, and the rules, regulations, and policies of the FCC, including the prohibition on unauthorized transfers of control.

10. Special Events:

Owner reserves the right in its discretion, and without liability, to preempt any of the broadcasts of the programs referred to herein, and to use part or all of the time contracted for herein by Broker for broadcast of special events of importance. In all such cases, Owner will use its best efforts to give Broker reasonable notice of its intention to preempt such broadcast or broadcasts, and, in the event of such preemption Broker shall receive a payment credit for the broadcasts so omitted.

11. Force Majeure:

Any failure or impairment of facilities or any delay or interruption in broadcasting programs, or failure at any time to furnish facilities, in whole or in part, for broadcasting, due to acts of God, strikes or threats thereof or force majeure or due to causes beyond the control of Owner, shall not constitute a breach of this Agreement and Owner will not be liable to Broker, except to the extent of allowing in each such case an appropriate payment credit for time or broadcasts not provided based upon the length of time during which the failure or impairment exists.

12. Right to Use the Programs:

The right to use the programs and to authorize their use in any manner and in any media whatsoever, shall be and remain vested in Broker.

13. Compliance with Law:

Broker agrees that throughout the term of this Agreement Broker will comply with all laws and regulations applicable in the conduct of Owner's business and Broker acknowledges that Owner has not urged, counseled, or advised the use of any unfair business practice.

14. Indemnification; Warranty:

Broker will indemnify and hold and save Owner harmless against all liability for libel, slander, illegal competition or trade practice, infringement of trade marks, trade names, or program titles, violation of rights of privacy, and infringement of copyrights and proprietary rights resulting from the programming furnished by Broker. Further, Broker warrants that the broadcasting of the programs will not violate any rights of others and Broker indemnifies Owner and its agents and agrees to hold them harmless from any and all claims, damages, liability, costs and expenses, including counsel fees (at trial and on appeal), arising from the production and/or broadcasting of the programs. Owner reserves the right to refuse to broadcast any and all programs containing matter which is, or in the reasonable opinion of Owner may be, or which a third party claims to be, violative of any right of theirs or which may constitute a personal attack as the term is and has been defined by the FCC. Broker's obligation to hold Owner harmless against the liabilities specified above shall survive any termination of this Agreement.

15. Events of Default:

The following shall, after the expiration of the applicable cure periods, constitute Events of Default under this Agreement:

a). <u>Non-Payment</u>: Broker's failure to timely pay the consideration provided for in ¶1.

b). <u>Default in Covenant</u>: Broker shall default in the material observance or performance of any material covenant, condition or agreement contained herein; or

c). <u>Breach of Representation</u>: Any material representation or warranty herein made by Broker, or in any certificate or document furnished to Owner pursuant to the provisions hereof, shall prove to have been false or misleading in any material respect as of the time made or furnished.

d). <u>Termination Upon Default</u>: In the event of the occurrence of an Event of Default, Owner shall be under no further obligation to make available to Broker any further broadcast time or broadcast transmission facilities and all amounts accrued or payable to Owner up to the date of termination which have not been paid shall immediately become due and payable.

e). <u>Liabilities Upon Termination</u>: Broker shall be responsible for all liabilities, debts and obligations of Broker accrued from the purchase of air time and transmission facilities including, without limitation, accounts payable, barter agreements and unaired advertisements but not for Owner's federal and local tax liabilities associated with Broker's payment to Owner as provided for herein. Upon termination, Broker shall retain all Accounts Receivable arising from the period of time during which this Agreement was in effect.

16. Termination by Governmental or Judicial Order:

In the event that the FCC or any other federal, state, or local governmental or judicial entity with jurisdiction in the premises orders or directs the termination of this Agreement or orders or directs an adverse curtailment in any manner material to this Agreement, either party, at its option and expense, may seek administrative or judicial relief and appeal from such order, or either party may terminate this Agreement in accordance with such order(s) or direction(s). Owner and Broker shall cooperate each with the other and comply with reasonable requests from each other to assemble and provide to the FCC information requested and relating to Broker's performance under this Agreement.

17. Representations:

Both Owner and Broker represent that they are legally qualified, empowered, and able to enter into this Agreement.

18. Modification and Waiver:

No modification or waiver of any provision of this Agreement shall in any event be effected unless the same shall be in writing, and then such waiver and consent shall be effective only in the specific instance and for the purpose for which given.

19. No Waiver; Remedies Cumulative:

No failure or delay on the part of Owner or Broker in exercising any right or power hereunder shall operate as a waiver thereof, nor shall any single or partial exercise of any such right or power, or any abandonment or discontinuance of steps to enforce such a right or power, preclude any other or further exercise thereof or the exercise of any other right or power. The rights and remedies of Owner and Broker herein provided are cumulative and are not exclusive of any right or remedies which they may otherwise have.

20. Construction:

This Agreement shall be construed in accordance with the laws of the State of Iowa, and the obligations of the parties hereto are subject to all federal, state or municipal laws or regulations now or hereafter in force and to the regulations of the FCC and all other governmental bodies or authorities presently or hereafter to be constituted.

21. Headings:

The headings contained in this Agreement are included for convenience only and no such heading shall in any way alter the meaning of any provision.

22. Successors and Assigns:

This Agreement shall be binding upon and inure to the benefit of the parties and their successors and assigns, provided, however, that neither shall assign their rights under this Agreement without written consent of the other party.

23. Counterpart Signatures:

This Agreement may be signed in one or more counterparts and/or by telecopy, each of which shall be deemed a duplicate original, binding on the parties hereto notwithstanding that the parties are not signatory to the original or the same counterpart, whether executed in ink or by telecopy.

24. Notices:

Any notice required hereunder shall be in writing and any payment, notice or other communications shall be deemed given when delivered personally, or mailed by certified mail or Federal Express, postage prepaid, with return receipt request, and addressed in accordance with the listing set forth in Attachment III hereto.

25. Entire Agreement:

This Agreement embodies the entire agreement between the parties and there are no other agreements, representations, warranties, or understandings, oral or written, between them with respect to the subject matter hereof. No alteration, modification or change of this Agreement shall be valid unless by like written instrument.

26. Severability:

The event that any of the provisions contained in this Agreement is held to be invalid, illegal or unenforceable shall not affect any other provision hereof, and this Agreement shall be construed as if such invalid, illegal or unenforceable provision had not been contained herein.

27. Section 73.3555 Certifications:

Pursuant to Section 73.3555(a)(ii) of the Rules and Regulations of the FCC, Owner hereby verifies that it will maintain ultimate control over the Stations' facilities, including, specifically, control over station finances, personnel and programming during the term of this Agreement; and Broker hereby verifies that the arrangement contemplated by this Agreement complies with the provisions of Sections 73.3555(a)(1) and (e)(1) of the Commission's Rules.

IN WITNESS WHEREOF, the parties have executed this Agreement as of the date first above written.

KILJ, Inc.

By: *[signature]*
John Kuhens, President

Paul L. Dennison

By: *[signature]*
Paul L. Dennison

30 Day Notice of Right to Cure Default of Stock Purchase Agreement (July 16, 2003)

30 DAY NOTICE OF RIGHT TO CURE DEFAULT OF STOCK PURCHASE AGREEMENT

July 16, 2003

TO:

MEDIA COMM., Inc. a/k/a MediaComm., Inc.
an Iowa Corporation
JOHN KUHENS
281 Radio Road
Mt. Pleasant, Iowa 52641

Pursuant to Section 12.6 of the Stock Purchase Agreement to Acquire KILJ, Inc. and KILJ-AM, Ltd., dated July 19, 1991, Paul L. Dennison and Joyce F. Dennison, hereby give notice that Media Comm., Inc. a/k/a MediaComm., Inc. materially breached said agreement. The material breach is the failure of Media Comm, Inc. a/k/a MediaComm., Inc. to make the following monthly payments, due Paul L. Dennison and Joyce F. Dennison, as required by said Agreement:

Monthly Payment due May 25, 2003 in the amount of $11,119.55
Monthly Payment due June 25, 2003 in the amount of $11,119.55
Monthly Payment due July 25, 2003 in the amount of $11,119.55

Pursuant to Section 12.6 of the Stock Purchase Agreement to Acquire KILJ, Inc. and KILJ-AM, Ltd., Media Comm, Inc. a/k/a MediaComm, Inc. has thirty (30) days from the date of service of this Notice to cure the above described material breach.

PATRICK C. BRAU   LI0008901
Brau Law Office
111 East Washington Street
Mt. Pleasant, Iowa 52641-1901
(319) 385-2511
(319) 385-2148 fax

ATTORNEY FOR PAUL L. DENNISON AND
JOYCE E. DENNISON

ACCEPTANCE OF SERVICE

The undersigned, on behalf of MEDIA COMM.; Inc. a/k/a MediaComm., Inc. an Iowa Corporation, hereby acknowledges service of the 30 DAY NOTICE OF RIGHT TO CURE DEFAULT OF STOCK PURCHASE AGREEMENT pursuant to Article XVI Section 16.1 of the Stock Purchase Agreement to Acquire KILJ, Inc. and KILJ-AM, Ltd.

DATED this ___ day of _____, 2003.

MediaComm, Inc. Board Meeting Minutes (August 18, 2003)

The MediaCom board of directors held a board meeting August 18th, 2003 at 1:37 p.m. at the KILJ studios.
A phone tele-conference was held with corporate Fred Beaver, concerning corporate by laws and the transfer of ownership of the KILJ AM & FM.
President John Kuhens named Mary Susanna Kuhens (Susie) to the Board of Directors.
The board then voted on a transfer of ownership agreement from Paul Dennison and Joyce Dennison. John and Susie voted in favor of the transfer with Dixie Burkhart casting a vote of no.
The measure passed.
John Kuhens then proceeded to sign the agreement.
The meeting was then adjourned at 2:10 p.m.

Submitted by:

John Kuhens
President MediaCom

Witnessed:

Dixie Burkhart   Mary Susanna Kuhens

BURKHART LETTER TO KUHENS cc DENNISON, BEAVER (AUGUST 18, 2003)

August 18, 2003

John Kuhens
2411 Radio Drive
Mt. Pleasant, Ia 52641

Dear John,

Just a note to inform you that I sincerely believe that there were adequate funds to cure the 30 Day Notice of Right To Cure Default of Stock Purchase Agreement. The funds in checking and the overpaid property tax would have easily satisfied the obligation to Paul Dennison, Inc. I would have put up funds of my own, had this not been my belief.

I would still be willing to put up personal funds to cure what the property taxes should have, in my opinion cured.

Please advise as to your thoughts.

[signature]

cc Dennison
   Beavers

BEAVER LETTER TO KUHENS
(AUGUST 18, 2003)

HANSON, BJORK & RUSSELL, L.L.P.
ATTORNEYS AT LAW
SUITE 1300
405 6TH AVENUE
DES MOINES, IOWA 50309

Thomas D. Hanson
Alan H. Bjork
Barry A. Russell
Robert B. Hanson
Lu Ann White
Dale A. Knoshaug
Fred E. Beaver
Clark G. McDermott
Michael D. Ensley
Richard Webster
Elisa E. Daniels

Telephone (515) 244-0177
Facsimile (515) 244-8254
E-Mail fbeaver@HBR-law.com

Johnston Address
6165 NW 86TH ST.
Johnston, IA 50131
(515) 727-1648

✗ Reply to Des Moines Office

August 18, 2003

Via Facsimile and Regular Mail
Mr. John Kuhens
MediaCom, Inc.
P.O. Box 311
Mount Pleasant, Iowa 52641

Dear Mr. Kuhens:

Mrs. Dixie Burkhart forwarded a copy of the minutes of a purported meeting of the MediaCom Board of Directors held today, August 18, 2003. Please be advised that the action reflected in those minutes is contrary to the advice I gave earlier in the day during a telephone conference among Mrs. Burkhart, you and me. You should also be aware that the appointment of Mrs. Kuhens as a Director by you in your capacity as President of MediaCom, Inc. is ineffective and contrary to Section 10 of Article III of the MediaCom By-laws. The vote by the Board of Directors to transfer ownership of KILJ shares is also ineffective and contrary to Article VI of the MediaCom By-laws. The vote to transfer ownership is also ineffective under Iowa law to authorize the action contemplated, since shareholder approval is also required. The meeting and the actions taken at that meeting are also legally flawed and ineffective for other reasons.

<u>Because of these and other legal deficiencies, you had not corporate authority whatsoever to act upon MediaCom's behalf when you signed and attempted to enter into the agreement referred to in the minutes. For this reason, the agreement in my opinion is not binding upon MediaCom, Inc. and is otherwise unenforceable.</u>

Please be advised that appropriate actions should be taken to remedy this situation as soon as possible. Also be advised that further reliance upon the agreement or upon the actions purportedly taken or the authority purportedly granted at the meeting would in my opinion be legally inappropriate and ineffective.

Sincerely,

Fred E. Beaver

WIEGEL LETTER TO SQUIRES (NOVEMBER 5, 2003)

GARY L. WIEGEL
Attorney at Law
114 E. Monroe
P.O. Box 488
Mt. Pleasant, Iowa 52641-0488

RECEIVED NOV 6 2003

Telephone (319) 385-2130
FAX (319)385-8667

November 5, 2003

Mr. Vernon P. Squires
Attorney at Law
BRADLEY & RILEY PC
PO Box 2804
Cedar Rapids, IA 52406-2804

RE: MediaComm, Inc. - Paul Dennison and Joyce Dennison

Dear Mr. Squires:

US Bank, NA has requested that I respond to your letter of October 31, 2003.

As you are aware, there are two different law suits now pending, one in Henry County District Court where the bank was named as a Defendant and the other, I believe, in Scott County. Both suits concern the transaction involving the Dennisons, MediaComm, Inc. and John Kuhens. There appears to be a dispute over whether or not the loan agreement is in default. I have advised US Bank to not comply with your request for the delivery of the stock under the Escrow Agreement until such time as there is a Court Order or determination in this matter.

Additionally, as a courtesy I call your attention to the fact that the Escrow Agreement apparently misstates who the Pledgees and Pledgors are on the signature page. If you should have any questions, feel free to contact me.

Yours truly,

Gary L. Wiegel
Attorney at Law

GLW:nlw
cc: US Bank, NA

PLAINTIFF'S EXHIBIT 23

30 Day Notice of Right to Cure Default of Stock Purchase Agreement (December 9, 2003)

30 DAY NOTICE OF RIGHT TO CURE DEFAULT OF STOCK PURCHASE AGREEMENT

December 9, 2003

TO:

MEDIA COMM., Inc., a/k/a MediaComm., Inc.
an Iowa Corporation
JOHN KUHENS
281 Radio Road
Mt. Pleasant, Iowa 52641

Pursuant to Section 12.6 of the Stock Purchase Agreement to Acquire KILJ, Inc., and KILJ-AM, Ltd., dated July 19, 1991, Paul L. Dennison and Joyce F. Dennison, hereby give notice that Media Comm., Inc., a/k/a MediaComm., Inc., materially breached said agreement. The material breach is the failure of Media Comm., Inc., a/k/a MediaComm., Inc., to make the following monthly payments, due Paul L. Dennison and Joyce F. Dennison, as required by said Agreement:

Monthly payment due May 25, 2003 in the amount of $11,119.55
Monthly payment due June 25, 2003 in the amount of $11,119.55
Monthly payment due July 25, 2003 in the amount of $11,119.55
Monthly payment due August 25, 2003 in the amount of $11,119.55
Monthly payment due September 25, 2003 in the amount of $11,119.55
Monthly payment due October 25, 2003 in the amount of $11,119.55
Monthly payment due November 25, 2003 in the amount of $11,119.55

Pursuant to Section 12.6 of the Stock Purchase Agreement to Acquire KILJ, Inc., and KILJ-AM, Ltd., Media Comm., Inc., a/k/a MediaComm., Inc., has thirty (30) days from the date of service of this Notice to cure the above described material breach.

VERNON P. SQUIRES (#LI0014929)
Of
BRADLEY & RILEY PC
2007 First Avenue, SE
PO Box 2804
Cedar Rapids, IA 52406-2804
Phone: 319-363-0101
Fax: 319-363-9824
Email: vsquires@bradleyriley.com

ATTORNEYS FOR PAUL L. DENNISON AND JOYCE E. DENNISON

PLAINTIFF'S EXHIBIT
12

DENNISON LETTER TO BURKHART (DECEMBER 31, 2003)

P.O. Box 311 • Mount Pleasant, Iowa 52641
Phone: 319-385-8728 • Fax: 319-385-4517

December 31, 2003

Dixie Burkhart
2693 Kentucky Ave
Mt. Pleasant, IA 52641

Dear Mrs. Burkhart:

This letter is to confirm our conversation of 8 AM this morning at which time I told you that I was enforcing the Time Brokerage Agreement dated 8/21/03. I also presented you with the opportunity to sell advertising for me at the usual radio station accepted commission of 20%.

For the Firm,

Paul L. Dennison

lr

LETTER OF AGREEMENT
(EFFECTIVE JANUARY 1, 2004)

LETTER AGREEMENT

Mr. Paul L. Dennison
2417 Lisa Lane
Mount Pleasant, IA 52641

Dear Paul:

As we discussed, KILJ, Inc. has agreed to hire you and/or your corporate nominee to serve as general manager of KILJ, effective January 1, 2004. The compensation will be $3,000 per month plus a 20 percent commission on all advertising sales revenue. The management duties include, but are not limited to, soliciting and selling advertising on behalf of KILJ. The term will be for ten years. This Letter Agreement will constitute our agreement until such time as you identify a corporate nominee and we execute an acceptable contract.

Sincerely,

KILJ, Inc.

By: *[signature]*
John Kuhens

Its: President

[handwritten annotation: No default at this time 10yr guarantee for Dennison to have control of my]

PLAINTIFF'S EXHIBIT 1

LETTER OF NOYES TO SQUIRES REQUESTING DENNISON TO VACATE (JANUARY 7, 2004)

LANE & WATERMAN LLP

Established 1854

220 North Main Street, Suite 600
Davenport, Iowa 52801-1987
Telephone (563) 324-3246
Fax (563) 324-1616

Writer's Direct Dial: (563) 333-6634
E-Mail Address: mnoyes@l-wlaw.com

January 7, 2004

VIA FACSIMILE
319-363-9824

Attorney Vernon Squires
Bradley & Riley PC
2007 First Avenue SE
P.O. Box 2804
Cedar Rapids IA 52406-2804

Vernon:

Today Dixie Burkhart is delivering to Paul and Joyce Dennison a check in the amount of $88,956.40 to cure those defaults listed in your Thirty Day Notice of Right to Cure Default of Stock Purchase Agreement dated December 9, 2003, and to pay the installment owing on December 25, 2003. I trust you will immediately file a dismissal of your lawsuit and will advise Mr. Dennison to vacate Mediacomm's premises. His presence on the Mediacomm premises is due to the premature execution of a turnover agreement whereby the Mediacomm assets were tendered to him. Aside from the improper board action, since the defaults have been cured that agreement is of no effect.

Respectfully,

LANE & WATERMAN LLP

By Michael Noyes

MLN/ct

PLAINTIFF'S EXHIBIT 13

BOGUS CORPORATE RESOLUTION TO PILOT GROVE SAVINGS BANK (JANUARY 8, 2004)

PILOT GROVE SAVINGS BANK

This Corporate resolution from KILJ INC. AND MEDIACOMM requests a change in the requirement of two signatures on the KILJ INC. and MEDIACO checking and savings.
John Kuhens will be the only authorized signature for KILJ INC. and MEDIACOMM.
Dixie Burkhart no longer works in the station or corporation.

Sincerely,

John Kuhens President
KILJ INC. & MEDIACOMM
2411 Radio Drive
Mt. Pleasant, Iowa 52641

Affidavit of Governor Thomas J. Vilsack

IN THE IOWA DISTRICT COURT IN AND FOR HENRY COUNTY

PAUL L. DENNISON AND JOYCE E. DENNISON,

    Plaintiffs,

v.

MEDIACOMM., INC. a/k/a MEDIACOMM., INC., U.S. BANK, N.A., successor in interest to FIRSTAR BANK, N.A., f/k/a FIRSTAR BANK IOWA, N.A., successor in interest to FIRSTAR BANK MT. PLEASANT, and JOHN KUHENS,

    Defendants.

No. EQEQ 003483

AFFIDAVIT OF
THOMAS J. VILSACK

STATE OF IOWA   )
) ss:
COUNTY OF POLK)

Thomas J. Vilsack, being first duly sworn, deposes and states:

1. I am an attorney licensed to practice before the courts of the State of Iowa. I have personal knowledge of all matters contained in this Affidavit.

2. I represented Paul and Joyce Dennison in 1991 when they sold KILJ radio station to Mediacomm, Inc. I prepared the transaction documents, including the Stock Purchase Agreement, Loan Agreement and Escrow Agreement.

3. These documents, taken collectively, were intended to provide the Dennisons with an immediate remedy if Mediacomm defaulted in its obligations under the agreements. The immediate remedy is the return of the KILJ stock to the Dennisons.

4. There are several reasons the transaction was structured to include an immediate remedy. First, the nature of the radio business is such that the identity and authority of

PLAINTIFF'S EXHIBIT 24

a station's owners must be certain at all times, both for licensing and advertising purposes. We anticipated that a default by Mediacomm could adversely affect the radio station, particularly if the default was accompanied by erratic efforts to keep the station operating. By negotiating and agreeing to an immediate remedy that would permit the Dennisons to resume control of the station, all parties agreed that this remedy was appropriate to maintain the viability of the radio station if an uncured default existed. [handwritten: BUT MUST BE POST-DEFAULT AGREEMENT]

5. The second reason for an immediate remedy involves the financial nature of the transaction. Mediacomm paid very little money down, and the parties anticipated that Mediacomm would pay only interest for several years. Given that Mediacomm would pay little, if any, principal during the initial years of the contract, the parties agreed that an immediate remedy upon default was appropriate to secure the Dennisons.

6. Finally, all parties agreed to an immediate remedy upon default in order to avoid protracted litigation if a default occurred. The Dennisons made several concessions to help make the deal viable for Mediacomm, and in return Mediacomm agreed that an uncured default would cause the stock to return to the Dennisons.

FURTHER YOU AFFIANT SAYETH NOT.

Thomas J. Vilsack
THOMAS J. VILSACK

Subscribed and sworn to before me by THOMAS J. VILSACK on this 8th day of March, 2004.

[Notary Seal: JUDI A. BROOKS, COMMISSION NO. 152800, MY COMMISSION EXPIRES 3-24-05, IOWA]

Judi A. Brooks
Notary Public in and for the State of Iowa

BUSINESS ACCOUNT AGREEMENTS WITH PILOT GROVE SAVINGS BANK

DIXIE BURKHART

Mar 09 04 03:37p   Pilot Grove Savings Bank   319 469 4905   p.22

CORPORATE AUTHORIZATION RESOLUTION

By: MEDIACOMM, INC
(Corporation)

600-600-717;

P O BOX 311
(Address)

86

MT. PLEASANT, IOWA 52641
(City, State and Zip Code)

A. I, DIXIE L. BURKHART, certify that I am Secretary (clerk) of the above named corporation organized under the laws of IOWA, Federal Employer I.D. Number 42-1371202, engaged in business under the trade name of MEDIACOMM, INC, and that the following is a correct copy of resolutions adopted at a meeting of the Board of Directors of this corporation duly and properly called and held on MARCH 23, 19___. These resolutions appear in the minutes of this meeting and have not been rescinded or modified.

B. Be it resolved that,

(1) The Financial Institution named above is designated as a depository for the funds of this corporation.
(2) This resolution shall continue to have effect until express written notice of its rescission or modification has been received and recorded by this Financial Institution.
(3) All transactions, if any, with respect to any deposits, withdrawals, rediscounts and borrowings by or on behalf of this corporation with this Financial Institution prior to the adoption of this resolution are hereby ratified, approved and confirmed.
(4) Any of the persons named below, so long as they act in a representative capacity as agents of this corporation, are authorized to make any and all other contracts, agreements, stipulations and orders which they may deem advisable for the effective exercise of the powers indicated below, from time to time with this Financial Institution, concerning funds deposited in this Financial Institution, moneys borrowed from this Financial Institution or any other business transacted by and between this corporation and this Financial Institution subject to any restrictions stated below.
(5) Any and all prior resolutions adopted by the Board of Directors of this corporation and certified to this Financial Institution as governing the operation of this corporation's account(s), are in full force and effect, unless supplemented or modified by this authorization.
(6) This corporation agrees to the terms and conditions of any account agreement, properly opened by any authorized representative(s) of this corporation, and authorizes the Financial Institution named above, at any time, to charge this corporation for all checks, drafts, or other orders, for the payment of money, that are drawn on this Financial Institution, regardless of by whom or by what means the facsimile signature(s) may have been affixed so long as they resemble the facsimile signature specimens in section C. (or the facsimile signature specimens that this corporation files with the Financial Institution from time to time) and contain the required number of signatures for this purpose.

C. If indicated, any person listed below (subject to any expressed restrictions) is authorized to:

	Name and Title	Signature	Facsimile Signature
(A)	JOHN KIMENS, PRESIDENT		
(B)	THERESA ROSE, EMPLOYEE		
(C)	DIXIE L. BURKHART, SEC/TES.		
(D)			

Iteals A, B, C and/or D

ABC (1) Exercise all of the powers listed in (2) through (6).
AC (2) Open any deposit or checking account(s) in the name of this corporation.
ABC (3) Endorse checks and orders for the payment of money and withdraw funds on deposit with this Financial Institution.
         Number of authorized signatures required for this purpose TWO
AC (4) Borrow money on behalf and in the name of this corporation, sign, execute and deliver promissory notes or other evidences of indebtedness.
         Number of authorized signatures required for this purpose TWO
AC (5) Endorse, assign, transfer, mortgage or pledge bills receivable, warehouse receipts, bills of lading, stocks, bonds, real estate or other property now owned or hereafter owned or acquired by this corporation as security for sums borrowed, and to discount the same, unconditionally guarantee payment of all bills received, negotiated or discounted and to waive demand, presentment, protest, notice of protest and notice of non-payment.
         Number of authorized signatures required for this purpose TWO
AC (6) Enter into written lease for the purpose of renting and maintaining a Safe Deposit Box in this Financial Institution.
         Number of authorized persons required to gain access and to terminate the lease TWO

D. I further certify that the Board of Directors of this corporation has, and at the time of adoption of this resolution had, full power and lawful authority to adopt the foregoing resolutions and to confer the powers granted to the persons named who shall have full power and lawful authority to exercise the same.

In Witness Whereof, I have hereunto subscribed my name and affixed the seal of this corporation on _____, 19___.

IMPRINT SEAL HERE

Attest by One Other Officer _____   Secretary _____

EXHIBIT Y-2

03/09/04 TUE 15:38 [TX/RX NO 7510] ☒022

Facts Don't Matter

Mar 09 04 03:33p   Pilot Grove Savings Bank   319 469 4905   p.15

5000-6537-4
5001-4036-3   6b

CORPORATE RESOLUTIONS AND AGREEMENT

I, the undersigned, do hereby certify that the following is a complete, true and correct copy of certain resolutions of the Board of Directors of (name of corporation in full) __KTLJ Inc_____, a corporation duly organized and existing under the laws of the State of (name of state where organized) __Iowa_____ (the "Corporation"), the address of which is __1816 Oakland Mills Rd Mt Pleasnt, Ia 52641__, which resolutions were duly adopted at a duly called meeting of the said Board held on (date of meeting) __Aug 1_____, __2800__, a quorum being present, and are set forth in the minutes of the said meeting; that I am the keeper of the corporate seal (if any) and of the minutes of the said Corporation; and that the said resolutions have not been rescinded or modified:

ENDORSEMENT FOR DEPOSITING CHECKS
Be it Resolved, that __Pilot Grove Savings Bank_____, Iowa, (the "Bank"), be and hereby is designated a depository in which the funds of this Corporation may be deposited by its officers, agents, and employees, and that the (title of officers and/or names of other persons authorized to endorse for deposit, etc.) _____ shall be and each of them hereby is authorized to endorse for deposit or negotiation any and all checks, drafts, notes, bills of exchange, or orders for the payment of money, either belonging to or coming into the possession of the Corporation. Endorsements for deposit may be by the written or stamped endorsement of the Corporation without designation of the person making the endorsement.

CHECK SIGNING SECTION
Be it Further Resolved, that the (titles of officers and/or names of persons authorized to sign checks, e.g. President, Treasurer, etc; also, indicate in what manner the above-named officers/persons are to sign—singly, any two, or jointly, amount limits, when more than one signature is required, etc.) __two_____
__John Kuhens   Dixie L Burkhart_____

(are) (is) authorized to sign any and all checks, drafts, and orders, including orders or directions in informal or letter form, against any funds at any time standing to the credit of the Corporation with the Bank, and/or against any account of the Corporation with the Bank, and that the Bank hereby is authorized to honor any and all checks, drafts and orders so signed, including those drawn to the individual order of any such officer and/or person signing the same, without further inquiry as regard to the authority of said officer(s) and/or other person(s) or the use of said checks, drafts and orders, or the proceeds thereof.

AUTHORIZATION FOR CASHING CHECKS
Be it Further Resolved, that (titles of officers and/or names of persons authorized to endorse) __same as above_____

or any of them (are) (is) authorized to endorse checks, notes, bills, certificates of deposit or other instruments, owned, payable to or held by the Corporation for the purpose of cashing the same or for any other purpose and to receive the cash or credit therefrom and the Bank is authorized to cash and give credit for any such instruments.

___ AN SECTION
Be it Further Resolved, that the (indicate in what manner the above-named officers/persons are to sign—singly, any two, or jointly, etc.) __two_____
__John Kuhens   Dixie L Burkhart_____

(are) (is) authorized, (1) to borrow from time to time on behalf of the Corporation from the Bank such sums of money for such times and upon such terms as may to them, or any of them, seem advisable; (2) to sign and deliver to said Bank, from time to time, notes or loan agreements evidencing such debts in such amounts, with such maturities, and of such rates of interest and upon such other terms and conditions as said officer(s) or person(s) deem(s) proper; (3) to pledge, assign, mortgage or otherwise grant a security interest in any or all real property, fixtures, tangible or intangible personal property, or any other assets of the Corporation, to execute and deliver to the Bank such security agreements, assignments, mortgages, financing statements, hypothecations, agreements not to encumber and other agreements as may be requested by the Bank from time to time with such promises, warranties, representations and conditions as said officer(s) or person(s) deem(s) proper to secure such borrowing and to guarantee and/or secure the obligations of others to said Bank, and may perform such acts required of the Corporation in such agreements or otherwise to perfect such security interests, including the deposit of such property with the Bank (and may withdraw and make substitutions of same from time to time); (4) to endorse or assign with or without recourse and deliver to the Bank for discount or negotiation notes, drafts, bills of exchange, checks, certificates of deposit, acceptances, chattel paper, accounts, commercial and other business paper, now owned or hereafter acquired by the Corporation; (5) to execute and deliver to the Bank applications, agreements and other instruments for the issuance by the Bank of commercial letters of credit for the account of the Corporation; and (6) to give subordinations, guarantees or other financial understandings to the Bank. The signature(s) of said officer(s) or person(s) appearing on any of the foregoing shall be conclusive evidence of this (their) approval thereof.

FACSIMILE SIGNATURES SECTION
Be it Further Resolved, that the Bank as designated depository of this Corporation be and is hereby requested, authorized and directed to honor checks, drafts or other orders for the payment of money drawn on the Corporation's name, including those drawn to the individual order of any person or persons whose name or names appear thereon as signer or signers thereof, when bearing or purporting to bear the facsimile signature(s) of any _____ of the following (please type or print; furnish specimens of each facsimile signature on the Bank's signature card): __n/a_____

and the Bank shall be entitled to honor and to charge the Corporation for all such checks, drafts, or other orders, regardless of by whom or by what means the facsimile signature or signatures thereon may have been affixed thereto, if such facsimile signature or signatures resemble the facsimile specimens duly certified to and filed with the Bank by the Secretary or any other officer of the Corporation. The Bank shall be held harmless by the Corporation against forgery or unauthorized use of facsimile signing equipment and/or devices.

IBA No. 2   IOWA BANKERS   (For reorders, please call 1-800-532-1423)

EXHIBIT
Y-3

Mar 09 04 03:34p   Pilot Grove Savings Bank   319 469 4905   p.16

6C

SAVINGS ACCOUNT SECTION
Be It Further Resolved, that the funds of the Corporation may be deposited in the designated depository into a savings account standing in the name of the Corporation, and the Bank be and is hereby authorized to pay withdrawal orders from said account, whether such withdrawal orders are deposited to the individual credit of the person so signing and/or countersigning such withdrawal orders or the individual credit of any of the other officers or not, signed in the name of the Corporation by any _____ of the following: (title and manner of signature—singly, any two, jointly, amount limits, when from one signature is required, etc.) __two__
John Kuhens   Dixie L Burkhart

TELEPHONE TRANSFER SECTION
Be It Further Resolved, that funds in the Corporation's deposit accounts in the Bank may be from time to time transferred between accounts or from accounts to Bank official checks upon telephonic direction by an officer or other person identifying himself as one of the following: (names and manner of request—singly, any two, jointly, amount limits, etc.) __one__
John Kuhens Dixie L Burkhart

Be It Further Resolved, that each of the foregoing resolutions shall continue in force until express written notice of its rescission or modification has been received by the bank, but if the authority contained in them should be revoked or terminated by operation of law without such notice, it is resolved and hereby agreed for the purpose of inducing the Bank to act thereunder that the Bank shall be saved harmless by the Corporation from any loss suffered or liability incurred by it in so acting after such revocation or termination without such notice.
I hereby certify that the following named persons have been duly elected to the offices set opposite their respective names, that they continue to hold these offices at the present time, that the signatures appearing hereon are the genuine, original signatures, and that the bank is entitled to continue to rely on this certification until otherwise advised in writing by an officer of the Corporation.

PRESIDENT - TYPED NAME	PRESIDENT - SIGNATURE
John Kuhens	*[signature]*
VICE PRESIDENT - TYPED NAME	VICE PRESIDENT - SIGNATURE
SECRETARY - TYPED NAME	SECRETARY - SIGNATURE
Dixie L Burkhart	
TREASURER - TYPED NAME	TREASURER - SIGNATURE
	[signature]
ASSISTANT SECRETARY - TYPED NAME	ASSISTANT SECRETARY - SIGNATURE
ASSISTANT TREASURER - TYPED NAME	ASSISTANT TREASURER - SIGNATURE

The undersigned acknowledges receipt of a copy of this instrument.
Witness Whereof, I have hereunto subscribed my name and affixed the seal of the said Corporation (if any), this _____ day of _____ A.D. 19 _____

AFFIX CORPORATION SEAL   OR   ☒ THE CORPORATION HAS NO SEAL

TO BE SIGNED SECRETARY
[signature]
Dixie L Burkhart

EXHIBIT
Y-4

03/09/04 TUE 15:26 [TX/RX NO 7510]

Mar 08 04 03:34p   Pilot Grove Savings Bank   319 469 4805   p.17

BUSINESS ACCOUNT AGREEMENT

PILOT GROVE SAVINGS BANK
1341 PILOT GROVE ROAD PO BOX 5
PILOT GROVE IA 52648

OWNERSHIP OF ACCOUNT
☐ SOLE PROPRIETORSHIP ☐ CORPORATION - NOT FOR PROFIT ☒ CORPORATION - FOR PROFIT
☐ PARTNERSHIP ☐ LIMITED LIABILITY CO.

DATE OPENED: 1-8-04
OPENED BY: jc
AUTHORIZATION DATED: 1-8-04
INITIAL DEPOSIT $
FORM: ☐ CASH
☐ VENDOR BANK

radio station
Henry Co, IA
319-385-8728

ADDITIONAL INFORMATION:
new card 1-8-04 to change auth. signers jc
Lotz Roth is authorized to get account balances
as requested. 1-8-04

[signature]

TYPE OF: ☐ NOW ☒ CHECKING ☐ SAVINGS ☐ MONEY MARKET ☐ TIME DEPOSIT
ACCOUNT NAME: KILJ Inc

ACCOUNT OWNER NAMES & ADDRESSES
KILJ Inc
2411 Radio Dr
Mt Pleasant IA 52641

ACCOUNT: 5000-6597-4
          5001-4896-3
NUMBER OF SIGNATURES: 1

[signature]
John Kuhens   482-68-4087

EXHIBIT
Y-5

TIN: 42-1094042

[signature] 1/10/04

Foreclosure Sale Ad

Advertisement to be placed in the legal advertising column of
the Mt. Pleasant daily newspaper

FORECLOSURE SALE

Pursuant to Orders of the Iowa District Court, in and for Henry County, Paul L. Dennison and Joyce E. Dennison, the secured parties, are offering for sale all of the capital stock of KILJ, Inc., an Iowa corporation, which holds licenses issued by the Federal Communications Commission, for the operation of AM Broadcast Station KILJ and FM Broadcast Station KILJ, Mt. Pleasant Iowa. This will be a cash transaction, and the minimum bid must exceed $1,105,230.18. The sale is being handled by The Connelly Company, a media brokerage firm, located in Effingham, New Hampshire, telephone number (603) 522-6462. Persons desiring to submit bids for this stock should contact The Connelly Company no later than August 9, 2004. Any sale of this stock will be subject to prior approval of the Federal Communications Commission.

PLAINTIFF'S EXHIBIT 30

Printed in the United States
216925BV00003B/23/P